Everyone Needs a Mentor
5th edition

David Clutterbuck

The Chartered Institute of Personnel and Development is the leading publisher of books and reports for personnel and training professionals, students, and all those concerned with the effective management and development of people at work.
For details of all our titles, please contact the publishing department:
tel: 020 8612 6204
email: publishing@cipd.co.uk
The catalogue of all CIPD titles can be viewed on the CIPD website:
www.cipd.co.uk/bookstore

Everyone Needs a Mentor
5th edition

David Clutterbuck

Chartered Institute of Personnel and Development

Published by the Chartered Institute of Personnel and Development
151 The Broadway, London SW19 1JQ

First published 1985
Second edition 1991
Third edition 2001
Fourth edition 2004
Reprinted 2006 (twice), 2008 (twice), 2009, 2010, 2011, 2012
This edition published 2014

Designed and typeset by Exeter Premedia Services, India
Printed in Great Britain by Bell & Bain, Glasgow

British Library Cataloguing in Publication Data
A catalogue of this publication is available from the British Library

ISBN 9781843983668

The views expressed in this publication are the author's own and may not necessarily reflect those of the CIPD.

The CIPD has made every effort to trace and acknowledge copyright holders. If any source has been overlooked, CIPD Enterprises would be pleased to redress this in future editions.

Chartered Institute of Personnel and Development
151 The Broadway, London SW19 1JQ
Tel: 020 8612 6200
Email: cipd@cipd.co.uk
Website: www.cipd.co.uk
Incorporated by Royal Charter. Registered Charity No. 1079797

Contents

	List of figures and tables	ix
	Author biography	xi
	Preface	xii
	Foreword	xv
Chapter 1	**The What and Why of Mentoring**	1
	Mentoring in employment	2
	Mentoring for entrepreneurs	2
	Mentoring in education	2
	Mentoring in the community	3
	The business case in brief	3
	Summary	4
Chapter 2	**Models and Methods of Mentoring**	5
	Sponsorship vs developmental mentoring	5
	A simple model of developmental relationships	8
	The two dimensions of 'helping to learn'	9
	Developmental mentoring vs developmental coaching	13
	Mentoring and coaching as reflective space	14
	Mentoring and coaching in the spectrum of learning	15
	Mentoring in the spectrum of supporting	16
	Mentoring as a series of dimensions	17
	Should mentors give advice?	18
	Can developmental and sponsorship mentoring work together?	18
	Summary	18
Chapter 3	**How Formal Should the Mentoring Programme Be?**	19
	The arguments for formal mentoring	20
	The arguments for informal mentoring	21
	What does a formal programme look like?	21
	Bridging the gap between formal and informal mentoring	22
	Summary	22
Chapter 4	**Making the Case for Mentoring**	25
	The case to top management	25
	Other organisational benefits	29
	Calculating the cost benefit of mentoring	30
	Convincing HR	31
	Benefits to the mentee	31
	Potential downsides for the mentee	35
	Benefits for the mentor	35

	Potential downsides for the mentor	37
	Benefits to the line manager	38
	Summary	38
Chapter 5	**What Makes an Effective Mentor an Effective Mentee?**	39
	Choosing mentors	39
	The mentor acronym	44
	Managing the relationship	45
	The mentor who encourages and motivates	45
	The mentor who nurtures	46
	The mentor who teaches	46
	The mentor who offers mutual respect	47
	Mentor motivations	47
	Checklist – ideal characteristics to seek in a mentor	48
	The mentor from hell	48
	Choosing mentees	49
	The effective mentee	50
	Summary	51
Chapter 6	**Matching Mentors and Mentees**	53
	Summary	60
Chapter 7	**Setting up the Mentoring Programme**	61
	The mentoring quadrangle	61
	Setting programme objectives	62
	Preparing the company for a mentoring programme	62
	How to prepare the mentor and the mentee	66
	The role of the line manager vs that of the mentor	67
	Testing the programme	67
	Training	68
	Some basic guidelines in the design of mentoring training	69
	Putting training and scheme management together	74
	Role of the mentoring programme manager	76
	Summary	78
Chapter 8	**Beginning the Mentoring Relationship**	79
	The mentoring contract	80
	Mentoring ground rules	81
	The first meeting	82
	Summary	82
Chapter 9	**Measuring and Monitoring the Programme**	83
	The measurement matrix	84
	What should be reviewed when?	84
	Summary	85
Chapter 10	**Standards for Mentoring Programmes**	87
	How to get the best out of programme standards	90
	Summary	90

Chapter 11	**Peer and Reverse Mentoring**	91
	Peer mentoring	91
	Reverse mentoring	93
	How to get the most from a peer learning alliance	96
	Summary	98
Chapter 12	**Phases of the Mentoring Relationship**	99
	How sponsorship mentoring relationships evolve	99
	How developmental mentoring relationships evolve	100
	The start of the relationship	100
	The middle period	102
	Dissolving the relationship	104
	Restarting the relationship	106
	Using the phases in training and programme management	107
	Summary	107
Chapter 13	**Problems of Mentoring Programmes and Relationships**	109
	Organisational issues	110
	Relationship issues	115
	Summary	117
Chapter 14	**Managing Multi-Country Mentoring Programmes**	119
	Creating a global mentoring strategy	119
	Adapting a global approach to local needs	120
	Some specific cultural issues	121
	Summary	122
Chapter 15	**Mentoring for Graduates and High Potentials**	123
	Graduate mentoring	123
	Mentoring 'high potentials'	125
	Summary	126
Chapter 16	**Diversity Mentoring**	127
	Same group, different group?	128
	Positioning diversity	129
	Potential problems with male–female mentoring	131
	Mentoring across racial/cultural divides	131
	Training mentors and mentees to manage diversity issues	133
	Summary	136
Chapter 17	**Maternity Mentoring**	137
	Summary	139
Chapter 18	**Professional and Executive Mentoring**	141
	The rationale for executive mentoring	142
	Small business mentoring	142
	What professional mentors do	143
	In-house or external mentor?	144
	Summary	146

Chapter 19 Virtual Mentoring 147
E-mentoring 147
Summary 153

Chapter 20 Cross-Organisational Mentoring 155
What should you look for in consortium partners? 156
Key roles 156
Key programme stages 156
Some FAQs 157
Summary 157

Chapter 21 Final Issues 159
All good mentoring relationships come to an end 159
Good mentees often make good mentors 159
Old-stagers can benefit from mentors too 159
Finding a mentor when there is no formal mentoring programme 160

Appendix 163

Bibliography 189

Index 199

List of figures and tables

Chapter 2

Figure 1	The context of mentoring	9
Figure 2	Two dimensions of helping to learn	9
Figure 3	Four basic styles of helping to learn	10
Table 1	Key differences between traditional coaching and mentoring	11
Figure 4	Developmental mentoring	12
Figure 5	Sponsorship mentoring	12
Table 2	Developmental vs sponsorship mentoring: the fundamental differences	13
Table 3	Developmental mentoring and developmental coaching compared	13
Table 4	The spectrum of learning relationships	16
Figure 6	The hierarchy of supporting behaviours	17

Chapter 5

Figure 7	The ten mentor competencies	40
Figure 8	Building self-awareness	41

Chapter 6

Figure 9	The hierarchy/experience gap between mentor and mentee	54
Figure 10	How experience and discipline affect rapport and learning potential	54

Chapter 7

Figure 11	The mentoring quadrangle	61
Table 5	Development roles of line manager and mentor	67
Table 6	A template for training over a 12-month programme	74

Chapter 9

Figure 12	Categories of mentoring measurement	84

Chapter 10

Table 7	The International Standards for Mentoring in Employment (ISMPE): an example	89

Chapter 11

Table 8	Benefits of reverse mentoring	93

Chapter 12

Figure 13 The phases of relationship development: a comparison of US and European approaches 100

Figure 14 The mentoring meeting 104

Chapter 14

Table 9 Issues in multi-country mentoring programmes 120

Chapter 16

Table 10 From equal opportunities to leveraging difference 127

Figure 15 Mentor–mentee relationship as perceived by expatriate mentors 132

Figure 16 Mentor–mentee relationship as perceived by mentees abroad 132

Table 11 The Diversity Awareness Ladder 133

Appendix

Figure 17 The dimensions of mentoring 167

Author biography

Professor David Clutterbuck is one of Europe's most prolific and well-known management writers and thinkers. He has written 55 books and hundreds of articles on cutting edge management themes. He co-founded the European Mentoring & Coaching Council, the primary professional organisation in the field with Europe, and is now its Special Ambassador, promoting good practice in coaching and mentoring internationally. He chairs the International Standards for Mentoring Programmes in Employment and is external examiner for the Ashridge coaching MBA. He was voted *Coaching at Work* magazine's first Mentor of the Year and one of *HR Magazine*'s top 15 HR influencers.

David is a serial entrepreneur, having built and sold two consulting businesses. He now works with an international network of mentor trainers, supporting organisations in developing capability in coaching and mentoring. He maintains a continuous programme of research into mentoring, coaching and leader development. He is an accomplished and controversial public speaker in high demand around the world. The broad scope of his work can be seen on his websites: www.davidclutterbuckpartnership.com and www.coachingandmentoringinternational.org. He likes to practise what he preaches, setting himself the goal of achieving at least one major learning challenge each year – these range from sky-diving to becoming a stand-up comic!

Preface

As I write this 5th edition of *Everyone Needs a Mentor*, it is sobering to reflect on how much has changed since the first mentoring programmes appeared a little more than 30 years ago. Of course, there had been informal mentoring for thousands of years, in all walks of life, but the idea that mentoring relationships could be stimulated and supported by organisations was new.

Those first mentoring programmes, originated in the United States, were heavily weighted towards career sponsorship, rather than learning; the mentor's authority and power to influence were important factors, and the learning that did happen tended to be one-way – from mentor to protégé. Mentors tended to be senior (usually much older) people, who were much further along the career path the protégé had recently embarked on. Boston-based academic Kathy Kram – the grande dame of mentoring, who introduced me to its potential and whose first book on the topic was published, without any collusion, at about the same time as the first edition of this book – now refers to this kind of mentoring as transactional mentoring. (In this book, I use the term 'sponsorship mentoring' to describe the same basic model.)

Then from Europe emerged a different concept of mentoring – one based on mutual learning, with more emphasis on self-development by the mentee. Rather than do things for the mentee, the mentor helped them with the quality of their thinking about issues important to them. The mentor still required relevant experience, but used it less to guide the mentee along the path they had taken, than to craft the questions that would help the mentee create their own path. Kathy Kram calls this 'relational mentoring'; I refer to it in this book with the more widely used term 'developmental mentoring'.

These two models of mentoring – and many hybrids of them – can be seen around the world in a wide array of contexts, from helping students with disability enter the University of Oxford, to supporting female entrepreneurs in developing economies, and from programmes aimed at fast-tracking and retaining 'high potential' employees, to programmes for the United Nations aimed at retaining climate change expertise in Ghana.

More recently, however, the world of mentoring programmes has seen another shift, which we have named 'Second Wave Mentoring'. The experience of organisations in trying to make mentoring work has led them to re-examine how they go about the design and management of their programmes. To some extent the International Standards for Mentoring Programmes in Employment (www.ismpe.org) has stimulated this analysis, but it is not possible to quantify the extent of influence of the standards.

Some of the drivers of Second Wave Mentoring include:

- The desire to make mentoring available to much wider audiences, at lower cost. From being a privilege for a selected few, mentoring has become an instrument for broad social change within organisations and societies.
- The need to link mentoring more closely with key HR processes – in particular, talent management, performance management, succession planning, and achieving diversity objectives.
- The need to demonstrate value for money, which is in turn leading to more effective measurement processes. Enterprise leaders want evidence that mentoring programmes are having a positive effect on the bottom line – which in well-managed programmes is fortunately relatively easy to produce!
- Increased frustration in developmental mentoring programmes, when mentors relapse into sponsorship behaviours. Solutions here include giving high potential employees

both a mentor and a sponsor, and providing mentors with longer-term educational interventions about the expectations of their role.
- Increasing expectation of some target groups (for example, the lesbian, gay, bisexual, and transgender (LGBT) community) of a greater role in the design and management of mentoring programmes intended to support them.

Characteristics of Second Wave Mentoring include:

- Appointing and training a mentoring programme manager, responsible for promoting and supporting mentoring in general, rather than just managing a single initiative.
- High-level engagement of top management in legitimising and promoting mentoring. In particular, having leaders as role models for being mentors and mentees sends a strong, positive message.
- Ensuring that both mentors and mentees are trained initially and that both are supported over the life of the mentoring relationship. A significant component of that support in some programmes is having a professionally qualified supervisor, similar to what is expected of professional coaches.
- Making full use of the range of distance media, rather than just relying on face-to-face meetings – telephone, Skype, e-mail and even texting have a role, as do centralised IT platforms. Increasingly, mentoring relationships are multi-media, using different methods according to circumstance.
- Putting considerably more thought and energy into matching processes, to ensure that the majority of relationships will 'gel'; and designing robust measurement processes at the beginning, both to assess the impact of mentoring and to be able to intervene and troubleshoot rapidly, when needed.
- A wider variety of programmes for different purposes and different groups, within the same organisation (as opposed to large, catch-all programmes).
- Greater integration between different mentoring programmes in the same organisation. For example, cascade mentoring takes the perspective that people who receive mentoring should also become mentors, in a chain of giving. One of the benefits of this approach is that it links employee development and corporate social responsibility agendas.
- Greater clarity and consistency in managing people's expectations of mentoring and coaching within the same organisation; along with increased flexibility to adapt programmes to specific functional and cultural needs. For example, IBM has identified four types of mentoring, aimed at different audiences and for different purposes. Central resources support all of these types of mentoring, but interpretation and programme management are customised.
- Taking greater account of the differences in expectations of mentoring from diverse cultures. For example, Chinese cultures tend to be less open to mutual challenge in mentoring conversations than do Dutch people. British, French, Scandinavian and US cultures all handle challenge in subtly different ways.
- Increased use of social media to help employees develop dynamic networks of mentors, rather than relying on one or two mentoring relationships. In these networks, there may be one or two close mentoring relationships focused on medium- to long-term career development, several medium-term relationships focused on development of specific (leadership) competencies, and ad hoc short-term relationships focused on transfer of skills or knowledge. Intrinsic in these mentor networks is that the traditional senior to junior hierarchy of relationships is often irrelevant – it is the learning exchange that is important and peer and reverse mentoring will play an increased role.
- A movement away from bureaucratic, top down approaches to mentoring. Many early programmes were quite directive towards participants and equated support for relationships with controlling them. Experienced programme managers now aim to achieve the openness and friendliness of informal mentoring, while providing enough

support and training to ensure that both mentor and mentee have the competence and confidence to achieve significant learning from their relationship.

In over 30 years of deep engagement with the fascinating world of mentoring, I might expect to have seen it all. Yet, as I travel the world working with people responsible for making mentoring work, I constantly encounter new applications, new approaches and new concepts that make me re-assess old assumptions. In this edition of *Everyone Needs a Mentor*, I try to reflect this new knowledge and incorporate both recent research and a wide range of new case studies, including some in cascade mentoring and maternity mentoring. Other new features include a training plan for initial participant training, a section on supervising mentors, and a discussion of the role of mentoring programme manager.

I hope *Everyone Needs a Mentor* continues to be a valuable resource for anyone engaged in mentoring, whether as a mentor or mentee, or as a programme manager. There are few roles more rewarding in life than helping others achieve their potential and their dreams – all of us involved with mentoring are immensely privileged!

David Clutterbuck

Foreword

Since the first edition of *Everyone Needs a Mentor*, the field of mentoring has experienced significant growth. Before the 1970s, the word 'mentoring' was rarely used. Nowadays, a Google search of the word will yield more than fifty million matches; a search in library databases such as EBSCO and Sage Premier will show more than fifty thousand articles on the subject, and the literature on mentoring has grown exponentially, with Amazon.com listing more than five thousand books related to the topic. Mentoring is emerging as a formal field of study with a group of research organisations, regularly scheduled conferences, its own literature base, journals, and special interest groups.

The International Mentoring Association (IMA), based at Western Michigan University, was created in 1987 to promote individual and organisational development through mentoring best practices in public and private institutions, businesses, and industry. Based in Marlborough, United Kingdom, the European Mentoring and Coaching Council was formed in 2002 as an independent organisation to promote effective practice in mentoring and coaching across Europe. Both organisations host annual international conferences, provide training and resources for practitioners, publish regular newsletters, and promote public forums and interest groups. Many other local and regional associations have been created in the past decade, including national, state, and university mentoring institutes and research center.

Many journals, primarily in the fields of education, psychology, management, and associated disciplines, continuously publish articles related to adult mentoring; similarly, mentoring articles have appeared in almost every professional field. At least two professional and specialised journals have survived for more than a decade. The *Mentoring & Tutoring* Journal by Routledge, a division of Taylor & Francis, published its first issue in 1993, and the *International Journal of Mentoring and Coaching* launched 1 December 2003.

This explosion in the mentoring field could not be possible without the seminal work of early researchers such as Kathy Kram in the United States and David Clutterbuck in the United Kingdom. Professor Clutterbuck has been instrumental in the development of the field by co-founding the European Mentoring & Coaching Council (EMCC) and the International Standards for Mentoring Programmes in Employment (ISMPE). His groundbreaking work *Everyone Needs a Mentor* continues to be one of the most cited publications in the field of mentoring; with more than fifty publications, Clutterbuck is one of the most prolific authors in the field worldwide.

This new edition of *Everyone Needs a Mentor* addresses contemporary issues and challenges. Due to globalisation and increasing complexity, organisations risk losing important elements such as intellectual capital and effectiveness. The aging, retirement, and attrition of personnel, the increasing diversity in the workplace, and the changes in processes and technology, have forced organisations to review their business practices and implement dynamic strategies to adapt and survive in more demanding environments. In this context, the establishment of formal mentoring programmes has become a popular strategy for addressing the complexity of work settings.

In the past 30 years, scholars and practitioners have embraced mentoring as a developmental approach that offers a range of individual and organisational benefits. Mentoring programmes have been proven to increase personnel retention and satisfaction, to accelerate the development of leadership, and to reduce the learning curve in response to a more demanding, competitive and global market. At the individual level, mentoring benefits include increased competence and career advancement, leading to an enriching job experience. Mentoring relationships also serve to ease the disparities that organisations experience.

Under these evolving circumstances, making sense of this dynamic and changing phenomenon can be a daunting task for novices, experienced researchers, and practitioners alike. *Everyone Needs a Mentor* alleviates this issue providing an organised framework for the practice of mentoring, making this volume an indispensable reading for both researchers and practitioners. Its content delivers a unique tribute to the foundational contributors to mentoring, building on previous research, adapting it, and expanding it to better fit the present day work environment in what the author has coined the 'Second Wave Mentoring'.

Clutterbuck's book provides a complete guide of the various facets of mentoring, allowing even those who are unfamiliar with mentoring a clear understanding of its origins, what it is today and why it is important. He touches on the many models and types of mentoring, and how the selection of an appropriate mentor is paramount to the success of any programme. The book discusses the complexity of the mentoring relationship, as well as the benefits and costs of using formal and informal mentoring approaches.

The author defines the characteristics of an effective mentor and mentee, and outlines the basic structure of setting up a mentoring programme, including how best to monitor and measure the success outcomes in the programme, how to match mentors and mentees, how to properly begin a mentoring relationship, and how to guide a mentee through the different phases of the relationship. Crucial to the success of any mentoring programme or mentoring relationship is to identify possible problems that those involved may face. *Everyone Needs a Mentor* explores potential issues, and uses case studies from a variety of disciplines to further communicate these possibilities, and how to avoid them.

Discussing the pros and cons of different forms of mentoring, the author provides a well-rounded manual useful for new and established programmes across a broad range of organisations, businesses and other entities. This book can be a great benefit to both mentees and mentors, as well as programme managers, co-ordinators and executives. An inclusive manifesto, the book also discusses the use of virtual mentoring, multi-country mentoring, cross-organisational mentoring and even mentoring during maternity, highlighting the importance of diversity as a way to promote access and inclusion, but also as an essential element for creativity and innovation.

I believe *Everyone Needs a Mentor* enables the reader to gain a broader perspective on the field of adult mentoring in the workplace, the importance and benefits of developing mentoring competences and applying international standards for the successful establishment of formal mentoring programmes and relationships to enhance our professional careers, while recognising the immense value it brings to organisations. I would recommend this book to both experienced mentors and mentees looking for a strong framework to maintain and improve established programmes, as well as to those who are new to the field of mentoring, and are looking for a straightforward guide to pioneering their own programmes.

Nora Dominguez
International Mentoring Association
President Elect

CHAPTER 1

The What and Why of Mentoring

I've been lucky enough to have had a number of mentors over the years, although it is only in recent decades that I have fully recognised and appreciated the role that some of these people played. I have also been fortunate to have been mentor to a wide range of people from different backgrounds and age groups. I'm grateful for the learning I have received from them and for the feeling of privilege in helping them achieve goals very different from my own.

Gratitude, learning and privilege are three terms we hear frequently when people talk about their experiences as mentor or mentee. The need to learn and the need to help others to learn are deep-seated emotional drives within most people. These drives were a part of human evolution. It seems that a distinguishing feature between Homo sapiens (us) and other species of great ape is the instinct on the one hand to pass on abstract learning or wisdom, and on the other to receive it. Our liking for story and anecdote – which are closely associated with depth and quality of learning – is no accident. As accumulated wisdom was passed from one generation to another, it expanded the range of human ability and opened up an ever-increasing gulf between humanity and the rest of the animal kingdom.

That instinct is a double-edged sword, however. It often occurs that the desire of the more experienced person (especially if they are much older) to pass on their wisdom exceeds greatly the desire of the less experienced person to listen. Most people may have the instinct to be a mentor, but to do the role well requires a capacity to hold back and allow people to learn for themselves.

To read much of the early literature on mentoring, it would be easy to conclude that the mentor is someone who gives wise advice – indeed, that is one of the common dictionary definitions. In practice, mentors provide a spectrum of learning and supporting behaviours; from challenging and being a critical friend, to being a role model; from helping build networks and develop personal resourcefulness, to simply being there to listen; from helping someone work out what they want to achieve and why, to planning how they will bring change about. A mentor may also be a conscience, a friend and – in certain definitions – a godfather or sponsor.

It is the holistic nature of the mentoring role that distinguishes it from other learning or supporting roles, such as coaching or counselling. We will explore the differences in detail in Chapter 2, but suffice for now to say that, while mentoring shares behaviours with some styles of coaching and some styles of counselling, the overlap of roles is only partial. Some sports now provide top athletes with a mentor as well as a coach. While the coach concentrates on technique and motivation, the mentor provides a very different kind of support; one based on reflective learning and something akin to pastoral care.

A key capability of the effective mentor is being able to adapt to a much wider range of behaviours.

There is also a remarkable width to the range of applications for mentoring. The following outline just some examples of mentoring programmes in recent years.

MENTORING IN EMPLOYMENT

- Rank Group is one of many companies that uses mentoring to support the development and retention of talented employees. One of the unusual aspects of its programme is that all the directors – including the non-executive directors – are actively engaged in the programme.
- A major London solicitor's practice uses mentoring to help people make the transition to partner. What it takes to be considered partner material is so difficult to explain or demonstrate that formal training doesn't really help. Mentoring provides a useful way of passing on this largely intuitive understanding.
- For many multinational companies, a major challenge is how to speed up the development of local nationals to take over from the expatriate engineers and managers. Mentoring provides a practical and culturally acceptable route to making this happen.
- Mentoring has been a major factor in the success of Norway's legislation to equalise male and female representation on company boards.
- The Institute of Chartered Accountants in England and Wales has a programme of 'ethical mentoring'. Mentors are experienced financial services people who help mentees tackle acknowledged ethical dilemmas and also help them develop their ability to recognise and work through ethical dilemmas and become agents for change in their organisations.
- The Institute of Practitioners in Advertising created a programme in which relatively young (under 40) entrepreneurs in the field were mentored by successful peers, mostly 15–20 years older, on issues such as how to sustain their businesses or build greater value in the business.

MENTORING FOR ENTREPRENEURS

- BOOST is an innovative project in Zimbabwe to help the brightest, most entrepreneurial graduates set up their own businesses, which will in turn hire other graduates. Against a background of political turmoil and very high unemployment among graduates, the scheme has received considerable backing at home and abroad. The mentors are all successful business people from the local economy.
- Mowgli and the Cherie Blair Foundation for Women are just two of a growing number of mentoring programmes targeted at supporting entrepreneurs in developing economies, by linking them with mentors in developed countries.
- A division of British Telecom selected a number of small businesses with high growth potential to take part in a programme with a dual purpose. On the one hand, the small businesses, which were selected through a competition process, gained access to the professional expertise of the mentors, who were all in the leadership team or one level below. On the other hand, the BT executives learned a great deal about the issues that small business customers faced.

MENTORING IN EDUCATION

- There are many programmes where volunteers from local companies or from the community in general spend time helping children with poor literacy and numeracy skills catch up. (There is some debate about whether this is really mentoring, even where there is an additional role of helping the young person think about life goals, but we'll avoid that for now.)
- Black students at risk of dropping out of university may have a mentor for the first year to help them settle in.
- Some schools now provide each newcomer with a peer mentor from two years above to help them settle in. The arrangement also helps build the self-respect and maturity of the young mentor. Another group increasingly targeted within schools as potential mentees is children at risk from bullying.

MENTORING IN THE COMMUNITY

- 100 Black Men is an international movement, started in the United States, which focuses on the mentor as role model and advocate for young black people at risk. It records major successes in keeping mentees out of trouble and helping them continue in education.
- Mentors help musically talented young people stick to it through the difficult teenage years when other attractions tug at their attention.
- Soldiers wounded in action and discharged from the armed forces have in some cases a mentor to support them in their journey back into work.

The notion that *everyone needs a mentor* is not so far from the truth. At key times in our lives, having a mentor can make a substantial difference to the choices we make, how confident we feel in making them, and how likely we are to achieve what we want. The concept of *lifelong mentoring* takes the perspective that we can be mentor or mentee (or both at once) at any stage of life, from the earliest ages. Key transitions include:

- starting school
- starting secondary school
- puberty
- leaving school
- going to university
- entering the workplace
- having a baby
- leaving prison, or the armed forces
- first role managing other people
- other transitions in 'the leadership pipeline'
- setting up a business
- moving job roles
- retiring
- dying (yes, there are even mentoring programmes for that, though it's not expected that the mentor will have previous personal experience!).

THE BUSINESS CASE IN BRIEF

We will explore the benefits to employers, mentees, mentors and third parties more fully in Chapter 4, so this is simply a brief summary. Employer organisations have found that having a well-run mentoring scheme has a significant, positive impact upon both recruitment and retention. In some cases, the loss of young graduates in their first year has been cut by two-thirds, simply because they have someone outside the authority structure who has the interest to listen, and the breadth of perspective to help the mentee make wise and confident choices.

Other employer benefits relate to having more effective succession planning, helping employees cope with the stresses of major change and increased productivity.

Mentees report a wide range of benefits, ranging from speed of settling into a new role, to deeper understanding of their own motivations. Recent research has led us to categorise the benefits to mentees in four ways:

- Development outcomes, which may include knowledge, technical competence and behavioural competence.
- Career outcomes, which may include the achievement (in part or whole) of career goals.
- Enabling outcomes, such as having a career plan, a (self-) development plan, a wider network of influencers or learning resources.

- Emotional outcomes – less tangible, but often powerful changes in emotional state, including increased confidence, altruistic satisfaction, reflective space, status and the pleasure of a different kind of intellectual challenge.

These same benefits seem to apply broadly to mentors as well. The principal benefit described by mentors in successful developmental mentoring relationships is the learning they acquire from the experience. This is not necessarily the case in sponsorship mentoring (see Chapter 2). A survey by Sandia Laboratories in the United States did not list 'own learning' as a benefit at all. Second comes the satisfaction from helping someone else – the vicarious pleasure of seeing someone else succeed.

Third parties, such as line managers and work colleagues, benefit because the mentee has someone with whom to discuss how they build and maintain better working relationships. One case reported to me by a colleague concerned a man who explained that his reason for seeking a mentor was to help him get out from under his boss, for whom he had very little respect. After six months, the mentoring pair agreed to change the objective. By reflecting on the relationship with his boss and working to improve it, he had eventually realised that this person had much to teach him and that they could get along together pretty well.

Outside of the work environment, mentoring has had a remarkable influence on the lives of a wide spectrum of disadvantaged or dispossessed people. When I originally wrote this book, I questioned whether *Everyone Needs a Mentor* was truly accurate as a title. After all, perhaps there were people who could live their lives without any recourse to such external help. I have yet to find anyone who is so self-sufficient not to benefit from having a mentor at some point in his or her life. What I have found is many thousands of people who wish they could have had a mentor at formative periods or times of critical personal transition. It is gratifying that most of these people are willing to give others what they did not have. Perhaps another definition of mentoring might be 'Man's humanity to Man' (in the generic sense of 'Man', of course!).

SUMMARY

Mentoring can bring benefits to mentors, mentees, organisations and society at large. In the past 30 years, the range of applications has multiplied.

EXPLORE FURTHER

CLUTTERBUCK, D. (2007a) An international perspective on mentoring. In: RAGINS, B.R. and KRAM, K. (eds). *The Handbook of Mentoring at Work*. California, SA: Sage. pp633–655.

CHAPTER 2

Models and Methods of Mentoring

One of the biggest problems in trying to understand the mentoring phenomenon is pinning down exactly what is meant by the term. The confusion has arisen for several reasons. Firstly, the development of mentoring concepts and behaviours has been strongly influenced by culture – both organisational and national.

Secondly, other forms of one-to-one developmental help, such as coaching, have also had a rapid evolution in recent years. The range of styles open to coaches has expanded from a traditional 'go try this and I'll give you feedback on how you performed' approach or a 'watch me, then you try it' approach to styles that place much more emphasis on questioning, stimulative techniques. It's not that coaching has invaded mentoring's territory, or vice versa. While the roles have remained broadly separate but overlapping, the behavioural repertoire available to each has increased over the past two decades.

A third reason for the confusion is that many of the academics who have studied mentoring have been – let's not mince words – pretty sloppy in their approach to defining what they are talking about. There seems to have been a general assumption that everyone knows what mentoring is, so why bother with defining it. The reality is very different. The purpose of the relationship, the expectations of the mentoring pair, the national and/or corporate culture, and the context in which they operate, all contribute to substantial differences in style and definition. A fundamental warning for anyone attempting to make sense of mentoring by reading the academic journals is *if it doesn't explicitly identify the type of relationship and the objectives of the relationship, it is likely to be at best misguided and probably misleading.*

SPONSORSHIP VS DEVELOPMENTAL MENTORING

In some cases, mentoring is seen as an activity which can take place within the line of command; in others this is seen as incompatible with the fundamental openness of the relationship. In some cultures, the exercise of authority and influence on the part of a protégé is seen as appropriate; in others, mentoring is seen as primarily a developmental activity, with the emphasis on empowering and enabling people to do things for themselves. Some people view mentoring as synonymous with coaching, or teaching; others see it as a form of counselling. Yet others view it as a kind of godfather relationship.

These different perspectives represent two competing models of mentoring. One, largely US-derived, emphasises sponsorship and hands-on help from the mentor. The mentor's power and influence are important to the relationship and the more junior partner is typically referred to as a protégé. Definitions of mentoring from this perspective include:

- A process in which one person (mentor) is responsible for overseeing the career and development of another person (mentee) outside the normal manager–subordinate relationship (Collin 1979).

- The basic model of mentoring is that one person passes their greater knowledge and wisdom to another (Hay 1995).
- A mentor is a professional person who is a wise, experienced, knowledgeable individual who 'either demands or gently coaxes' the most out of the mentee (Caruso 1992).
- A one-to-one relationship in which a senior manager oversees the development and progression of a more junior manager (Anon, Equal Opportunities Review 1995).
- A special type of colleague who informally guides, counsels and teaches the techniques of survival and success to a protégé (Bajnok and Gitterman 1988).
- An experienced, objective sounding board with the power to influence events (Conway 1995).

Words like 'oversee' and 'responsible for' project an image of a hands-on kind of relationship with a clear sense of senior and subordinate. The word 'protégé' also carries distinct overtones of applied power (a protégé is someone who is protected).

The second model, which owes its origins to Europe, and particularly the UK and Scandinavia, emphasises helping people to do things for themselves. It is concerned with co-learning and helping someone make better decisions and grow in wisdom, as a result of deeper self-awareness. Instead of protégé, this kind of mentoring uses the term 'mentee', or sometimes simply 'learner', to place less emphasis on any difference in power.

Definitions that reflect this model of mentoring include:

- To help and support people to manage their own learning in order to maximise their potential, develop their skills, improve their performance, and become the person they want to be (Parsloe 1992).
- A protected relationship in which experimentation, exchange and learning can occur and skills, knowledge and insight be developed (Mumford 1993).
- A one-to-one relationship between two people, where one individual is prepared to assist in the professional and personal development of the other (Gardner 1996).
- Someone who encourages, challenges and supports the learning and development of others (Darwin 1998).
- A relationship between two people with learning and development as its purpose (Megginson and Garvey 2001).
- An expression by the mentor of wisdom through intuition in guiding another, a mentee, toward more self-awareness and freedom in the mentee's journey in pursuit of happiness (Hughes 2003).
- From the perspective of the participants, mentoring is a learning partnership between two people with different levels of experience, where both can achieve new learning, new insights and personal growth. Mentoring creates synergy between two people. [From the perspective of the organisation] mentoring is a strategic development activity that supports the organisation's vision, goals and values and the participant's own development needs and wishes (Poulsen 2008).
- A relationship in which there [is] a high degree of trust and mutual regard, [and in which] the mentor helps another person become what that person aspires to be [and] helps the mentee realize his or her potential (Alred *et al.* 1998 (adapted)).
- Off-line help from one person to another in making significant transitions in knowledge, work or thinking (Megginson and Clutterbuck 1995).
- A confidential one-to-one relationship in which an individual uses a more experienced person as a sounding board and for guidance. It is a protected, non-judgemental relationship, which facilitates a wide range of learning, experimentation and development. It is built on mutual regard, trust and respect (Business Wales 2013).

- Helping someone with the quality of their thinking about issues important to them (Clutterbuck 2012).
- The role of the mentor is one of support to the mentee. The mentor will listen and give advice and guidance, when it is appropriate. Mentoring focuses on developing capability by working with the mentee's goals to help them realise their potential. The mentee is responsible for their learning and development and setting the direction and goals for the relationship. The flow of learning is two-way in a mentoring relationship and the mentor often gains as much as the mentee (unpublished summary by Lis Merrick, Sheffield Hallam University).

Let's look in a bit more detail at the fourth from last of these, which has become the most commonly used definition of developmental mentoring. The rationale behind the component words and phrases of the first of these is as follows:

- *Off-line* is appropriate because it is difficult to be fully open in a relationship where one person has authority over the other. In the few cases where mentoring relationships have been set up between individuals and their managers, the managers in particular have found a conflict of role – either the mentee holds back information, or the managers find themselves in possession of confidences which they cannot use without damaging the relationship. There are rare occasions when an off-line mentoring relationship becomes an inline relationship and, if it is sufficiently strong, may continue informally. However, most schemes would withdraw support for a formal mentoring relationship in these circumstances.
- *Help* is a weak term, but it covers a wide range of resources for which the mentee can turn to the mentor – from direct advice, to simply listening. A key skill for the effective mentor is to be able to adapt the nature of the help given to the mentee's needs at the time.
- *One person to another:* In developmental mentoring, the hierarchy is not important – it is the experience gap that matters. Peer mentoring is increasingly common, as is upward mentoring, where the mentor is more junior in terms of the hierarchy. Top management at General Electric (GE) all have young e-literate mentors who keep them abreast of new technology.
- *Significant transitions:* Mentoring schemes and mentoring relationships need some sense of purpose if they are to achieve benefits for the participants. We will explore some of this in Chapter 11. One of the most common problems with formal mentoring schemes is that mentor and mentee meet, each hoping the other will define what they should be talking about. This is not a recipe for success!

The second, simpler definition reflects the non-directive nature of developmental mentoring. When the goddess Athena conversed with Telemachus in the original story of Mentor, she focused not on telling him what to do, but on helping him a) understand the context of what was happening within him and around him and b) to develop his own judgement and ability to make wise decisions. In effect, she was using her wisdom to stimulate the growth of his.

A relatively concise description of the essentials of a developmental mentoring relationship comes from a website, designed by my colleague Jenny Sweeney, as follows:

- Mentoring is a partnership between two people built upon trust. It is a process in which the mentor offers ongoing support and development opportunities to the mentee. Addressing issues and blockages identified by the mentee, the mentor offers guidance, counselling and support in the form of pragmatic and objective assistance. Both share a common purpose of developing a strong two-way learning relationship.

- Mentoring helps mentees and mentors progress their personal and professional growth. Its primary focus tends to be on the acquisition of people skills which enable individuals to operate effectively at high levels of management. The aim of mentoring is to build the capability of the mentees to the point of self-reliance while accelerating the communication of ideas across the organisation.
- The mentoring relationship is confidential. The mentor offers a safe environment to the mentee within which they can discuss work-related issues and explore solutions to challenges. For this reason, in a formal mentoring scheme mentors are rarely in a line relationship; they are off-line. In this way, the mentors are not required to evaluate the current work performance of the mentees. They are there to help the learner manage his or her own learning.
- Mentors can help individuals reach significant decisions about complex issues. Through skillful questioning, they help clarify the mentee's perspective while bringing an additional view to bear on the issues. Mentors are not there to solve problems but rather to illuminate the issues and to help plan ways through them.
- Mentoring is a positive developmental activity. Mentors can discuss current issues relating to the mentee's work, offering insights into the ways the organisation works, how the informal networks operate and how they think about the challenges and opportunities they encounter.
- Mentors can advise on development and how to manage a career plan; they can challenge assumptions and, where relevant, they can share their own experience. Mentoring has proved to be very effective in transferring tacit knowledge within an organisation, highlighting how effective people think, take decisions and approach complex issues.
- Sharing views and ideas builds understanding and trust. The mentor and mentee relationship often evolves into a key friendship, invaluable when difficult decisions arise.

A SIMPLE MODEL OF DEVELOPMENTAL RELATIONSHIPS

Understanding the dynamics of mentoring relationships isn't necessarily straightforward, as Figure 1 indicates. Every relationship operates within a *context*, which for formal mentoring involves the culture and/or climate of the organisation, the structure and purpose of the scheme, and the background of the mentor and mentee. Each mentoring pair brings to the relationship a set of *expectations* about the purpose of the relationship, about their role and the behaviours they should adopt, and about the likely outcomes. Many or all of these expectations will be influenced by the context. The interaction between the mentor and mentee is a self-reinforcing system – each party's *behaviour* will influence the behaviour of the other. This in turn will influence the *process*, eg how frequently they meet, how deeply they explore issues. And finally, the effectiveness of the process will have a strong influence on the *outcomes*, which can be categorised as either supporting (often referred to in the literature as 'psychosocial') or career oriented.

Outcomes will normally need to be positive for both sides in order for the relationship to continue much beyond the short term – if either mentors or mentees feel they are getting nothing for their efforts, the relationship will falter and die. The challenge is to provide ways of describing what we mean by mentoring that are both academically sound and simple for people to understand and apply. In this chapter, we explore a basic model that fits these criteria, then some alternative perspectives on mentoring that help to distinguish it from other forms of helping others to learn and grow.

Figure 1 The context of mentoring

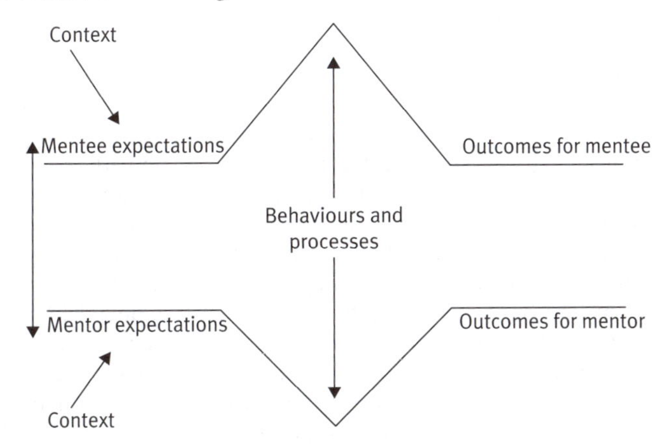

THE TWO DIMENSIONS OF 'HELPING TO LEARN'

One way of looking at the whole spectrum of mentoring is through two key relationship variables.

The first of these is 'who's in charge?' If the mentor takes primary responsibility for managing the relationship (by deciding the content, timing and direction of discussion, by pointing the mentee towards specific career or personal goals, or by giving strong advice and suggestions), then the relationship is directive in tone. If he or she, by contrast, encourages the mentee to set the agenda and initiate meetings, encourages the mentee to come to his or her own conclusions about the way forward and generally stimulates the development of self-reliance, then the relationship is relatively non-directive (see Figure 2). Support for this dimension of helping behaviour comes from a variety of resources both within the mentoring literature and in the parallel literatures on counselling and coaching, as well as interviews and appraisal.

For example, Barham and Conway's (1998) study of the influence of cultural factors on mentor behaviour concludes that, where managers expect their normal role to be that of expert, 'The style of the mentoring relationship will be more didactic and less empowered from the mentee's perspective'. Where the culture expects managers to be facilitators, however, 'The balance of the relationship will be more equal and it will be about mutual learning and sharing. There will be an empowered 'feel' to the mentoring relationships'.

Various studies suggest strongly that the most effective relationships, in which personal development is the desired outcome, are those in which the mentee is relatively proactive and the mentor relatively passive or reactive. The opposite is probably true for relationships that are more focused on sponsorship behaviours.

Figure 2 Two dimensions of helping to learn

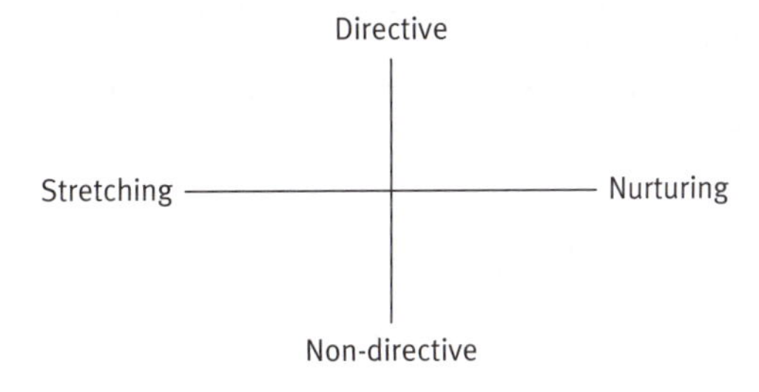

The second dimension relates to the individual's need. Is it primarily about learning – being challenged and stretched – or about nurturing – being supported and encouraged? Again, this is a dimension well established in the general psychological literature, and in particular that on leadership.

Blake and Mouton (1964), Schriesheim and Murphy (1976), Likert (1961) and others emphasise the importance of both task orientation and consideration/social support in achieving group goals. The effective mentoring relationship similarly requires a mixture (often shifting with the needs of the mentee) of task focus (for which read challenge or stretching) and supporting behaviours (for which read nurturing). Authors such as Darling (1984) refer to both types of behaviours in their descriptions of what mentors do. The stretching/nurturing dimension also reflects the complex duality of the goddess Athena – the real mentor in the Greek myth. She is at the same time the macho, fearsome huntress and the nurturing earth mother. Athena, who was closely associated with the owl as a symbol of wisdom, was frequently depicted in full armour and even was supposed to have been born fully armed! Yet she was also closely associated with handicrafts and agriculture. It is tempting to view these as masculine/feminine characteristics and some writers have done just that. However, in my experience this can all too easily lead people into styles of mentoring behaviour based on gender stereotypes. The essence of effective mentoring is that mentors have the facility to move along the dimensions, in any direction, in response to their observation of the learner's need at the time. The beauty of this model is its combination of simplicity and inclusiveness. All 'helping to learn' behaviours fit within these broad dimensions. ('Teaching' is not necessarily a helping to learn behaviour *per se* – being taught is something done to you, while learning is something you do yourself, or with someone else.) We can isolate four primary 'helping to learn' styles based on the dimensions (see Figure 3).

Figure 3 Four basic styles of helping to learn

TRADITIONAL COACHING

Traditional coaching is a relatively directive means of helping someone develop competence. It is relatively directive because the coach is in charge of the process. Although there are, in turn, four basic styles of coaching, which range from the highly directive to more stimulative learner-driven approaches, it is common for the learning goals to be set either by the coach or by a third party. In the world of work, coaching goals are most frequently established as an outcome of performance appraisal. The issue of learner commitment (is this really what matters to them?) is therefore relevant. Some of the useful behaviours effective traditional coaches may display include challenging the learner's assumptions, being a critical friend, and demonstrating how they do something the learner is having difficulties with.

Table 1 describes some of the key differences between traditional coaching and mentoring.

Table 1 Key differences between traditional coaching and mentoring

Traditional coaching	Mentoring
• Concerned with task. • Focuses on skills and performance. • Primarily a line manager role. • Agenda set by, or with, the coach. • Emphasises feedback *to* the learner. • Typically addresses a short-term need. • Feedback and discussion primarily explicit.	• Concerned with implications beyond the task. • Focuses on capability and potential. • Works best off-line. • Agenda set by the learner. • Emphasises feedback and reflection *by* the learner. • Typically a longer-term relationship, often 'for life'. • Feedback and discussion primarily about implicit, intuitive issues and behaviours.

COUNSELLING

Counselling – in the context of support and learning as opposed to therapy – is a relatively non-directive means of helping someone cope. By acting as a sounding board, helping someone structure and analyse career-influencing decisions, and sometimes simply by being there to listen, the mentor supports the mentee in taking responsibility for his or her career and personal development.

NETWORKING

To function effectively within any organisation, people need personal networks. At the very least, they need an information network (how do I find out what I need to know?) and an influence network (how do I get people, over whom I have no direct control, to do things for me?). The same is true for the unemployed young adult in the context of community mentoring, for newly recruited researchers at university, and people in many other situations where mentoring can be applied. Effective mentors help their mentees develop *self-resourcefulness* by making them aware of the plethora of influence and information resources available to them – people, organisations and more formal repositories of knowledge. They may make an introduction to someone they already know, or talk the mentee through how he or she will make his or her own introduction to that person, or help the mentee build entire chunks of virgin network.

Recent research into networks finds that the quality and scope of a person's networks are highly correlated with performance at work. It also seems that effective networks have strong, frequent interactions with a core of people in their network who are instrumental in getting things done, and occasional more ad hoc interaction with a wider, more distant network of people, who bring different perspectives and new thinking (King 2012).

GUIDING

Guiding (being a guardian) is another relatively hands-on role and is the one most managers find easiest because it is closest to what they do normally. Giving advice comes naturally. It is unfortunate that so many managers who have attended coaching courses or read well-meant books on the developmental role of the supervisor, come away feeling guilty, or worse, that they have to constantly restrain themselves from giving straight answers to their direct reports. The reality is that there are many situations where asking 'what do you think you should do?' is not an appropriate response. Using the tools of reflective analysis at inappropriate times is likely to have a far greater demotivating effect than simply leaving well alone. Equally, however, always providing the answer isn't going to help someone grow. Because being a guide/guardian tends to carry with it a relatively strong element of being a role model – an example of success in whatever field the learner has chosen to pursue – their behaviours, good or bad, are likely to be passed on to the learner, along with more practical support. At an extreme, guardians become sponsors or godfathers taking a very direct interest in the learner's development, putting the learner forward for high-profile tasks, tipping him or her off about opportunities and actively moulding the learner's career. This can be very stifling for the recipient, who may not be in a position to resist this largesse, should the learner prefer to succeed by his or her own resources. If learners comply with the mentors' manipulations, a subtle psychological contract often emerges, in which career progression is traded for loyalty and respect. Some cultures regard this more positively than others.

MENTORING

Finally, mentoring draws on all four other 'helping to learn' styles. Indeed, the core skill of a mentor can be described as having sufficient sensitivity to the mentee's needs to respond with the appropriate behaviours. Thus, the effective mentor may use the challenging behaviours of stretch coaching at one point and the empathetic listening of counselling a short while later.

Where an organisation, a national culture, or a mentoring pair decide to draw the boundaries of what is appropriate behaviour for a mentor may vary substantially. What we call *developmental mentoring* assumes a diamond across the middle of the diagram (Figure 4). Traditional US mentoring, by contrast, is concentrated on a circle centred in the top right-hand corner (Figure 5), and often encompasses a high level of sponsorship behaviours.

Figure 4 Developmental mentoring

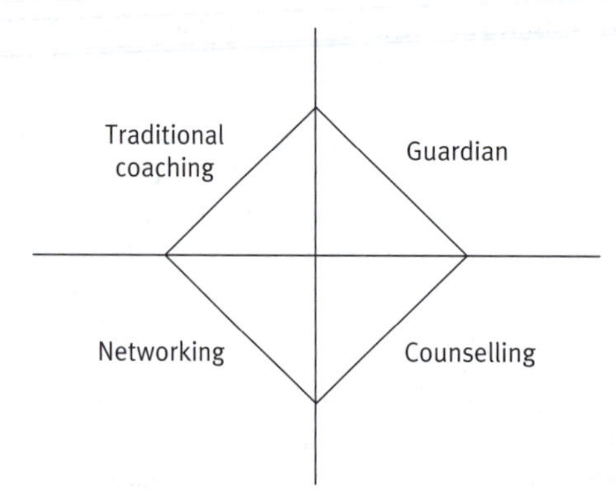

Figure 5 Sponsorship mentoring

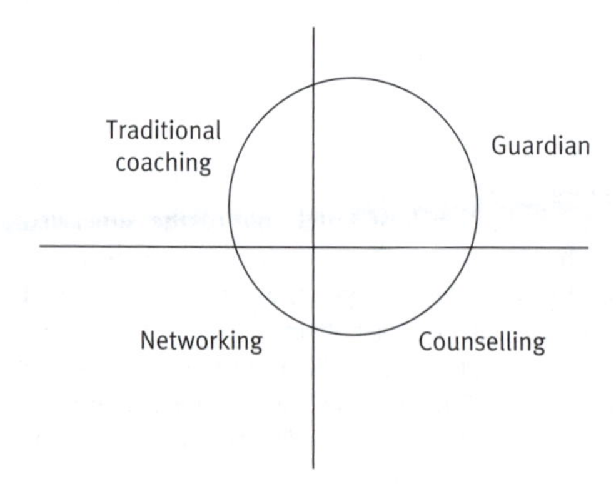

Table 2 explains the distinction between developmental and sponsorship mentoring in more detail. Essentially, one emphasises empowerment and personal accountability, the other the effective use of power and influence.

Table 2 Developmental vs sponsorship mentoring: the fundamental differences

Developmental mentoring	Sponsorship mentoring
• Mentee (literally, one who is helped to think). • Two-way learning. • Power and authority of mentor are 'parked'. • Mentor helps mentee decide what he or she wants and plan how to achieve it. • Begins with an ending in mind. • Built on learning opportunities and friendship. • Most common form of help is stimulating insight. • Mentor may be peer or even junior – it's relative experience that counts.	• Protégé (literally, one who is protected). • One-way learning. • The mentor's power to influence is central to the relationship. • Mentor intervenes on mentee's behalf. • Often ends in conflict, when mentee outgrows mentor and rejects advice. • Built on reciprocal loyalty. • Most common forms of help are advice and introductions. • Mentor is older and more senior.

DEVELOPMENTAL MENTORING VS DEVELOPMENTAL COACHING

If the role of developmental mentor and developmental coach seem remarkably similar, it's because they are. Attempts by the European Mentoring & Coaching Council (EMCC) to establish clear boundaries established that there is no clear consensus. Virtually every factor that we might put forward as a source of difference can be countered with exceptions to the rule. For example, there are schools of coaching thought that say that coaches need no understanding and knowledge of the client's world, and others that say that such knowledge is essential; approaches to mentoring that emphasise access to the mentor's knowledge and experience in a specific career path and approaches that emphasise being able to take an objective view, based on wider life experience.

Organisations and people like to place stakes in the ground (even if the ground is shifting). So some sense of the shades and nuances that might colour the practice of developmental mentoring and developmental coaching has a pragmatic utility within the kaleidoscope of different purposes, cultures and theories. Table 3 represents one way of looking at similarity and difference – it is, in essence, another snapshot in time. The characteristics described under Similarities will frequently, but not always, be shared between the two constructs. Equally, the characteristics in the Differences column will only represent a difference of emphasis that is frequently observed, but is by no means ubiquitous. And because this is a snapshot in time in an evolving picture, the map of praxis may look very different in, say five years' time.

Table 3 Developmental mentoring and developmental coaching compared

Similarities	Differences
• Focus on the quality of the learner's thinking. • Coach/mentor uses their experience to craft powerful questions.	• Mentors more likely to make introductions, help develop networks. • Mentors more likely to help explain politics of a particular organisation or profession.

Similarities	Differences
• Advice-giving is permissible, but not as a first resort and only in specific circumstances. (A common complaint about ineffective coaches is their over-rigid adherence to never giving advice.) • Much of the learning occurs in the reflections of the coachee/mentee between or long after sessions. • Coach and mentor both have a duty of care towards the coachee/mentee.	• Coaches (in the workplace context of line manager to direct report) more likely to give feedback. • Coaching tends to be a short- or medium-term *assignment or activity* focused on performance in a defined field or role. • Mentoring tends to be a medium- to long-term *relationship* focused on career or on more holistic, less well-defined issues. • Coaching more often a paid arrangement… *or not, depending on context!*

MENTORING AND COACHING AS REFLECTIVE SPACE

On average, knowledge workers cannot acquire greater than ten minutes at a time to focus without interruption on a specific task or issue. Although people are often working longer hours than a decade ago, they have less and less time to stop and think deeply. In experiments with hundreds of managers and professionals, less than 3% claim to find their deep thinking time at work, and of these, the majority do so by coming in very early in the morning. For most people, however, deep thinking time happens on the journey to and from work, in the bath or shower, taking exercise, doing the ironing, lying awake at night, or in other parts of their 'free' time.

Deep, reflective thinking is as essential to the effectiveness of our conscious brain as REM sleep is to our unconscious. In both cases, we become dysfunctional if our minds do not carry out the essential task of analysing, structuring, organising and storing. When we allow ourselves to enter personal reflective space (PRS), we put the world around us largely on hold. (Even if we are doing a complex physical movement, like jogging or driving the car, we allow our internal autopilot to take over.) Often unbidden, although with practice it is possible to control the process, one issue of concern rises to the surface of our consciousness and we start to examine it with a depth and clarity we have not previously been able to apply to it. There are many comparisons for this process – I like the analogy of the mine disposal engineer gingerly examining a sea mine washed ashore. Another analogy is peering through the windows of a doll's house before gradually disassembling it. Whatever metaphor you use, the process is the same: you ask yourself questions about the issue in an attempt to better understand it and its impact on you. The more questions you ask from different perspectives, the more likely you are to achieve some level of insight, which allows you to position the issue very differently and consider new ways of dealing with it. For me, a remarkably high proportion of excursions into reflective space result in being able to combine two difficult and until then separate situations in a way that achieves a positive outcome for both. Some people find that PRS takes them to a better understanding of the dynamics of their situation and gives them the confidence to take actions they had been avoiding. Possibly everyone is different, but there are at least two factors common to everyone who enters PRS regularly:

1. They emerge with renewed energy to tackle the issue they have been considering.
2. Whether vocalised or not, the person has been having a dialogue with him- or herself. (This is *not* a sign of madness, I hasten to add.)

When you engage in similar dialogue with a mentor, you are in effect inviting them to join you in your PRS. The dialogue becomes a trialogue, with the mentor asking you similar questions, but more rigorously, more objectively from a wider range of perspectives, and more intensively. The effective mentor therefore takes you down the path from analysis, through understanding and insight to plans for action in a faster, more thorough manner.

AN EXAMPLE

The owner/manager of a 65-employee company was forced by a minor but significant health warning to consider throttling back on his hours and responsibilities. He was frustrated, however, by a complete failure to delegate key tasks to his three direct reports. After a while he gave up, until the next heart twinge brought the issue back to the fore. This time he sought help, asking a mentor to help him think the issues through. The mentor asked the kinds of question that put the behaviours of both sides into perspective – a set of unconscious collusions that would always result in problems being passed up to the boss. Whatever the conscious expectations the owner and his managers had of each other, the unconscious ones were those driving both sides' behaviour. Teasing these expectations into the open allowed the owner to design and implement a whole new range of tactics, which broke the fixed, negative cycle of behaviour and changed the relationship with two out of the three managers. (You can't win all the time!) One solution was to stop getting angry when the managers asked him to take a decision within their authority. Instead, he now patiently explained what they should do. When they arrived back at their office, however, they found an invoice 'for doing your job' and an appropriate sum deducted from their departmental budgets!

MENTORING AND COACHING IN THE SPECTRUM OF LEARNING

People learn from others in a variety of ways and one sign of learning maturity is that a person has a wide network of different learning relationships. In many ways, the journey to adulthood is one of widening one's range of learning relationships.

Table 4 details the key style differences in helping others to learn. First, really good teachers are able to operate across the spectrum, although the structure and organisation of modern school systems makes it increasingly difficult for them to do so. Second, each of these approaches is both valid and valuable, but they represent a spectrum from the highly impersonal to the highly customised and personal. Third, one can also plot an evolution in the quality of the learning in two ways. One is that the closer one gets to mentoring, the more the learning is shaped and encapsulated by the individual's own experiences. The other is the cascade from data through information (a product of teaching), knowledge (tutoring), and skill (coaching), to wisdom (mentoring). At each stage of this cascade the level of usefulness increases: data becomes interesting (except to trainspotters) only when it is organised into information; information allows people to pass examinations, but it requires further structure and context to turn it into knowledge, at which point it can be applied more widely. Having the knowledge of what a good manager should do doesn't mean that you are any good at it, however. For that, knowledge has to be applied and re-applied until it becomes skill. Finally, wisdom is the ability to apply accumulated knowledge and skill more widely again, having the judgement to draw meaningfully on experience in one or more situations to completely new contexts.

Table 4 The spectrum of learning relationships

Role	Relationship	Dominant style	Affinity	Learning transfer	Power management
Teacher	Pupil	Tell	Aloof	Explicit data and information	High exerted power (parental)
Tutor	Student	Discuss		Knowledge	
Traditional coach	Learner	Demonstrate/ give feedback		Skills	
Developmental coach	Client	Raise self-awareness		Performance	
Mentor	Colleague	Encourage/ stimulate	Close	Intuitive data and wisdom	Low exerted power (collegial)

The implications of this for mentors are considerable. Whose wisdom are we talking about? Effective mentors tend to treat their wisdom like a nuclear arsenal – they very rarely let it fly. Instead they use their experience to inform the questions they ask and to challenge assumptions the mentee may be making. They also recognise that the greatest value to the mentee is to develop his or her own wisdom, not to borrow that of the mentor. Inevitably, in a successful and enduring mentoring relationship, there will be nuggets of observations by the mentor that the mentee will savour and perhaps pass on in turn, but the prevailing message of developmental mentoring is, 'Look into your own experience. Learn your own lessons. Build your own wisdom.' (This is heavily in contrast with the sponsorship mentoring view of, 'Listen to my experience. Learn from my triumphs and mistakes. Value my advice and judgement.')

MENTORING IN THE SPECTRUM OF SUPPORTING

Given that mentoring – and all other developmental styles – addresses needs for both learning/stretching and supporting/nurturing, it's not surprising that we can identify a similar hierarchy of supporting roles and behaviours (see Figure 6). The most directive or hands-on role is that of sponsor.

Giving advice is a key supporting role, especially for those occasions when the learner simply doesn't know what to do or how to move forward on an issue. Sometimes the advisor is simply a sounding board. Being sought out for one's knowledge or insight is one of the strongest compliments people can receive – it raises one's self-esteem and encourages future helpfulness.

Being a counsellor is in many ways similar, but the satisfaction comes from the use of one's knowledge and skills to help someone reach their own conclusions and solve their own problems. The counsellor is also much more likely than the advisor to reflect on how the issues considered relate to them and their own circumstances.

Friendship is the least directive of roles and the one – in its most beneficial manifestations – that demands least from the participants. Friends may sometimes act in the other supporting roles, where circumstances make it appropriate. *Critical friends* are a valuable source of feedback, which the individual might not otherwise receive.

Figure 6 The hierarchy of supporting behaviours

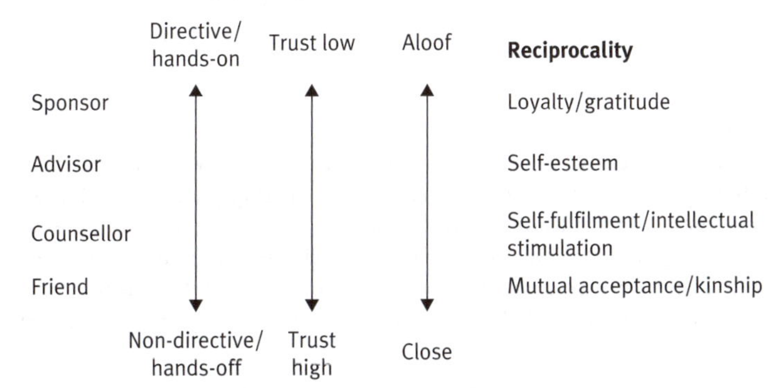

Mentors might adopt any or all of these roles, depending on the style of mentoring agreed. A traditional sponsorship mentoring approach would place more emphasis on sponsoring and advising; a developmental mentoring approach would avoid sponsoring and would concentrate on a mixture of advising and counselling behaviours. Either model of mentoring could result in the development of friendship, but friendships tend to be deeper and longer lasting in developmental mentoring, perhaps because both parties in successful relationships learn to be very open with each other.

Many organisations have recognised that high flyers need a portfolio of relationships. In particular, they benefit from having:

- A coach – to focus upon performance issues, especially for the current job role (this may or may not be the line manager).
- A mentor – to challenge them, provide the bigger picture and concentrate on longer-term development.
- A sponsor – to ensure they are placed in the right assignments to develop their potential (this is generally a much longer-term relationship than either coach or mentor).
- Peer learning relationships – both within and across the organisational boundaries.
- Access to traditional learning resources – such as business school courses and new media, such as e-learning, at times when they have a specific learning need.

MENTORING AS A SERIES OF DIMENSIONS

One of the most useful insights into the complexity of mentoring comes from Bob Garvey, now at the University of York. His model views mentoring relationships as being on a spectrum of five dimensions, with their position on each spectrum open to change as the relationship evolves or the external context changes. The dimensions are:

- Open vs closed – is the discussion on a set agenda of specific issues, or determined by what is on the mentee's mind at the time?
- Public vs private – who knows whether mentoring is going on?
- Formal vs informal.
- Active vs passive – does the mentor or the mentee drive the relationship and the agenda?
- Stable vs unstable – how much trust is there in the relationship and how consistently do mentor and mentee meet each other's expectations?

These dimensions can apply to both developmental and sponsorship mentoring. The success of the relationship may depend upon how able mentor and mentee are to adjust where they are on each dimension as the relationship evolves.

SHOULD MENTORS GIVE ADVICE?

One of the apparent big differences between developmental and sponsorship mentoring is that giving advice is central to the latter and to be avoided in the former. In practice, it's more complex than that. Developmental mentors do give advice, but they do so only when they are sure the mentee can't work things out for themselves and they broadly limit their advice or guidance to helping the mentee understand the context of a situation, rather than telling them what to do. So they provide missing pieces of a situational jigsaw, or clarify the implications of alternative courses of action. So, for example, sharing the consequences of a poor decision they have observed elsewhere can assist the mentee to avoid making a similar error. But the core question the mentor needs to keep asking themselves is: 'Is this going to help the mentee work out what is the right solution for them?'

CAN DEVELOPMENTAL AND SPONSORSHIP MENTORING WORK TOGETHER?

It's inevitable that some formal developmental mentoring relationships will lead to longer-term, close friendships that will evolve into some form of informal sponsorship. The problem is that this can damage the core mentoring programme, by creating expectations that this will be a normal outcome from the relationship. Lis Merrick and Paul Stokes at Sheffield Hallam University have found that senior leaders in some companies are keen to shift their mentoring relationships in this direction, in order to speed up the progression of talent.

A practical solution is to be very clear about the separate roles of mentor and sponsor. Mentoring focuses on helping mentees decide what they want from their lives and careers and planning how they will make that happen for themselves. Sponsorship focuses on direct intervention to support the process – for example, through making sure there is a plan for exposing the employee to formative experiences and ensuring that line managers do not block their progress. With this clarity, mentors can be encouraged to hold back from a transition to sponsorship, until the mentoring relationship has wound up. At this stage a broader discussion may take place in terms of whether the mentee will benefit from sponsorship at this point, and who the best sponsor would be. While the result may be that the former mentor and former mentee now become sponsor and protégé, it is a new and separate arrangement, with different purpose, style and intended outcomes.

SUMMARY

This has been a very short introduction to fundamental but relatively straightforward ways of thinking about and describing the mentoring phenomenon. There are other descriptive models well worth a look – in particular, Carter's (1994) notion of mentoring contexts – and some of these are to be found in the Bibliography. From my experience, however, the three models described in this chapter provide a very effective means of focusing both mentor and mentee on pragmatic expectations, both of each other and of the mentoring process.

CHAPTER 3

How Formal Should the Mentoring Programme Be?

Some years ago, a petrochemicals company asked me to examine its two pilot, high-profile mentoring schemes – why weren't they working? Although launched with great enthusiasm and a considerable effort to train mentors, many of the relationships had simply never taken off. Others had faded away, often because the pair had run out of interesting things to talk about.

The problems stemmed from a variety of failings, not least insufficient clarity about roles and objectives. However, one of the most interesting results of our analysis of data gathered through focus groups was that the relationships that worked best and most often were generally those where the mentees themselves selected their mentors. Those relationships where the mentors were effectively imposed by the organisation were less effective and less likely to be continuing. This distinction was particularly marked among a group of high-flyers, who had one mentor of each kind, with the allocated mentor being from the same general area of the business and the personally selected mentor coming from another department.

Yet experiences in other companies show that encouraging people to select mentors entirely at their own choice leads, in a high proportion of cases, to relationships that deliver few, if any, benefits. Left to their own devices, people often choose someone they get on with extremely well and have known for a long time; or they approach a more senior high-flyer with a view to hanging on to their coat-tails. In the first case, while there is high rapport, there is typically very little opportunity for learning – growing pearls of learning requires at least some measure of grit in the oyster. When the chosen mentor is a high-flyer, he or she is often uninterested in helping to develop others; even if the high-flyer is interested, he or she is unable to create the necessary time.

It's as a result of this kind of contradiction in experience that emerging good practice in dealing with selection and matching centres around 'guided choice'. This can mean providing the mentee with strong guidance on how to find and use a mentor; or it can involve giving them a limited number of options, selected by the scheme co-ordinator against criteria, which the mentee has provided or at least been involved in. The second of these approaches requires an existing pool of people who have volunteered and ideally been trained to be mentors. There is, however, an even bigger conflict about mentoring, which is starting to be resolved and to which I referred to in passing in Chapter 2. Put briefly, while most practitioners – both in-company and consultants – maintain that formal mentoring (ie a structured programme in which mentoring relationships are established and supported) is far more effective than informal, most academics, particularly in the USA, say that their studies show the opposite to be true. The clash between scientific observation and the experience of practitioners is not unique to mentoring – it happens in almost every aspect of endeavour – but understanding the reasons for the differences almost always stimulates a leap forward in practical implementation. And that is what is beginning to happen in mentoring right now.

THE ARGUMENTS FOR FORMAL MENTORING

SOCIAL INCLUSION

The main arguments in favour of a formal structure for mentoring centre around the need for some control of a process that, left alone, may not always work to the advantage of the organisation or the majority of the people in it. Social inclusion is an issue of increasing importance in most large organisations – how do we ensure both equal opportunities and the effective use of the diversity of talent, experience and backgrounds of our people? There are many well-documented cases of programmes aimed at a specific group, breaking the glass ceilings in gender, race or disability. The Cabinet Office, for example, runs a highly successful mentoring scheme aimed at people with severe physical (and sometimes mental) disability, who have ambitions to progress. The mentors are all very senior civil servants who see the relationship as a stimulating challenge.

Some of the most dramatic figures on mentoring for social inclusion come from the programme Big Brothers Big Sisters, which links young people at risk in North America (and more recently in the UK) with a mentor in the community. The 10–16 year old mentees in this programme are:

- 46% less likely to begin drug abuse (70% for minorities)
- 27% less likely to begin underage drinking
- 30% less likely to hit someone else.

They also skip 80% fewer school days than non-mentored peers and have better relationships with parents, peers and teachers. By contrast, informal mentoring appears to reinforce social exclusion, because the scarce pool of mentors tends to be snapped up by those who are from the dominant social group, who are better educated, and more obviously ambitious. In Europe and North America this means that white male graduates are far more likely to find an informal mentor than any other group. Because mentor and mentee are so similar, an additional negative is that relatively little learning takes place on the part of the mentor. Diversity in a mentoring relationship stimulates participants to examine issues from different perspectives.

POSITIVE MENTORING

Formal mentoring also helps ensure that the relationship has clear purpose. The most common reason why so many mentoring relationships fail is that neither mentor nor mentee is quite sure what they are aiming for, so there is no sense of direction. A formal scheme provides an umbrella purpose for the organisation, which helps mentor and mentee establish more specific goals for their own relationship.

Formal mentoring also ensures that there is a practical framework of support for mentor and mentee, including initial training and, in good practice environments, some form of continuing review, where mentors can address any further skills needs they identify. Training ensures both parties understand what is expected of them – not least who manages the relationship and what the boundaries are. The formal process also helps to weed out 'toxic' mentors. People who have manipulative goals, who represent values the organisation is trying to move away from, or who have so many problems of their own that they end up transferring these to the mentee, are all common characters who can damage both the mentee and the organisation and who may actively seek to find mentees in an informal environment.

THE ARGUMENTS FOR INFORMAL MENTORING

A variety of highly analytical studies, mostly in the USA, suggest that people in informal mentoring relationships are much more satisfied with them. Among the reasons suggested for this are:

- Informal relationships take longer to get off the ground and tend to last longer overall, so there is more opportunity to create strong trust and to achieve medium-term goals. Formal relationships are often under considerable time pressure. Informal mentors are less likely to be in the role out of some form of obligation; they are there because they want to be. (There is evidence that altruistic mentors are less effective than those who see benefits for themselves in the relationship.) Many companies with formal schemes put subtle pressure on managers to become mentors as a way to demonstrate their commitment to people development.
- Informal mentors tend to have better communication and coaching skills than formal. (This is a matter of numbers – formal schemes often create increased demand that can be filled only by relaxing the competence criteria. In informal mentoring, the people most likely to put themselves forward – toxic mentors excepted – are those who have confidence in their own competence to perform the role.)

Broadly, these studies suggest that informal mentors offer stronger elements of friendship and empathy than formal mentors. Most of the other differences identified relate to the mentor's willingness to act as a sponsor to the mentee – something seen as a positive in traditional US mentoring, but as a practice to avoid in European, developmental mentoring, which places much more emphasis on helping the mentee become more self-resourceful.

WHAT DOES A FORMAL PROGRAMME LOOK LIKE?

Formal programmes (and especially those designed in line with the International Standards for Mentoring Programmes in Employment (ISMPE)) tend to have the following characteristics:

- a designated programme co-ordinator or manager
- visible sponsorship from the leadership team (important in legitimising mentoring, in providing senior level role models for mentoring behaviours, and ensuring the programme is adequately resourced)
- clearly defined purpose (how mentoring will benefit mentors, mentees, the organisation and other stakeholders)
- processes to select and match participants
- training for both mentors and mentees
- continued support for mentoring pairs
- processes for measurement, review and continuous improvement.

Many formal programmes now also include:

- education for line managers in how to support their direct reports, who are in mentoring relationships
- education and engagement processes for HR
- steering groups for each programme (especially useful in the context of diversity mentoring and mentoring for graduate recruits)
- an online portal of supporting materials on mentoring.

Some formal mentoring programmes take the support process even further, by providing periodic group supervision for mentors. The benefits of this are that it builds their knowledge and skills, helps them overcome problems they may meet in their mentoring relationships, and identifies any issues of concern.

BRIDGING THE GAP BETWEEN FORMAL AND INFORMAL MENTORING

As more and more people become comfortable with the formal mentoring approach and more confident in their roles as mentors and mentees, the quantity and quality of informal mentoring increases. But is it possible to get the best of both worlds, by having just enough structure and support to allow informal mentoring to flourish? Experience from around the world suggests exactly that, with the key elements being:

- An online registration and matching system, where people can seek and make their own pairings. The system needs to have very good guidance as to how to go about selecting an appropriate partner and, ideally, a resource, which prospective mentees can go to for personal advice.
- Sufficient, visible role models of good mentoring practice to demonstrate what quality mentoring looks and feels like and to provide a voluntary, informal advisory resource for mentors. If top management can be among those role models, it provides a very strong message to the organisation.
- A mixture of voluntary training resources. These might include; a regular open training programme, run in-house or externally with a consortium of other organisations; an e-learning package to run on PC or online; and a library of wider reading materials on mentoring and related disciplines. It may also be useful to provide an option for people who have a strong interest in developing their mentoring skills, to take a certificate or degree course through one of the several providers now available.
- An understanding that the quality of mentoring rests to a considerable extent on the amount and relevance of the training both parties have received. While an informal process can't insist that mentors and mentees are trained, the desire to have an effective relationship should drive both parties away from matching with someone who is not sufficiently committed to be trained in the role.
- An opportunity for mentors (or developers in general) to meet informally as a mutual support and learning group through an online chat room and/or self-organised gatherings. In this scenario, mentors may request some help from HR in arranging venues and perhaps finding external speakers on specific learning topics, but the impetus has to come from them. Some organisations already run 'lunch and learn' events – perhaps monthly – along these lines.
- Good practice 'snippets', sent monthly to all managers (or indeed all employees) on developmental behaviours, from both the learner and the developer perspectives. This is perhaps the closest the organisation may go to a formal arrangement. These short advisory bulletins (no more than a few hundred words each time) would be generated by HR, with the aim of stimulating awareness, discussion and incremental improvements in people's behaviour to mentor and be mentored, coach and be coached, and so on.

SUMMARY

Getting the best from a mentoring scheme involves building in the best aspects of both formal and informal approaches. A formal structure is essential because it provides meaning and direction for relationships and support where necessary. But individual relationships will flourish best when allowed to operate as informally as possible. Successful formal relationships very frequently go on to become successful informal ones. There is also an increasing body of field evidence that the quality and extent of informal mentoring improves dramatically once a critical mass is achieved of people who have been effective mentors and mentees under formal arrangements.

An organisation that manages to create a mentoring/coaching culture can increasingly relax the level of formal intervention it imposes. What structures it does provide, in terms of educational materials and training, for example, become regarded as support mechanisms rather than controls. Meetings between mentors to develop their skills can become informal, self-driven support networks. And the range of people from whom the mentees learn can gradually be extended as they learn to build and manage their own learning nets.

CHAPTER 4

Making the Case for Mentoring

Like all developmental interventions, making the case for investment in mentoring is not necessarily straightforward. The chain of cause and effect may be distorted, especially if the mentoring programme is just one part of a larger initiative or package of initiatives – for example, as one of a number of support measures for promoting diversity, or as part of a graduate induction programme.

Nonetheless, there are sufficient cases of very specific benefit from mentoring programmes and relationships to produce a very strong case to all four of the key internal audiences:

- top management
- prospective mentees
- prospective mentors
- key third parties such as line managers and the HR community.

For all of these, the two basic questions are:

- How do I know the investment (of time, energy and/or money) is worthwhile?
- Why do I need to invest in a formal support structure or relationship, rather than let mentoring happen naturally and informally?

THE CASE TO TOP MANAGEMENT

Every company needs some form of career development programme to produce a succession of motivated, upward-moving employees. Even employees who are destined to remain at the same level may need career development as the jobs they are in change or become obsolete. Managers with high potential should identify and improve their skills, set career goals and know how to achieve those goals in the most practical and efficient way. Conventional career development courses provide some of the answers, but all too often fail to provide adequate follow-up. The results, too, are often hard to define. Schemes involving selection by assessment centres of high-flyers or frequent job rotation to gain wide experience probably offer the nearest thing to tangible results, but are extremely expensive, not least because at each change the young person has to start again at the beginning of the learning cycle of the new job.

Leaving career development solely to managers, while cheaper, tends to be singularly ineffective. A manager may lack the ability to recognise a potential high-flyer or, if he or she does, be reluctant to lose that employee by counselling him or her to move to another area of the company. Managers who are unavailable, uncommitted, or who dislike particular subordinates can effectively block the career paths of talented employees and prevent them from realising their potential. Diversity objectives also tend to be marginalised, unless there is a structured programme to promote and monitor them.

A mentoring programme, as a formal method of recognising talent in a company, is a viable alternative to both these approaches. It can be carried out in tandem with traditional career development methods and has reasonably good predictability in its results. It may be run for as long as the employee benefits from it. As in many other relationships, both mentee and mentor have to work hard to make it succeed; both can draw substantial benefits.

Mentoring can work in most organisations, regardless of size, culture or market sector. It can communicate to employees far more fully the complexity of procedures and the unique nature of the company than any formal training course, induction booklets or company manual.

Mentoring enhances the abilities of both the mentor and mentee, so the organisation gains through increased efficiency. Companies with formal, longstanding mentoring programmes claim tangible increases in productivity and efficiency. Intangible benefits include improved staff morale, greater career satisfaction, and getting up to speed more quickly when mentored managers are inserted into a new job.

Another significant impetus behind mentoring is the cost – not in cash terms (mentoring is *not* a cheap alternative when you take into account the value of management time) – but in saving expensive off-site courses, which take employees away from productivity activity for weeks on end.

The primary rewards to a company of a mentoring programme are:

- easier recruitment and induction
- improved motivation
- management of corporate culture
- leadership development
- succession planning
- improved communication
- improved retention of employees.

EASIER RECRUITMENT AND INDUCTION

A formal mentoring programme eases the sometimes difficult process of assimilating new recruits. Companies such as BAE Systems and National Grid, for example, have found graduate induction has become less of an ordeal since they began mentoring. Enthusiasm has been productively channelled and graduates are taking on greater responsibility as their commitment grows.

Most staff turnover occurs during the first six to twelve months with a new employer and a major cause is inability to adjust rapidly enough. Assigning a mentor to a new arrival helps overcome the counterproductive problems of culture shock and the uncertainty most people feel as they find their feet in the new environment. Employees become productive more quickly and are likely to stay with the company longer. Some surveys of the effectiveness of executive new hires suggest that as many as 80% fail to fulfil the expectations of them. Whatever the true figure, anecdotal evidence indicates strongly that mentoring can help by speeding up the acculturation of the new recruit, by helping them build the networks they need to be effective in a new environment, by raising their political awareness, and by generally sensitising them to both their external environment and their internal reaction to it.

Mentoring also cultivates in the mentee an increased sense of commitment and loyalty to the organisation. The mentor is the mediator between the mentee and the company. Through close interaction with the mentee, the mentor creates a personal atmosphere in what might otherwise seem a faceless bureaucratic organisation. The mentee receives through the mentor a positive perception of the company. The mentee can be made to feel he or she is participating in the inner operations of the company and this in turn generates a closer identification with the organisation's goals.

Many companies experience difficulties in attracting the right kind of graduates, even in times of severe unemployment. Even top financial services companies in the City of London are finding that graduates – and especially those with advanced degrees – will turn down employers who don't offer a mentoring programme. A mentoring programme can be a significant inducement for graduates to join less glamorous firms or industries because it demonstrates commitment to management development and staff retention. It is particularly attractive if it offers a fast track to middle management.

IMPROVED MOTIVATION

Mentoring can help reduce managerial and professional turnover at other critical stages, too. Young, ambitious people often undergo a period of frustration and impatience when they realise their progress up the company career ladder is slower than they initially expected. If mentees have a mentor who is taking an active interest in their career and who explains the reasons for and ways round current blockages, they are more likely to persevere. The mentor helps them understand and recognise the long-term plans the company has for them and helps the mentee make the most of the learning experiences inherent in the current job. Hence mentoring lessens the threat of other companies luring away promising young employees with offers of speedier career advancement.

A mentoring relationship also motivates the middle and senior managers involved and can be a valuable means of delaying 'plateauing'. A manager is less likely to retire mentally in the job if he or she is constantly faced with fresh challenges arising from a mentoring relationship. Mentors are forced to clarify and articulate their own ideas about the company's organisation and goals in order to explain them to their mentees. They may feel they have to improve their own abilities to justify the mentee's respect. Cultivating potential in the company becomes a significant opportunity for the mentor to demonstrate that the old dog is still capable of learning and showing new tricks. As a result, mentors may find new purpose and interest in their jobs.

MANAGEMENT OF CORPORATE CULTURE

In the original edition, I titled this section *A Stable Corporate Culture*. Almost every mentoring programme I examined then had as part of its objectives passing on the nuances of the corporate culture. In the intervening years, the emphasis has changed dramatically. Instead of preserving cultures, companies are desperately trying to change them. This poses a number of problems – not least that it makes it even more difficult to identify mentors with the 'right' values.

Mentor and mentee in an effective developmental relationship are able to explore the differences between espoused corporate values and actual behaviour. At the same time, the mentor helps to clarify in the mentee's mind which aspects of the culture are fixed and not open to challenge, and which are open for dialogue. At one of the world's largest and most successful merchant banks, for example, new recruits soon learn that near obsessive honesty is an immutable part of the culture, but that maintaining a work–life balance (on a par with integrity in the corporate values statement) is honoured more often in the breach. The mentee is able to use the mentor as a role model for selected aspects of the culture, while the mentor is able to use the mentee's constructive challenge to inform the continuing senior-level debate on how the culture should evolve.

Bringing mentors together from time to time to continue their skills development and review relationship progress (within the bounds of confidentiality) has proven valuable in changing how the organisation tackles important issues relating to culture. For example:

- An international IT services company had, as a basic assumption about how people's careers should evolve, that they should move as early as possible into positions of junior supervision and thence to manage small projects, until they began to climb the management ladder. The mentors revealed, however, that a significant proportion of the workforce just wanted to become better and better techies. One of the main reasons talent was leaving the company was that these people felt the culture was incompatible with their needs. The result was that the company introduced a dual-path career system.

- A financial services company had stifled discussion about work–life balance issues for years. With the introduction of a mentoring programme, people had an opportunity to open up about their anger with regard to the long-hours culture. Suddenly, top management could no longer pretend the problem didn't exist and it committed to making changes happen.

LEADERSHIP DEVELOPMENT

It's common for programmes to use mentoring to help emerging leaders, or people moving between levels in the leadership pipeline, recognise and work on the behavioural skills and the contextual knowledge they need to acquire. Role modelling plays a big part here.

At the same time, mentoring gives existing leaders a safe space in which to practice developmental behaviours and approaches, which they can transfer to their relationships with their direct reports.

SUCCESSION PLANNING

An increasingly common benefit reported by larger companies is an improvement in succession planning. Widespread mentoring, especially where the duration of formal relationships is limited to one or two years, ensures that senior managers are familiar with the strengths, weaknesses and ambitions of a relatively large cross-section of more junior talent.

IMPROVED COMMUNICATION

In a traditional, senior-to-junior mentoring relationship the mentee's unique position in the organisation can aid informal communications because he or she straddles several levels.

For example, through the relationship with the mentor the junior management mentee has access to and is accepted by middle management. At the same time he or she is accepted in the lower managerial levels. Since the mentee is familiar with the language and mannerisms of both, he or she can efficiently communicate each group's ideas and opinions to the other. Rich informal communication networks improve productivity and efficiency in a company since they lead to more action, more innovation, more learning and swifter adjustment to changing business needs.

It can be lonely at the top. The chance to pass information to lower levels of management restores interdependence between management levels and eases the flow of ideas and information. This special communication network also facilitates easier working of other areas of management development.

Improved communication between headquarters and the field has been a significant result in a number of mentoring schemes. In one UK public sector organisation, headquarters was trying to rein in the regional barons, who had virtually declared independence and who actively discouraged their people from getting too close to headquarters employees. Headquarters had at the same time allowed itself to become somewhat aloof and disconnected. Deliberately pairing mentors and mentees across this divide increased understanding and established a quality of dialogue that overcame most of the hostilities.

Mentoring can sometimes benefit an organisation in unexpected ways, too. In one company a mentee was being mentored with the ultimate objective of helping him leave. A spokesman explained:

> This highly talented individual has gone as far as is possible in this company. We have no appropriate position for him so we are grooming him to take over a small corporation outside this company.
>
> In the meantime, for the three to five years that he stays with us, we benefit from his productivity and enthusiasm. In the future we will have a very useful ally.

A similar case arose in the north-west region of ICI's engineering department. The company explains:

> A sponsored mechanical engineering student began training with us and met her mentor for about three hours on her first day. Two weeks later, she left us and decided to go up to university, forsaking her engineering ambitions. During this time the mentor had provided support, primarily in a counselling mode, to a person living away from home for the first time, in a strange environment. He helped her rethink her ambitions and come to a decision on her future.

The most recent large-scale study of mentoring programmes in the UK (Industrial Society 1995) found that the most common intention behind introducing a mentoring programme was to provide help and encouragement for those taking qualifications (56%), followed by familiarising new recruits with the organisation (50%), 'providing growth for any employee who requests a mentor' (46%), developing senior managers (31%), and fast-tracking (31%). A handful of schemes addressed issues of equal opportunities.

Another study, this time from North America (CMSI 2001), asked programme co-ordinators how satisfied they were with the return on investment from mentoring. Some 52% said they were moderately satisfied, and 29% said they were highly satisfied.

IMPROVED RETENTION OF EMPLOYEES

Keeping the good people you have is increasingly being regarded as a core competitive advantage. In the war for talent, any reduction in employee turnover is a major benefit and mentoring has been shown to play a major positive role in retention.

A key indicator is 'intention to quit'. US studies of employees in large companies indicate that 35% are thinking of leaving within the next 12 months. However, among those who have a mentor, the figure falls to 16%. When it comes to actual resignations, the figures are even more startling. In SmithKline Beecham's finance division, staff turnover in 1999 was 27% – except among people who had a mentor, where it was 2%! Some allowance must be made in these figures for sample bias (people who have given up on the company are unlikely to seek a mentor within it) but that is only likely to have had a minor effect. More recently, analysis of workforce statistics by Sun Microsystems (now part of Oracle, having been acquired by the company in 2010) found that mentees were 23% less likely to quit and mentors 20% less likely to do so than peer control groups (Holincheck 2006). A US study of mentoring's impact on knowledge transfer and retention found that the mentoring relationship had a positive impact on employment commitment to their employer organisation (Fleig-Palmer 2009).

With graduates, opportunity to improve retention appears to lie in the transition period between the end of their formal induction and getting settled into their first supervisory job. Many mentoring schemes stopped when the graduate induction stopped. Good practice now seems to be to carry on for six months plus, to bridge this period of uncertainty and relatively low self-confidence.

OTHER ORGANISATIONAL BENEFITS

The benefits described thus far are relatively generic, but in most cases organisations will have very specific goals for introducing and maintaining a mentoring programme.

For example, it may have a very strong need to tackle diversity issues by opening up access to disadvantaged groups. Or it may wish to deal with the problems of stress and absenteeism by providing a safety valve for people's concerns. Other goals have included:

- helping 'invisible' people in finance become better known and demonstrate their abilities
- supporting managers in a bureaucratic culture to become more commercially minded
- establishing a professional development network for members of an engineering association
- helping entrepreneurs grow their management abilities in line with the demands of their businesses
- raising overall appraisal scores across a division
- helping new project teams gel more rapidly so they can achieve the assigned task ahead of the competition
- increasing creativity and the quality of risk taking.

Community organisations will have different goals again – from helping young people stay at school to helping long-term unemployed find permanent work. The one common factor we can find across all the goals of successful mentoring programmes is that they aim to achieve an important organisational objective by assisting people to achieve their potential.

CALCULATING THE COST BENEFIT OF MENTORING

How can you put a monetary value on the benefits of mentoring? In a community context, it is relatively easy to compare social expenditure on, for example, keeping young people at risk out of trouble with the costs of dealing with them when they do get into trouble. One study, for example, puts the return on investment for social services budgets at 272% (Anton and Temple 2007).

In the world of business and employment, it is possible to calculate approximate returns in respect of, for example, volume of sales by mentees versus unmentored counterparts. It's worth noting that many measures need only be done once, or at long intervals – once a credible ratio is identified, it can be applied over a number of years.

The most common measurements relate to retention. First, you can establish the turnover among people who are part of a mentoring relationship (both mentors and mentees), and among a peer group who are not. A minimum sample size of 12 is needed in each group. Typical ranges may be between 10% and 40% higher retention among the mentees. Now establish as best you can the following, bearing in mind that the numbers may vary considerably with job role and hierarchical level:

- cost of recruiting and/or training a replacement
- losses from the hiatus between departure of the employee and when their replacement becomes fully operational. (There may be several months with no-one in the role and even when the newcomer starts, they may need several more months before they are contributing at full strength. Typical losses here include work not done and loss of customers)
- systemic losses (impact on the work of other departments or functions).

If all this seems like too much work, you can use a rule of thumb to calculate the retention return on investment. A quick Internet search found a range of estimates of employee replacement costs, most falling between 50% and 200% of total annual employment cost. This kind of 'research' doesn't have high validity in general, so it is advisable to take a conservative view. Even then, the savings of a mentoring programme *always* greatly exceed the costs!

CONVINCING HR

The assumption that the entire HR community will be actively supportive of mentoring is seductive, but often wrong. HR business partners, for example, have a great many pressures on them and it's not unusual for some to resist the introduction of mentoring, because it's one more responsibility they have to take on. It's important, therefore, to engage with the HR community generally at an early stage of planning and to have a continuing dialogue with them about how each mentoring initiative will support other priorities they have. Creating a mentoring programme within HR itself can be a practical way of developing their appreciation of mentoring as an important part of their toolkit.

BENEFITS TO THE MENTEE

Most of the early literature on mentoring assumed that the beneficiary would normally be a career-minded graduate, with ambition and a desire to tap into the power sources of the organisation. The reality, of course, is that mentees come from a wide range of circumstances and that the benefits they seek are equally diverse.

Among the most common benefits we find across groups are:

- obtaining opportunities to network and advice on how to grow their networks
- having someone sympathetic who will understand difficult situations and help you work your way through them
- someone to believe in you and your ability
- help to work out what you want from your life and work, and how to make the appropriate choices and sacrifices
- help in developing greater confidence
- working through tactics to manage relationships with other people
- becoming more comfortable in dealing with people from unfamiliar backgrounds
- making sense of feedback from other sources – putting it into context and deciding how to deal with it
- being given an opportunity to challenge the organisation's thinking and be challenged in one's own.

Although promotion to a more senior level is often a goal for the mentee, for many people the aim is to develop as a person and open up wider possibilities.

For example, Liz sought a mentor to help her through the transition from full-time employment with a construction company to being a self-employed consultant. She sought from the mentor reassurance that she had the capability to fulfil the new role and assistance in planning how to make the switch in career. Hal, by contrast, wanted to stay in the same company, but become more effective in integrating his work and non-work lives. (In practice, he didn't have much of a life outside work.) For him, the mentor was someone who gave him permission to let go of responsibilities – even though, as someone outside the company, the mentor had no formal authority to do so. The mentor also provided a resource with whom Hal could talk when he found the going difficult.

EASIER INDUCTION FOR THOSE COMING STRAIGHT FROM UNIVERSITY OR MOVING TO A NEW COUNTRY

One mentor comments: 'Mentoring is a means of smoothing out graduates' transition from an educational environment – one of the major changes of their life – and enabling them to settle in more quickly.' According to the NHS in Wales, it 'provides exceptional opportunities and the unique status of having someone to trust in a bewildering environment', who can direct the mentee's learning opportunities.

A French mentee working in England stresses how important her mentor has been: 'My mentor has worked abroad and can speak French. He has helped me to adapt to the

British way of life. The scheme has definitely helped me to settle into this country and the company.'

The same principle can be applied at a much more senior level – expatriate managers taking on roles in a new country need to learn the business and social culture rapidly. They often value having a local person, perhaps from another company, helping them through this transition.

IMPROVED SELF-CONFIDENCE

The mentee gains a sense of self-worth and importance. The one-to-one relationship between the mentor and the mentee helps the latter feel that the company values him or her as an individual rather than as a cog in the managerial wheel. A mentor gives mentees (in particular graduates) undergoing frequent job rotation and management change a point of stability in what may seem an unpredictable environment. By helping them explore their own potential, the mentor also enables them to gain the self-knowledge necessary for well founded self-confidence. This aspect of mentoring is particularly relevant in the context of diversity – for example, some gender-based mentoring programmes recognise explicitly that women can sometimes be less self-confident than their male peers.

LEARNING TO COPE WITH THE FORMAL AND INFORMAL STRUCTURE OF THE COMPANY

Through the mentor, the mentee learns about the formal culture of an organisation, its values, its company image, objectives and predominant management style.

The mentor advises the mentee on self-presentation and behaviour so that he or she can fit into the company's formal culture. Mentees learn how to promote themselves within the organisation, when to be noticed as an individual, and when to be seen working collaboratively. In one large multinational, the primary aim of the mentoring scheme was to help 'invisible' people in the finance department manage their reputation within the organisation in general.

A mentee learns how to operate successfully within the informal culture. The mentor helps the mentee work through the internal company politics by identifying the key decision-makers in the company and which executives have the real power. As one senior executive comments: 'If you do not know the rules of the game, you cannot operate. The only way to know these rules is to be invited by an insider to participate.'

CAREER ADVICE AND ADVANCEMENT

A mentor can act as a role model – a tangible symbol of what the mentee can achieve in the future. As a role model, the mentor helps the mentee to focus career aspirations and turn them into realistic objectives. This is a double-edged sword, of course. The mentee has to beware he or she does not adopt the mentor's weaknesses as well as his or her strengths!

The mentee learns how to move up the promotion ladder. When the mentor is more senior and more experienced in corporate politics, he or she can help the mentee choose which jobs or projects to take and when to take them.

A female mentee in the social services sector was advised by her mentor to apply for a position she felt was unattainable. She comments:

> Before the internal interviews my mentor kept dropping my name to other senior administrative officers. He also frequently mentioned me to his own superior. Two other people in the department also applied for the vacancy. There was a woman on my level who had four years' experience and a man a grade higher. Everyone was very surprised when I got the promotion, since it was virtually unknown for someone of my age and experience to jump three levels.

Sometimes the mentor may suggest a total reorientation of career direction and may recommend a decrease or increase in the pace of advancement. One young manager recalls his attitude before he had a mentor:

> I was never sure about the timing of my career; when I should try to move upward or when I should stay in one position. I thought I ought to understand a job completely before I applied for promotion. Then a senior executive took an interest in my career and told me that if I stayed too long in one job I would probably get stuck there since I would not be recognised as a high-flyer. He advised me to apply for a post two grades above my current one. I didn't think I'd get it, but I did.

In traditional US mentoring, the mentor acts as a kind of sponsor, increasing the visibility of the mentee at executive levels by frequently describing how well his or her charge is progressing. The mentor may involve the mentee in his or her own projects and bring the mentee into executive meetings, inviting him or her to speak up. The mentor will brief the mentee beforehand on how to behave and give background on other subjects scheduled to be discussed.

Within the context of developmental mentoring, the mentee gains a sounding board who will help also him or her think through the decision-making process, through which the mentee selects between career options. The mentor helps the mentee identify what he or she values and to assess each option against his or her personal values and goals. As a result, the mentee gradually becomes more self-confident in making career choices and more adept at turning down those that are likely to lead to blind alleys.

MANAGERIAL TUTORAGE

A mentee may gain an insight into management processes through observing his or her mentor closely. The mentor provides an example of effective management and successful leadership and so accelerates the mentee's learning pace. This will apply only where the mentor and mentee are close enough in location/function for the mentee to observe in the normal course of work – or when the mentor specifically invites the mentee to shadow him or her (for example, in making a presentation).

An American mentee at Unisys comments:

> A mentor teaches the invaluable lesson of people management to a mentee who is often straight out of management school. He may know all about cost-benefit analysis and be an economic wizard, but he needs to be shown, for example, the importance of building support teams. A mentor has the experience to teach this.

A mentor is able to use his or her knowledge of the organisation to facilitate the mentee's access to areas otherwise closed. As a result, the mentee better understands how the organisation functions. Interviews with 'graduated' mentees reveal that one of the most valuable parts of the relationship is frequent discussion of how the business works and why middle and senior management do not do things the way the mentee would.

My own experience of being guided in this way remains fresh in my mind, although it happened some 25 years ago. As a young junior manager in the publishers McGraw-Hill, I was convinced my boss's boss, the publisher, had no idea what he was doing. So many decisions he made appeared to be irrational. Then he retired and his successor took me under his wing. Although there was a reporting line through my boss, we developed a strong rapport, especially as we travelled together on sales calls to major advertisers. John spent much of the time asking me about my job, but also talked to me about his own role and the context of the decisions he had to make. After a while, I realised that his predecessor wasn't as stupid as I'd thought; he had simply been operating at a level of management more complex than I had previously been exposed to. As I understood this more deeply, I applied what I was learning to my own department, and soon found myself promoted. I had, in effect, graduated to a new level of thinking that opened new doors for me.

A mentee has a legitimate source of advice and information in the mentor. For example, Jenny Blake found:

> It was very difficult to sell to the Middle East, especially since I was a woman and not allowed to go there. My mentor was in charge of the Middle East marketing section and was able to give me invaluable advice. He made me aware of important cultural differences and expectations when I was dealing with foreign marketing representatives – for instance, how they expected to be treated with respect and to be made a fuss of.

A junior manager describes the problem he faced without such a figure:

> Often a young manager has to try to gather information without betraying his ignorance. It is a very risky business. To get ahead you have to supply the right answers and not ask the wrong questions.

In a mentoring relationship, the mentee can ask naïve questions in an unthreatening atmosphere.

Helen Martin, a mentor at BP Chemicals, feels:

> A mentor is not an agony aunt or a miracle cure for all problems. We are simply people who have probably experienced similar situations in the past. We can therefore help the individual to find the best way to tackle an issue themselves.

LEADERSHIP DEVELOPMENT

Besides teaching managerial and people management skills, mentoring between senior and junior people reveals to the mentee how power is gained and wielded within the company. This is frequently a crucial lesson and is one of the most powerful sources of motivation for a young manager. A business school education may teach valuable theoretical skills but it cannot normally teach a manager how to exercise and feel comfortable with power, nor can it give him or her the confidence to make a major deal on his or her own initiative, take calculated risks or launch a new product. The mentor becomes a valuable sounding board for difficult decisions and for developing the skills of judgement.

A CONSCIENCE AND GUIDE

One of the behaviours that has impressed me about many of my mentees, particularly those at senior levels in organisations, is how easily I become a kind of conscience for them. Often, a week or so before our next meeting, they will recall all the actions they said they were going to take. Not wanting to admit they haven't dealt with them, they tend to switch focus from more day-to-day issues, so they can report progress to me. It's not that I have any authority over them, or seek to give approval or disapproval; what drives them is their own self-image and self-esteem.

Even when the mentor is not there, some mentees find they can use the mentoring process to address issues which they need to deal with. Here's a quote from one of my mentees:

> I do try to have conversations with you in my thoughts, to see if I can imagine what you'd say to me if told you some of this stuff. Occasionally, it sort of works, because I start to see things from the point of view I envisage you might take, and think about the kinds of questions you might ask me, to make me consider other perspectives (like: Who am I trying to prove things to and why?). Needless to say, when I do actually write to you, your reply always contains the unexpected and unpredictable.

TAPPING INTO EXPERIENCE

In leadership roles, particularly, it's valuable to have an independent sounding board – someone who has enough accumulated experience to empathise and help contextualise difficult issues. Says Richard McCord, Head of Finance at Centrica Energy Renewables, a participant on the Institute of Chartered Accountants in England & Wales' programme that links potential finance directors with experienced finance directors:

> My mentor is a former FTSE100 CFO, and I can talk to him confidentially about issues I am grappling with in the office. He has been there and done it himself, so he really understands where I'm coming from, and he can talk to me about how he dealt with similar challenges in his own career.

POTENTIAL DOWNSIDES FOR THE MENTEE

Having a mentor isn't always a blessing. Mentors who want to relive their own careers through their mentee, who 'want to stop you making the mistakes I did' or who have their own agenda for the mentee, can be stifling. Indeed, there is some evidence that having an overbearing mentor is a relatively common cause for young graduates to move employer. Conflict between mentor and line manager in another context can sometimes spill over into the mentee's relationship with either or both; conversely, having a line manager and mentor who are too cosy can also leave the mentee feeling exposed and reluctant to be too open in mentoring discussions.

Although it is rare in developmental mentoring, in sponsorship mentoring it is common for the relationship to develop unhealthy levels of dependence and for mentor and mentee to end up competing with each other for positions.

Finally, mentors who are locked into advice-giving mode may sometimes give the wrong advice. Mentees need to have the personal strength and awareness to make their own mind up about what they should do, even if the mentor is unhappy about it.

In general, the downsides of mentoring for the mentee emerge only when the mentors are poor or the programme is poorly designed and/or implemented.

BENEFITS FOR THE MENTOR

All the surveys and reviews I have conducted in recent years to evaluate the outcomes of mentoring programmes have indicated that the most frequent and most powerful benefits for mentors are:

- the learning they take from the experience, both in having to explain intuitive reasoning and in listening to a different perspective (ie problems mentees have with their bosses often cause mentors to reflect on similar issues their direct reports may have with them!)
- the opportunity to take reflective space in a hectic daily schedule
- the satisfaction of knowing you have made a difference to someone else
- the intellectual challenge of working on issues for which you do not have to take personal responsibility and that may take you into unfamiliar territory
- increased skills base and reputation.

Mentors questioned in the Industrial Society survey (1995) list the main benefits as prompting reassessment of their own views, leadership style, awareness of views of more junior staff, broader perspective, and discovering talent. Other benefits recorded were 'useful role for plateaued managers' and 'good for their own career progression'. Field experience suggests that when mentees are unaware of how much their mentors are getting out of the relationship, they are constrained in how much use they make of it.

LEARNING BY THE MENTOR

Mentors learn from mentees in a variety of ways. Firstly, it often occurs that the problems the mentee describes with their own manager sound horribly like the mirror image of issues the mentor has with one of his or her direct reports, prompting the mentor to reflect on his or her own behaviour. Secondly, explaining concepts to someone else is a good way to reinforce good practice in oneself. (Being seen as a role model also puts some pressure on the mentor to live up to his or her own values.)

Thirdly, the mentee is a superb resource of different experience, from which the mentor can extract learning. So much so that some companies now encourage mentoring pairs to be as different as they can tolerate. A good example is the following, recounted to me by the head of diversity in a public sector organisation:

> We had a senior manager, who simply wouldn't take the diversity message on board. He wasn't hostile, but he was dismissive – it simply wasn't enough of an issue to warrant his time or that of his direct reports. I took the gamble of asking him to become the mentor of a younger black man, who had potential to go far in the organisation. Shortly after that, he was promoted to become a regional manager. I met him on a train about six months into the mentoring relationship. He sat down beside me and said: 'My region is a hotbed of racism. What can I do about it?' The transformation had been achieved through listening to his mentee and seeing the world for the first time through black eyes.

Finally, the process of climbing the corporate ladder often means missing out on new ideas, techniques and technologies. There never seems to be the time for catching up and at a certain stage it becomes embarrassing to admit ignorance. Directing the learning experiences of the mentee gives the mentor the excuse he or she needs to devote the time to developing his or her own knowledge, too. It is also often acknowledged that the best way to learn is to teach. Some companies see mentees as a source of practical help for the mentor, while Midland Bank (now HSBC) has found that 'mentors have identified a need to increase their own business awareness of Midland Group in order to be better placed to respond to mentees'.

OPPORTUNITIES TO REFLECT

The more senior people become in an organisation, the less thinking time they seem to have. Many mentors regard their mentoring sessions as a welcome opportunity to adopt a change of pace. Some also report that the discipline of doing so helps them take reflective space to consider their own issues, too.

INTELLECTUAL CHALLENGE

The most successful mentoring relationships almost always evolve into a heightened level of mutual challenge, based upon the quality of both trust and respect between the two partners. Says one mentor:

> I wouldn't say I'm coasting in my job, but there's not a lot of intellectual stretch in it for me. But the problems my mentee brings me don't have straightforward answers. It's clear he relishes the discussions and lately we've branched out into wider areas of company policy. As a result, I've taken some ideas for change to my director and there's a high chance my job will expand to take some of them forward.

PERSONAL SATISFACTION

Helping a promising younger employee make progress can be a challenging and stimulating experience for a mentor, especially if his or her own career has reached a temporary or permanent plateau. Some managers, whose careers have reached a real or perceived plateau, find the challenge of mentoring both rewarding and stimulating and have been motivated to put new effort into their own career planning.

Mentors often find the mentoring relationship rewarding in many other ways – for example, in the sense of pride when the mentee achieves personal goals. Mentors also gain a sense of purpose in seeing the values and culture of an organisation handed to a new generation and in thinking more carefully about company policies. Says an industrial company with a long-running mentoring programme:

> Mentoring has made us question traditional thinking and practices, firstly to clarify them in our own minds before explaining them to our mentees, but also in not just defending them when challenged through the innocent, unadulterated eyes of the newcomer who has not yet been influenced by our culture.

INCREASED SKILLS BASE AND REPUTATION

A mentor who identifies promising employees acquires a reputation for having a keen insight into the needs of the company. This enhances his or her status with peers. The international accounting firm Merrill Lynch constructed a formal system of rewarding its mentors. Mentors' names are included in regularly circulated reports about mentees' accomplishments. Mentors are personally thanked by top management and are invited to be presenters at mentor briefing sessions, which are run for new participants. A spokesman for the firm explains: 'We feel we need to reward our mentors visibly and link their success publicly to the success of the mentoring programme.' One thing the mentor does not receive, and should not be led to expect from the scheme, is a direct payment or bonus to compensate him for his time and effort. One argument against such payments is that developing others is an integral part of every manager's job. A more powerful argument is that mentorship has to be built on friendship and is a close and personal relationship. Hence, turning it into a paid service is likely to hinder the relaxed and informal atmosphere necessary between mentor and mentee. In theory, this can become a problem if the company links human development objectives to a bonus scheme as part of the annual performance appraisal. In practice, the trick is to ensure that the mentor is neither especially rewarded nor penalised for this part of his job.

A few companies reward their mentors with status, inviting them to attend annual or bi-annual lunches or dinners with top management, where people strategies are discussed in open forum. Access to top management thinking – the inside track – is a prized commodity in most organisations!

Mentors at Pilkington Glass, one of the earliest graduate mentoring schemes in Europe, perceived the following benefits:

- We clarify and question our perception of the company.
- We see the company through fresh eyes.
- We improve our abilities so we have more to offer the mentee.
- We see people work in different ways depending on whether they are theorists, activists etc.
- It offers a new challenge.
- It offers a new learning experience.
- We understand the trauma new recruits experience and can be more sympathetic to others undergoing change.

POTENTIAL DOWNSIDES FOR THE MENTOR

As with the mentee, there are few significant downsides for mentors in carrying out the role if they do it well, other than that this is yet another demand on their time. For this reason, I generally advise new mentors to think very carefully before committing to more than one or two relationships, or they may not do them justice. Some of the other downsides I have observed over the years include:

- the breaking of confidentiality by the mentee (largely the mentor's fault)
- resentment from direct reports that they are not receiving similar time and effort invested in their development to that the mentor spends with the mentee
- loss of face when a succession of mentoring relationships fail (usually a sign of poor mentoring, but occasionally the result of a run of circumstances)
- having an over-demanding mentee (my favourite is the young graduate who came to see his mentor several times a *day* for reassurance – it took a threat by the mentor to throw the graduate through the window to stop this behaviour – by which time the relationship had nowhere to go!).

BENEFITS TO THE LINE MANAGER

It is surprising how little attention is paid to the line manager as a stakeholder in the mentoring relationship, yet he or she can make or break it. All too often, line managers only see the downsides of having a direct report mentored – the mentee will be taking more time away from his or her work for mentoring meetings, and *what are they saying about me?* The latter is a very valid concern. As a good working estimate, at least 90% of mentoring pairs spend some time discussing the mentee's relationship with his or her boss. This seems to hold broadly true at all levels, from new recruit at the lowest levels to chief executive.

Where the line manager sees the positives, however, it benefits everyone. When the mentee can discuss relationships with his or her boss and other working colleagues within the mentoring meeting, it allows the mentee to put his or her own and other people's behaviour and expectations into perspective. The mentee develops, with the mentor's help, better strategies for tackling issues around these relationships. If the mentee has a difficult conversation to initiate, he or she can practise it first with the mentor. As a result, relationships between the line manager and the mentee, and between the mentee and other colleagues, can be substantially improved.

The line manager also has access to a second opinion. If he or she feels the mentee isn't understanding or committing to something important, the line manager can recommend the mentee to take it up with his or her mentor. It sometimes happens that the line manager sees this as a great opportunity to dump all that troublesome development stuff on someone else. This is a wasted opportunity that could be used to invest more time into the coaching role and raising the performance of the whole team.

SUMMARY

Listing the benefits of mentoring is useful in developing the general argument in favour of the process. There is a deeper reason, however, for developing a clarity about the expected outcomes of any mentoring programme. Where people have high clarity about the organisation's expectations from a mentoring programme, they are more likely to be clear about the objectives of their own relationship and this, in turn, appears to lead to more productive pairings. As we shall examine in subsequent chapters, knowing what you want out of mentoring is critical to getting what you want!

CHAPTER 5

What Makes an Effective Mentor an Effective Mentee?

One of the problems with so much of the research literature on mentoring is that it assumes that the qualities required of mentors are the same in all contexts. Yet simple observation tells us this isn't so. The qualities that are relevant for mentors and mentees in a programme aimed to help at-risk teenagers are not the same as those for people engaged in a mentoring programme aimed at those undertaking their first general manager job overseas. Mentoring virtually requires different skills to mentoring face-to-face. Yes, there will be generic similarities – for example, the mentees' need to understand and come to terms with their respective environments and the mentors' need to be able to empathise with the situations the mentees describe – but the circumstances and the purpose of the relationship defines the required behaviours and competencies. In circumstances such as reverse mentoring, diversity mentoring or cross-cultural mentoring (see Chapters 11, 16 and 14), a raft of additional competences come into play.

Mentoring is a disciplined process, although it has few rules. A starting point in selection is that the organisation should decide and explain carefully who it wants to mentor and why, the criteria for selection, and who will do the selecting. The criteria will vary from company to company, but should always be drawn against the background of some key questions:

- How much will this person gain from a mentoring relationship? (Mainly for mentees, but also relevant for mentors.)
- What is the transition that we expect mentees to make?
- What is the experience exchange we aim to achieve?
- What attributes in the mentor will be most likely to make the relationship a success?
- What attributes in the mentee will contribute to a successful mentoring relationship?

In this chapter we explore some of the competencies of mentors and mentees and set out some principles for managing selection and matching processes.

CHOOSING MENTORS

In theory, at least, the mentee should be the starting point for selecting the mentor. In practice, some organisations have begun by creating a pool of mentors and gone looking for suitable mentees for them (or sent them off to find their own!). This has the disadvantage of creating some level of obligation to find a mentee for any would-be mentor, no matter how incompetent they may be in the role, and risks making the whole process mentor-driven.

Every manager's job should entail a significant amount of developing other people and indeed some companies make it a virtual condition of each manager's advancement. In practice, however, some people are better cut out for it and more motivated towards doing so than others. Moreover, the ability to act as a mentor will often vary according to the manager's own stage of career development. For example, someone seeking or undergoing a major change in their own career development may not have the mental energy to spare for someone else's issues.

In selecting mentors, a good starting point is having a clear sense of the qualities that make a good developer of other people's potential. These qualities may differ from company to company, even from division to division. Equally, the ideal mentor for one person may be a disaster for another. It's important to have a reasonable level of diversity among mentors (level, discipline, experience, gender, culture and so on) to provide requisite variety and flexibility to meet mentees' different needs. The smaller or less diverse the pool of mentors, the harder it is to ensure that people have a good match. Sometimes organisations make the mistake of trying to be over-specific about the person specification for mentors. The result is that they miss out on people who, with the right support, may be a good fit for mentees, who also don't fit the mould.

There have been numerous attempts to define the competencies of a mentor, most of them flawed by a failure to define to begin with what role is being measured. There is also a great deal of confusion in the literature between practical skills or competencies (what mentors do/how they do it) and outcomes (the results of the mentoring relationship). My own view of the skill set has evolved significantly over the years and is now most succinctly summarised in Figure 7.

Figure 7 The ten mentor competencies

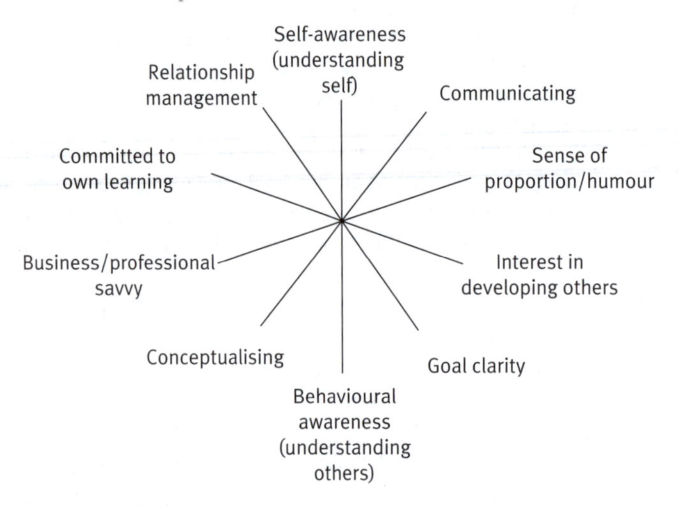

Source: This diagram first appeared in CLUTTERBUCK, D. (2000a) Ten core mentor competencies. *Organisations & People*. Vol 7, No 2, November. Reproduced by kind permission of The Association of Management Education and Development (AMED), www.amed.org.uk

SELF-AWARENESS (UNDERSTANDING SELF)

Mentors need high self-awareness in order to recognise and manage their own behaviours within the helping relationship and to use empathy appropriately. The activist, task-focused manager often has relatively little insight into these areas – indeed, he or she may actively avoid reflection on such issues, depicting them as 'soft' and of low priority. Such attitudes and learned behaviours may be difficult to break.

Providing managers with psychometric tests and other forms of insight-developing questionnaires can be useful *if they are open to insights in those areas*. However, it is easy to dismiss such feedback, even when it also comes from external sources, such as working colleagues.

Some managers actively seek psychometric analysis, yet fail to internalise it through the inner dialogue essential to carrying knowledge through to action. Not that all personality insights should necessarily lead to action; in many cases, the role of internal dialogue may be to help the person accept that a behaviour pattern or perceived weakness can reasonably be lived with.

Interviews with mentors and mentees indicate that having some level of personality and motivational insight is useful for building rapport in the early stages of a relationship. 'This is me/this is you' is a good starting point for open behaviours. People who have low self-awareness can be helped in a number of ways. One is through dialogue with a trained counsellor/facilitator, helping them relate psychometric and other behavioural feedback to specific actions and behaviours. By learning how to think through such issues for themselves, they may become more effective at doing the same for others. Figure 8 shows a useful way of looking at this kind of approach to building self-awareness. If nothing else, the model helps open up some of the hidden boxes in the Johari window!

An important debate here is whether low self-awareness is the result of low motivation to explore the inner self (disinterest), or high motivation to avoid such exploration, or simply an inability to make complex emotional and rational connections (in which case there may be physiological aspects to consider as well). The approach in helping someone develop self-awareness will be different in each case and is likely to be least effective in bringing about personal change.

Figure 8 Building self-awareness

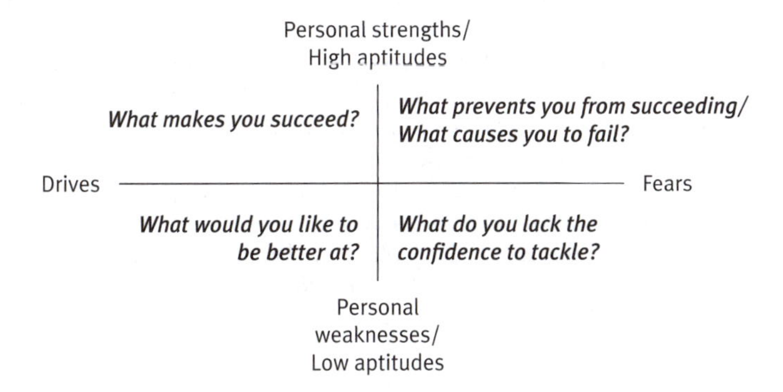

BEHAVIOURAL AWARENESS (UNDERSTANDING OTHERS)

Like self-awareness, understanding how others behave and why they do so is a classic component of emotional intelligence. To help others manage their relationships, the mentor must have reasonably good insight into patterns of behaviour between individuals and groups of people. Predicting the consequences of specific behaviours or courses of action is one of the many practical applications of this insight.

Developing clearer insight into the behaviours of others comes from frequent observation and reflection. Supervision groups can help the mentor recognise common patterns of behaviour by creating opportunities for rigorous analysis.

BUSINESS/PROFESSIONAL SAVVY

There isn't a great deal to be done here in the short term – there are very few shortcuts to experience and judgement. However, the facilitator can help the potential mentor understand the need for developing judgement and plan how to acquire relevant experience.

Again, the art of purposeful reflection is a valuable support in building this competence. By reviewing the learning from a variety of experiences, the manager widens his or her range of templates and develops a sense of patterns in events. The more frequently he or she is able to combine stretching experience with focused reflection – either internally or in a dialogue with others – the more substantial and rapid the acquisition of judgement.

A useful method of helping people develop business savvy is to create learning sets, where a skilled facilitator encourages people to share their experience and look for patterns.

SENSE OF PROPORTION/GOOD HUMOUR

Is good humour a competence? I would argue strongly that it is. Laughter, used appropriately, is invaluable in developing rapport, in helping people to see matters from a different perspective, in releasing emotional tension. Laughter is also closely associated with creative thinking (an essential component of the mentoring conversation) and with general stress-reduction and well-being. It's also important that mentor and mentee should *enjoy* the sessions they have together. Enthusiasm is far more closely associated with learning than with boredom!

Can adults develop a good sense of humour if they do not already have one? Probably not easily. However, a good deal of pessimistic attitude and cynicism derive from a feeling of disempowerment and a perception of lack of control over one's circumstances. Such attitude changes can be created by helping people become more at ease with themselves, with their role in the organisation and their potential to influence their environment. The most obvious way to make that happen – apart from wholesale culture change within the organisation – is for the individual to have his or her own mentor.

In practice, good humour is a vehicle for achieving a sense of proportion – a broader perspective that places the organisation's goals and culture in the wider social and business context. People acquire this kind of perspective by ensuring that they balance their day-to-day involvement with work tasks against a portfolio of other interests. Some of these may be related to work – for example, developing a broader strategic understanding of how the business sector is evolving; others are unrelated to work and may encompass science, philosophy or any other intellectually stimulating endeavour. In general, the broader the scope of knowledge and experience the mentor can apply, the better sense of proportion he or she can bring.

COMMUNICATION COMPETENCE

Communication isn't a single skill; it is a combination of a number of skills. The generic skills include:

- *Listening* – opening the mind to what the other person is saying, demonstrating interest/attention, encouraging him or her to speak, holding back on filling the silences.
- *Observing as receiver* – being open to the visual and other non-verbal signals, recognising what is *not* said – parallel processing – analysing what the other person is saying, reflecting on it, preparing responses. Effective communicators do all of these in parallel, slowing down the dialogue as needed to ensure that they do not over-emphasise preparing responses at the expense of analysis and reflection; equally, they avoid becoming so mired in their internal thoughts that they respond inadequately or too slowly.
- *Projecting* – crafting words and their emotional 'wrapping' in a manner appropriate for the situation and the recipient(s).
- *Observing as projector* – being open to the visual and other non-verbal signals as clues to what the recipient is hearing/understanding; adapting tone, volume, pace and language appropriately.

- *Exiting* – concluding a dialogue or segment of dialogue with clarity and alignment of understanding (ensuring message received in both directions).

Other specific communication competencies for mentors that are useful to include in training are:

- use of metaphor and analogy
- visual communication (using diagrams, pictures etc)
- use of silence
- use of body language.

Some tools to help develop these competencies come from neurolinguistic programming (NLP) and situational communication. NLP has many good techniques, which a competent communicator can incorporate into their portfolio of responses, but a lot of the theory remains at best unproven – and NLP cannot make a poor communicator into a naturally good one. (They tend to become robotic and prone to conscious or unconscious manipulation of the client.)

Situational communication, developed from research at Birkbeck College, helps people understand the communication requirements of different commonplace situations and focus on the development of specific skills in those situations. It thus has a very high utility factor. Alongside situational communication is a very practical method of diagnosing communication styles, which enables the individual to become more self-aware of his or her own style preferences and recognise the preferences of others. Good mentors will generally need a strong sense of situation and a high degree of adaptability between styles.

CONCEPTUAL MODELLING

Effective mentors have a portfolio of models they can draw upon to help mentees understand the issues they face. These models can be self-generated (eg the result of personal experience), drawn from elsewhere (eg models of company structure, interpersonal behaviours, strategic planning, career planning) or – at the highest level of competence – generated on the spot as an immediate response.

According to the situation and the learning styles of the mentee, it may be appropriate to present these models in verbal or visual form. Or the mentor may not present them at all – simply use them as the framework for asking penetrating questions.

Developing the skills of conceptual modelling takes time, once again. It requires a lot of reading, often beyond the normal range of materials that cross the individual's desk. Training in presentation skills and how to design simple diagrams can also help. But the most effective way can be for the mentor to seize every opportunity to explain complex ideas in a variety of ways, experimenting to see what works with different audiences. Eventually, there develops an intuitive, instinctive understanding of how best to put across a new idea.

COMMITMENT TO OWN CONTINUED LEARNING

Effective mentors become role models for self-managed learning. They seize opportunities to experiment and take part in new experiences. They read widely and are reasonably efficient at setting and following personal development plans. They actively seek and use behavioural feedback from others. They see the mentoring relationship itself as a significant opportunity for their own learning.

STRONG INTEREST IN DEVELOPING OTHERS

Effective mentors have an innate interest in achieving through others and in helping others recognise and achieve their potential. This instinctive response is important in establishing and maintaining rapport and in enthusing the mentee, building confidence in what he or she could become.

BUILDING AND MAINTAINING RAPPORT/RELATIONSHIP MANAGEMENT

The skills of rapport-building are difficult to define. When asked to describe rapport in their experience, managers' observations can be distilled into five characteristics:

1. **Trust:** Will they do what they say? Will they keep confidences?
2. **Focus:** Are they concentrating on me? Are they listening without judging?
3. **Empathy:** Do they have goodwill towards me? Do they try to understand my feelings, and viewpoints?
4. **Congruence:** Do they acknowledge and accept my goals?
5. **Empowerment:** Is their help aimed at helping me stand on my own feet as soon as is practical?

To a considerable extent, the skills of building and maintaining rapport are contained in the other competencies already described. However, additional help in developing rapport-building skills may be provided through situational analysis – creating opportunities for the individual to explore with other people how and why they feel comfortable and uncomfortable with them in various circumstances. This kind of self-knowledge can be invaluable in developing more sensitive responses to other people's needs and emotions.

The mentor can also be encouraged to think about the contextual factors in creating rapport. Avoiding meeting on the mentor's home ground (eg in his or her office) may be an obvious matter, but where would the mentee feel most comfortable? Sensitivity to how the meeting environment affects the mentoring dialogue can be developed simply by talking the issues through, both in formal or informal training and with the mentee.

GOAL CLARITY

The mentor must be able to help the mentee sort out what he or she wants to achieve and why. This is quite hard to do if you do not have the skills to set and pursue clear goals of your own.

Goal clarity appears to derive from a mixture of skills including systematic analysis and decisiveness. Like so many of the other mentoring competencies, it may best be developed through opportunities to reflect and to practise.

One of my areas of particular focus in research in recent years has been the role of goals in coaching and mentoring. There is an assumption in much of the literature on mentoring that it is important for the mentee to start with a clear and specific goal. In reality, that is largely untrue. In my own doctoral research (Clutterbuck 2007b), I found that there was no significant correlation between having or committing to a clear goal at the beginning of the relationship and either relationship quality or outcomes for either mentor or mentee. Other studies bear out the same theme – goals in mentoring are largely emergent. The mentoring relationship is to a large extent a vehicle for helping people work out what they want to achieve (or who they want to become) and how this meets their internal values, before working out how they will progress.

THE MENTOR ACRONYM

In the first edition of this book, back in 1985, I incorporated a useful acronym from a North American article, which maintained that the mentor:

- **M**anages the relationship
- **E**ncourages

- **N**urtures
- **T**eaches
- **O**ffers mutual respect
- **R**esponds to the mentee's needs.

MANAGING THE RELATIONSHIP

Once again, views have moved on. While the notion of the mentor managing the relationship still holds favour in some US companies, the wider global expectation is for the mentor to assist the mentee in taking over the management of the relationship. Similarly, when it comes to responding to the mentee's needs, it is no longer seen as a good idea for the mentor to be more than minimally interventionist. Rather, the mentor helps the mentee work out his or her own solutions. The concepts of encouragement, nurturing, teaching and offering mutual respect remain largely unchanged, however, and we repeat those notes here (with minor amendments) for background information.

THE MENTOR WHO ENCOURAGES AND MOTIVATES

The ability to encourage and motivate is another important interpersonal skill that the mentor must have in abundance, if the relationship with the mentee is to reach its full potential.

The mentor must be able to recognise the ability of the mentee and make it clear to the mentee that he or she believes in the mentee's capacity to progress in their career. The mentor must be willing to let the mentee turn to him or her for as long as needed, as well as be willing to help the mentee to eventually become independent.

The mentor encourages the mentee through recognising the different roles he or she can play. For example, in relationships between a young person and an older, more senior colleague, for a certain period the mentor can be a reassuring parental figure to whom the mentee can turn for support and sympathy. The mentor must also at this stage be willing to let the mentee identify with him or her and use him or her as a role model. At other stages of the relationship, the mentor can encourage the mentee to become more independent and make individual decisions.

One mentor in a civil service department recalls how difficult it was to learn this lesson:

> I had this intelligent individual who was highly motivated. I expected his progress to be extremely rapid, but was surprised to find that he seemed to depend on me for quite some time. I was worried about it and considered whether I ought to try to force him somehow to make his own decisions unaided by me. Eventually I decided to go at his pace and not the pace I expected. He is now at a higher level than me in the company, but recently came to me to thank me for not rushing him in that first year. He explained he had found it very difficult to adjust to his new job and had found the new pressure especially hard to cope with. Apparently, my support and encouragement had kept him going through it all.

The ability to encourage and motivate is an especially important skill for the mentor if the company has a deliberate policy of not promoting high-flyers until they have a broad base of experience. If these people are to be prevented from seeking faster promotion elsewhere, the mentor has to help them extract a high degree of job satisfaction from their experiences now and let them know they will reap the rewards for their patience later in their career.

One corporate mentor explains:

> We get so many MBAs coming straight from college who expect to race up the promotion ladder. Without a mentor to explain the system to them, few of them

> realise that this is just not the way we operate. If we discover a talented individual, we allocate them to different areas of the company before we promote them so that they understand and have been directly involved in all aspects of the business.

A young manager in a small British defence firm emphasises the point with reference to the difference the support of a senior manager made to his career:

> I graduated with an engineering degree and immediately took my MBA. I then successfully applied for the position of technical manager, which had just been newly created in a defence firm. I found my new job extremely difficult because I was dealing with engineers who were obviously far more experienced than I and whose technical knowledge far outmatched mine. They plainly resented my presence. A few were even openly hostile to me. Fortunately, since my position was new to the company itself, a senior manager had been asked to help me as much as possible. He supported and encouraged me. Sometimes it was only this which stopped me from leaving. More importantly, he helped me to recognise that my difficulties were not caused by my own incompetence or failure, as I had originally thought, but that in fact the engineers' hostility had another cause and was aimed at my position rather than at me personally. He explained that the company had been trying to get the structure of the technical side of the company more into line with central management. I was just unlucky to be caught in the middle of a war between management and the engineers.

Armed with the knowledge that he was fully supported by top management, this young manager was able to ride the storm until he won the respect of the engineering staff.

THE MENTOR WHO NURTURES

The mentor must be able to create an open, candid atmosphere that will encourage the mentee to confide in and trust him or her. The mentor is there to draw out the mentee and help discover his or her identity and how they fit into the organisation, profession or society. With the help of the mentor, the mentee undertakes self-assessment and discovers where his or her skills, aspirations, values and interests lie. Most importantly, the mentor must be able to listen to the mentee and ask open-ended questions that will draw the less experienced person out.

One key test of the mentor who nurtures is a track record of bringing along subordinates. If his or her department has provided a consistent breeding ground for talented young supervisors and managers, then the chances are high that he or she will make a good mentor for people from other departments.

THE MENTOR WHO TEACHES

This is a skill that the mentor may need to be taught, because being a really good teacher does not come naturally to many people. Highly ambitious, self-motivated people (and the description applies to most people who make it to top management) often lack the patience to teach. Yet the mentor must know how to help the mentee maximise his or her opportunities to learn. The mentor does this by creating a stimulating environment that consistently challenges the mentee to apply theory to the real world of management.

A mentor may teach his or her mentee using the following methods:

- The mentor holds 'what if?' sessions where he or she guides the mentee in problem-solving discussions to encourage him or her to discover as many alternatives as possible.
- The mentor discusses with the mentee real problems the mentor is currently dealing with or has recently dealt with. Rather than expand upon the cleverness of his or her own solutions, the mentor asks the mentee what course of action he or she would take.

The mentor can often complete the analysis by telling the mentee the solutions he or she actually devised and why they were chosen. In this way, through mini internal case studies, the mentor gives the mentee an insight into decision-making in higher-level jobs.

- The mentor plays devil's advocate. In a protective environment, the mentor teaches the mentee how to assert his or her opinions and influence the listener in difficult situations.
- The mentor plays aggressive and threatening roles so that the mentee learns to handle stressful and potentially explosive situations. A vice-chairman in an advertising company was helped in his career by a senior executive in the corporation. This mentor invited opposition from his mentee and frequently acted in a domineering and brusque manner. The mentor's aim was to help develop in his mentee an aggressiveness that he considered was essential for success in that field. The vice-chairman comments:

> Before I met my mentor I was not particularly forceful. However, when I talked to him I found I had the choice either to be chewed up, or to assert myself. He constantly pushed me in these one-to-one confrontations so that now when I talk to a client I have developed a way of expressing my opinions with weight and force.

THE MENTOR WHO OFFERS MUTUAL RESPECT

An essential ingredient in any mentoring relationship is mutual respect between the two partners. If the mentee does not respect and trust his or her mentor's opinions, advice and influence – and vice versa – the benefits from the relationship will be severely limited. Programme managers must remember that a mentee's attitude towards the mentor will inevitably be influenced by the mentor's general reputation within the company. Is he or she respected by their peers, for example?

Within sponsorship mentoring, mentees tend to assess:

- the mentor's professional reputation. For example, if the mentor has been associated with too many failed projects, the protégé is unlikely to feel that a close and visible relationship will benefit his or her career
- the mentor's interpersonal skills. For example, a protégé may feel that a rewarding relationship might be difficult to establish with someone who communicates mainly through memos and e-mails
- the mentor's status amongst their peer colleagues
- the mentor's corporate alliances and networks, both inside and outside the organisation. The protégé must believe that the mentor has enough influence and sufficiently wide connections to make a tangible difference to his or her career.

Within developmental mentoring, respect comes less from an appreciation of what the mentor can do for the mentee than from what he or she can help the mentee do on his or her own – what they can learn from conversations with them mentor. Inevitably, many of the same reputational factors will apply, because these will affect the mentee's perception of the nature and scope of learning from the mentor.

MENTOR MOTIVATIONS

Investigations into mentor motivations (Engstrom 1997/8) indicate that the mentor's motivations have an impact on how effective they are. It seems that the more a mentor is motivated by altruism (eg giving back, preventing the mentor from making the same mistakes as I did), the less effective they are. From the experiences of mentees who have had deeply altruistic mentors, it seems that the mentor may often slip automatically into a mindset that is mostly about them – 'I have all this knowledge, experience and goodwill and advice to give, and I want you to take it'. Other negative motivations arise from making mentoring an obligation. While ideally all managers should become mentors to people outside their teams, pushing this expectation too hard raises the risk that people will sign up just to tick the box. When this happens, the quality of mentoring diminishes considerably.

Positive motions for mentoring seem to focus around personal learning and the joy that comes from discovery (both their own and the mentee's).

So it's important to clarify upfront what motivates potential mentors. A brief interview is usually enough to gain a pretty good idea of this. If someone comes with a high altruistic motivation, the interview may be enough to make them rethink, and it is common for them to return some time later with a different and more appropriate mindset.

CHECKLIST – IDEAL CHARACTERISTICS TO SEEK IN A MENTOR

Look for someone who:

- already has a good record for developing other people
- has a genuine interest in seeing younger people advance and can relate to their problems
- has a wide range of current skills to pass on
- has a good understanding of the organisation, how it works, and where it is going
- combines patience with good interpersonal skills and an ability to work in an unstructured programme
- has sufficient time to devote to the relationship
- can command a mentee's respect
- has his or her own network of contacts and influence
- is still keen to learn.

THE MENTOR FROM HELL

The mentor from hell exists – at least in the minds of mentees who have been unfortunate enough to encounter him or her. Consider this story from a young manager, recalling his days as a graduate mentee:

> Once every six months I'd be summoned to the great man's presence. I'd come slightly early and he would always be running late. I'd sit in the ante-room, where his secretary made sure I didn't steal any paper clips. As I was shown in, he'd always be putting away my file – reminding himself of who I was. Then he'd talk at me solidly for over an hour. Finally, he'd ask if I'd found it useful. I never had the courage to tell him the truth ... !

This mentor hadn't a clue and probably didn't want to know how to do the job properly anyway; it might have spoiled the ego trip. He might have been horrified to be told that good mentors speak for less than 20% of the time, address issues raised by the mentee, and expect to engage in quality dialogue on a much more frequent basis than once every six months.

Some other common toxic mentors include:

- people who rush around 'helping' others in order to avoid addressing their own issues and often end up transferring their problem into the mentee's situation
- people who have an alternative agenda
- people who take umbrage when the mentee adopts a different solution from the one they have proposed
- people who are not switched on to their own learning.

CHOOSING MENTEES

'So what's the business problem?' That's the first question I typically ask when working with an organisation to design a mentoring programme, because without a clear target group with a specific issue to manage, it may be difficult to establish whether the project has been worthwhile. Very often there is a mixture of objectives, but the most common seem to be:

- to retain key staff
- to overcome institutional barriers to progress for disadvantaged groups
- to build bridges between parts of the organisation
- to support culture change, especially after a merger or major acquisition
- to support a competency programme.

Defining the business (or community) issue largely defines the selection criteria for mentees, whether these are used to identify people through some central co-ordinating mechanism or to enable people to decide for themselves whether to apply.

Mentoring schemes for high-flyers often have some element of initial evaluation or assessment built in to ensure that they have the commitment and potential to make effective use of the opportunity they have been given.

Some ground rules, which have been learned the hard way in a wide variety of organisations (but that doesn't stop other companies repeating the mistakes), include:

- Don't assume that everyone in the target group wants to have a mentor. A large financial services company in the City dutifully followed orders from New York and set up mentoring pairs for all its middle-level women, matching them either with more senior women or male executives. In interviews, many of the women reported that they were bemused by the project. While they had had very pleasant lunches, neither they nor the mentors were clear about what the purpose of meeting was, and many felt patronised by what they saw as a heavy-handed approach. Others saw the initiative as some kind of mark of inferiority – 'Somebody has decided I have a problem, but they haven't the balls to tell me what it is,' said one woman.
- Don't assume that any target group sees itself as a group. One company, concerned that hardly anyone had signed up for a mentoring programme for people from ethnic minorities, discovered that the intended beneficiaries saw themselves either in their professional status or from much smaller communities – Muslims and Hindus saw their issues as very different and resented being lumped together.
- Accept that some people may have less need of a mentor at some points in their career than others. Giving the individual some say in when he or she becomes involved increases personal commitment to the process. An example I encountered involved a small group of middle managers who had not met their assigned mentors more than once or twice over almost a year. When quizzed about their reluctance, they explained that the mentor was fine, but not currently needed. Each of them had an excellent and productive developmental relationship with their line manager and with the tutor on the leadership course they were taking. 'Right now, I'm concentrating on applying what I'm learning to my current job and my performance in a couple of skills areas,' explained one. 'I can't cope with any more help at the moment. But I'd expect to make use of my mentor when I need to put all this into the bigger picture and establish some longer-term development goals.'
- Sometimes a mentor is not the most appropriate form of help. In the early days of mentoring programmes it was common for companies to pair graduate entrants with a mentor from day one. Practical experience shows this is usually a mistake. It typically takes three to six months in the organisation before the mentee understands enough of the systems and culture to ask insightful questions, but by this time one or both parties has often become bored and the relationship struggles to get back on course.

Organisations are increasingly opting instead for a six-month buddy system, where the graduate is teamed up with a recruit from the previous year who can show him or her the ropes.

THE EFFECTIVE MENTEE

At first sight, it may seem invidious to set out criteria for 'good' mentees. After all, surely the purpose of mentoring is at least partially to help people become more effective. However, how the mentee behaves can have a substantial impact on the quality and type of help he or she receives.

Most of the research into mentee attributes comes from the sponsorship mentoring literature. For example, an early study by US author Michael Zey (1984) listed the following attributes that helped mentees attract mentors:

- *Intelligence* – the mentee must be able to identify and solve business problems rapidly.
- *Ambition* – the mentee must be gifted and have the ambition to channel his ability into career advancement. The mentor also wants to further his career and looks for a mentee who will advance through the organisation with him.
- *Succession potential* – the mentor also wants a mentee who demonstrates that he is capable of performing the mentor's own job. The mentor wants to be sure that he has groomed a replacement.
- *Strong interpersonal skills* – the mentee must be able to make new alliances for the mentor as well as retaining the ones the mentor has already established.

Other studies have found that:

- Employees who performed visible, risky and important tasks were three times as likely to form mentoring relationships of their own accord as those who took few risks.
- Mentoring relationships are more mutually rewarding, if the mentee has a general, all-round reputation for hard work, enthusiasm and ability.

In developmental mentoring, analysis of the case study literature and experience from a wide variety of programmes suggest that desirable qualities include being:

- realistically ambitious for the relationship, having clear expectations of what it can do for them
- unambiguous about their own role in selecting and bringing issues for discussion
- prepared to take the prime responsibility for meeting arrangements and the agenda
- possessed of a personal sense of purpose, at least in embryo
- willing to challenge and be challenged
- able to approach the relationship with respect, good humour and openness
- aware of the obligations the relationship places on them, with regard to their behaviour towards the mentor and to interested third parties, such as their line manager
- proactive – Scandinavian studies of mentoring relationships suggest that the most effective are those where the mentee is highly proactive and the mentor relatively reactive
- able to articulate their issues clearly and explicitly
- emotionally self-aware and capable of reflection
- able to give and receive critical feedback
- balanced in terms of self-respect and self-confidence.

In theory, the more closely the mentee meets these characteristics, the more he or she (and the mentor) is likely to get out of the relationship. This is generally fine in the context of mid-career high-flyers. However, in practice, in many cases the objective of the mentoring may be to enable people to *acquire* some of these characteristics. For example, programmes for young, inner-city teenagers at risk start with the handicap that they have little self-belief or sense of purpose, cannot articulate their issues, and have low self-awareness. Increased self-confidence is also a common outcome of diversity-based mentoring programmes.

For the mentoring programme manager it's important to establish how prepared for mentoring the potential mentees are. If some mentees lack too many of the qualities above, it may be appropriate to offer them other forms of support, such as remedial coaching or other focused development opportunities, such as awareness, assertiveness or communication training before they join the programme, or as an additional simultaneous resource.

SUMMARY

No-one expects mentors or mentees to be perfect. Indeed, the mentoring relationship is one where developing skills and positive personal characteristics are both the goal and the core of the process. However, in selecting participants in a mentoring programme, it is important to consider what each is able and willing to learn and to contribute. One of the gratifying aspects of the introductory briefings I have given in many companies about to launch mentoring programmes is that so many people who have come with the intent of becoming a mentor decide instead (or as well) to be a mentee; and vice versa!

CHAPTER 6

Matching Mentors and Mentees

One of the advantages of informal mentoring is that would-be mentees can have as many bites at the cherry as they like until they find a relationship that works for them. In formal, structured programmes that isn't so easy. Experience has led to some practical ground rules that avoid some of the worst problems:

- **Avoid 'shotgun marriages' wherever possible**. The least successful matches are typically those where the mentor and mentee feel they have been imposed upon each other. Next least successful are those where pairings are nominated by top management. If you cannot allow people some element of choice, at least make sure that participants understand how the matching process has been made. It's now relatively common for programmes to include match-making procedures based on a variety of information about the mentee's learning needs, the mentor's experience, and some general psychometric data, intended to avoid strong clashes of values or learning styles. (See the case studies at the end of this chapter.)

  The greatest level of buy-in from participants seems to come from giving the mentee a selection of three potential mentors they can meet, if they wish. It is very rare for anyone to ask for more than the original three. Making it clear that mentees will make their selection according to the degree of rapport they feel and the closeness of match with their learning need seems to overcome most of the potential problems of mentors feeling turned down. When I first suggested to programme managers that mentees should explain their choice in person to each of the potential mentors, there were understandable concerns that mentees would feel intimidated. In practice, the honesty of this approach is usually much appreciated by both the chosen and non-chosen mentors. It is common for the mentee to end up with one formal mentor and one or more informal, ad hoc ones!
- **Equally, avoid giving people an unguided choice**. Experience suggests that many people will select as a mentor someone whom they know well and get on with. Alternatively, they will seek a high-flyer on whose coat-tails they can hang. Neither is likely to lead to a successful mentoring relationship. Too much familiarity allows little grit in the oyster – the amount of learning potential is relatively low. Seeking a high-flyer starts the relationship off with a set of unhealthy expectations. Moreover, the high-flyer may be too preoccupied with his or her own career to give much time to someone else.
- **Avoid too great a hierarchy or experience gap between mentor and mentee**. Figure 9 illustrates the point.

If the experience gap is too narrow, mentor and mentee will have little to talk about. If it is too great, the mentor's experience will be increasingly irrelevant to the mentee. Whereas once upon a time we could broadly say that there should not be more than two layers of hierarchy between mentor and mentee, organisation structures are now so complex and a single layer of management may hide such a wide variation in status, experience and ability that such a simple rule no longer suffices. It is up to the mentee and the programme manager to establish an appropriate learning distance.

Figure 9 The hierarchy/experience gap between mentor and mentee

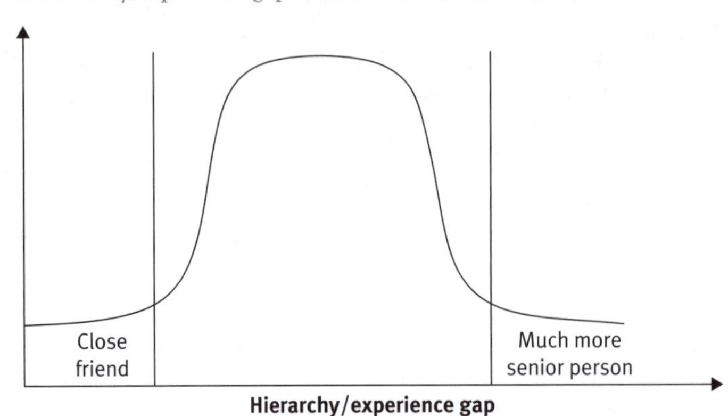

The issue is made more complex by the question of how important the experience gap is in terms of relationship purpose. In some programmes and relationships the mentor's specific knowledge and experience in a field is a key driver of learning; in others, it plays a relatively minor role, with broader life experience being more important. The relationship will also be strengthened if the mentor perceives that they have something to learn from the mentee's experience. An extension of the same principle is shown in Figure 10.

Figure 10 How experience and discipline affect rapport and learning potential

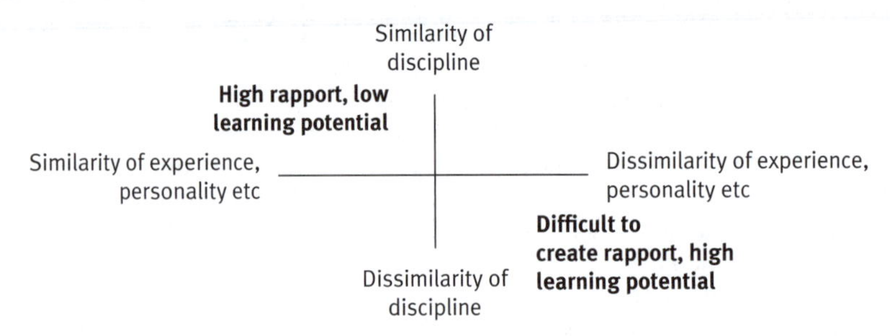

In the top right corner, the relatively immature learner or the person lacking confidence will often feel more comfortable with someone who shares a similar functional background and perhaps common interests and views outside of work. At the other extreme, a highly self-confident, mature learner may welcome the challenge of learning with someone with whom they have very little in common.

Learning maturity is the term we have co-opted to describe the extent to which mentors and mentees are able to accept and reflect upon challenges, to the assumptions they make about how things work – what is right and so on – along with a number of other factors, such as ability to think rationally, apply different information-gathering and learning strategies, and their level of emotional intelligence (EI). In short, how much difference can the mentor or mentee take in the relationship, before it interferes and undermines the quality of the learning dialogue? (A very simple form of measuring learning maturity is described in the case study at the end of this chapter, from Middlesex University.) This can be an important factor in matching people who have substantially different cultural backgrounds – too many points of difference and the relationship simply won't gel.

Although this approach seems rather mechanical, it does seem to be how well-informed HR professionals make their instinctive choices about who they should recommend to pair. It also helps in decisions about how close the mentor should be to the mentee in organisation terms. In many modern programmes, the mentor's different perspective is a critical element of the relationship. At a large UK retailer, for example, mentees in the finance division were divided into two groups: those who needed to become more effective in their functional responsibilities, for whom a mentor from finance was provided, and those who were technically proficient but who needed greater commercial awareness, who were given mentors from sales, merchandising and marketing. In another case, mentees were given two mentors: one in their own division and one in another division and function. Over 80% of mentees found the mentor from the other division most useful and easiest to talk with.

Research by Richard Hale (Hale 2000) reinforced the view that effective matching is largely about balancing building rapport and creating the conditions for learning challenge. He also emphasised the importance of values compatibility as an underpinning for rapport in mentoring relationships. (See the case study of values-based matching at the end of this chapter.)

Avoid entanglements between line and off-line relationships. Most companies with mentoring programmes aimed at managers, for example, prefer to establish the relationship outside the normal working hierarchy. One reason for this is that there are times in the mentoring relationship when both sides need to back off. This is something much easier to do if there is a certain distance between them, either in hierarchical level or departmental function, or both. In addition, the boss–subordinate relationship, with all its entanglements of decisions on pay rises, disciplinary responsibilities and performance appraisal, may work against the openness and candour of the true mentoring relationship. The line manager may also not have a sufficiently wide experience of other job opportunities. Moreover, unless the line manager mentors all his or her direct reports – which would involve a very substantial time commitment – there is likely to be resentment from those people who are not mentored, while those who are become cast as favourites. This doesn't help build team unity!

Ensure that mentors are committed to the programme. A manager who is outstanding in his or her field may at first glance seem to be an ideal candidate for a mentor. It is just this sort of flair and expertise the company needs to pass on. However, if this manager's communication skills are extremely poor, or the manager resents being taken from his or her work because of mentorship obligations, he or she is unlikely to function well in the role. The company, the mentor and the mentee may all suffer in these circumstances.

Such a situation arose in one company where the programme managers attempted to assign mentors to mentees instead of allowing them to volunteer. They picked the most talented employee in research, who reluctantly agreed to act as a mentor. However, the mentee found his mentor was usually inaccessible and rarely spent time with him. The programme managers were reluctant to assign the mentee to another person for fear of offending his mentor. Trapped by the company politics, the mentee felt his career was being sacrificed to cover up the mistakes of senior management. Not surprisingly, he left to seek his career development elsewhere.

The moral of this story is clear. Companies should choose mentors who not only have useful experience, but who are also actively committed to the programme. A volunteer mentor is worth a dozen press-ganged ones. The mentor must be ready to invest time and effort into the relationship, so his or her interests will probably already lie in people development. The mentor must be ready to extend friendship to the mentee and be willing to let the relationship extend beyond the normal limits of a business relationship. The mentor should not participate in the programme unless he or she is willing to consider the relationship as a relatively long-term commitment.

Allow for a 'no-fault divorce clause'. It is standard good practice now for mentors and mentees to be required to review the progress of the relationship after two or three meetings, with a view to assessing how suited they are to each other. If the conclusion is that they are not, the mentor can help the mentee think through what sort of mentor – if any – he or she needs at this time. We now have a small number of cases of relationships that have been dissolved in such a process, but that have subsequently resumed – perhaps years later – when the mentee's circumstances and needs have changed.

Must the mentee share the same qualities as the mentor? There is a common assertion that in order for a mentoring relationship to succeed, the mentee must have a similar personality to the mentor's. Elizabeth Alleman and her colleague Isadore Newman (Alleman 1984) attempted to establish whether a similarity of personality or background was indeed the basis of rewarding mentor relationships. Alleman and Newman studied 100 managers, 29 pairs reporting a mentoring relationship and 21 pairs reporting a typical business relationship. The two compared the relationship between the mentor and the mentee to the relationship between a manager and his or her superior. Through personality tests and questionnaires they discovered:

- Mentoring pairs have no more similarities in personality or background than non-mentored pairs. When participants described themselves and their partners, their profiles contained few shared traits.
- Mentoring relationships are not based on complementary personality traits. Newman and Alleman did not find evidence to support the suggestion that mentors choose mentees whose strengths and skills offset the mentor's weaknesses.
- Mentors do not believe there are any special similarities between themselves and their mentees.
- Mentees view their mentors as similar to ideal workers and identify with them to a greater extent than managers who have a non-mentoring relationship with their supervisor.

In short, Alleman and Newman maintain that it is not essential for the mentor and mentee to have similar personalities or backgrounds. Indeed, if a cultural readjustment is needed in the organisation, then it may pay to avoid deliberately too close a match.

So how do we explain the apparently contradictory conclusions of Hale (2000) and the case study of values-based matching below? The answer seems to be that standard personality tests aren't subtle enough to predict whether people will 'hit it off'. In some situations, opposites attract. When people connect at a values level, however, the ground is set for much deeper levels of trust and personal disclosure.

In another more recent study of using personality tests in the context of mentoring, Engström (1997/1998) examined 30 pairs of mentors and mentees within a Swedish multinational company. The pairs included all gender options except female to female. He based his analysis of personality on five factors, which he describes as 'generally accepted in the field of personality and [which] include most other personality factors presented in the field'. These will be familiar to many readers: extroversion, emotional stability, agreeableness, conscientiousness, and openness to experience.

Among Engström's conclusions are that mentoring relationships are seen as most successful when:

- both mentor and mentee demonstrate high extroversion
- both demonstrate a high level of agreeableness (defined as encompassing likeability, friendliness, social adaptability, altruism, affection, compliance)

- the mentee demonstrates much greater conscientiousness than the mentor (ie the mentee assumes ownership of the process)
- in the mentee's perception, the mentee demonstrates high openness to experience and the mentor high emotional stability.

An unexpected conclusion from the research was that men-only mentoring pairs were always perceived by both parties as more successful than mixed gender pairs, whether the woman was mentor or mentee. (Without a female-to-female comparison, this conclusion should be treated with some caution, insofar as drawing any implications is concerned.)

CASE STUDY

VALUES-BASED MATCHING

The Project Leadership Experience at Norway's Statoil (an oil company operating in 35 countries and employing some 29,000 people) is an intensive executive education programme, run with the University of California, Berkeley in the United States, aimed at project managers. It addresses topics related to strategy, leadership and management, team dynamics and team development, and culture from organisational and global perspectives. All participants are helped to create a personal development plan based on their learning and their individual areas of continued developmental need as project leaders. They are also supported with a formal mentoring programme for the year after the programme to help them put learning into practice and to maintain the pace of their self-development.

Mentees receive several day-long peer support sessions and 10–12 sessions with their mentor. The programme managers felt that they had a very good knowledge of the mentees by the time they had to think about matching with a mentor, but they knew relatively little about the mentors and certainly not enough to be sure that all the relationships would build rapid and sustainable rapport. Some relationships had failed to work in the pilot programme, apparently because of 'lack of chemistry' between mentor and mentee.

The matching was designed to have two stages: one to filter out obvious factors, such as where mentor and mentee were too close in their daily work; and one to assess values capability, which they assessed using an approach designed by Swiss consultancy Value Based Matching® GmbH, based on the Reiss Motivation Profile® (RMP). Highly validated as a tool for understanding people's innate drives and motivations, the RMP questionnaires provided a pragmatic way to assess the level of common-feeling and respect potential mentors and mentees would have for each other.

Since introducing values-based matching, there have been no cases where re-matches were required, other than where mentors or mentees have moved to new roles within or outside the company. It was necessary to reassure participants that their data would not be shared apart from with the programme management team and in the mentoring pairs. Sharing this data may have contributed to strengthening the relationships, as people understood each other better and were able to discuss values issues more openly.

Source: Contributed by Gianella Daniele.

CASE STUDY

PUBLIC SECTOR DEVELOPMENTAL MENTORING SCHEME, MIDDLESEX UNIVERSITY AND THE FIRST DIVISION ASSOCIATION (FDA) AND LIVERPOOL JOHN MOORES UNIVERSITY

The aim of the Public Sector Diversity Mentoring Scheme (PSDMS) is to develop public sector graduate entrant mentors who will support the goal of increased employability for a diverse set of undergraduate student mentees who aspire to a career within the public sector. The key project partners are Middlesex University (MU), First Division Association (FDA) and Liverpool John Moores University (LJMU). The project aims to have a longer term impact for the future employment of students in the public sector and will establish a nationwide relationship between Higher Education Institutions (HEIs) and public sector employers. The International Standards of Mentoring Programmes in Employment (ISMPE) were used as the basis to develop the programme strategy, protocols and framework.

The programme has two strands. The first is a mentoring programme for undergraduate students and public sector graduate entrants; the second is the facilitation of Development Centres, offered to all mentees on the programme. The purpose of the Development Centres was to encourage the mentees to experience a public sector-style assessment centre, based on a number of the core competencies used to recruit civil service graduate fast-stream applicants.

The project launched in October 2012 with 126 participants on the scheme. All participants attended one of five compulsory training days in November 2012, consisting of an overview of the project aims and objectives, detailed programme content and expectations briefing, core skills workshops, mentor/mentee matching, and programme evaluation. The mentees and mentors were paired and commenced their relationships in December 2012 with a view to bringing them to close by July 2013. The minimum time commitment for each participant was eight to ten hours.

A robust approach to matching was needed to cater for the disparate locations and multiple organisations. The mentees were drawn from a broad suite of programmes, university-wide in London and Liverpool, while the mentors came from over 30 public sector organisations from the South of England to Scotland. This presented a challenge in terms of mentoring mode of communication and employability 'fit'.

The matching process was designed and incorporated alongside the training day. The training day was used as an aid to support the matching process (Klasen and Clutterbuck 2002). At the beginning of the day, mentees and mentors were informed that there would be a number of paired skills exercises, providing the opportunity for mentees to work with at least five different mentors. Participants were asked to think about the importance of rapport in all relationships, and the learning potential there may be when perceived or actual similarities and/or differences present themselves.

Towards the end of the day, participants were presented with a matching document; this was explained by the training day facilitator. The purpose of the process was to capture the participants' preferences, both positive and negative, and so to facilitate the matching process. The matching document was split into four sections. First, the document collected profile information about the participant including their subject discipline, organisational role and work-related area as appropriate for mentees and mentors. Second, the document enabled the participants to state a number of preferences including gender, age, mode of communication (telephone, e-mail,

Skype and face-to-face). Third, participants were asked to identify their personality/value characteristics and select three that might have the greatest impact on rapport. Finally, participants were given the option to identify up to three mentees/mentors they would like to be paired with and three they would not. All participants were made aware that the project team would attempt to match all preferences but that it would not be possible in all cases.

The matching documents were reviewed by the project team at MU and LJMU. One member of the team from each institution created each pair which was then evaluated by a second member of the project team. The matching documents were overlaid with a summary sheet which captured the rationale for each pairing (see Appendix).

Following this process, all participants received an e-mail from the Project Lead at each HEI, confirming the pairing, attaching the programme handbook and training day slides, providing guidance on first point of contact and attaching a link to an electronic survey to collect participant feedback.

Outcomes

The 63 participants were matched with people from their region. Five months after the matching took place, of the 63 pairings, five relationships had come to an early close, and two mentees had been re-matched with new mentors. An interim survey looked at the matching process to determine what had happened and how it could be improved.

Interim survey results

One of the key aims of the interim survey was to evaluate the matching process, identifying the extent to which mentees and mentors felt that they were able to influence the process; identify matching criteria priorities and the potential to include additional matching criteria.

In total 52 mentees and 51 mentors completed the survey, which found that:

- almost all participants understood the purpose of the matching process and felt they could influence it
- the most significant criterion for both mentors and mentees overall was the personality characteristics of the other person
- other factors participants considered relevant included the mentor's capacity to devote time to the relationship, proximity of location, and specific career experience.

Comments from participants included:

> I wanted to mentor a girl to be able to share my experience of working in a male-dominated environment and encourage more women to join the civil service.

> If a preference was stated then this would clearly demonstrate a connection between mentor and mentee.

> To enable a person to exercise a choice helps them to feel more confident that they will be matched with someone who they would feel comfortable working with.

> Because I wanted to be able to communicate face-to-face.

> This criterion is fundamental to the success of the mentoring relationship, in a way that the others are not. The relationship depends upon interpersonal interaction; and method of interaction is therefore of fundamental significance in a way in which the other criteria are not.

> This is because I had the opportunity to interact with the person I chose, therefore building a relationship.

> I think it would be useful for mentors and mentees to provide a

brief profile of themselves, which can be shared with the group prior to the training/matching event. This would not be an additional criteria but would provide additional information on which to base preferences. The day is quite intense, with mentors and mentees profiling one another as well as attempting to absorb the training and undertake the role-playing exercises, and it is very difficult if not impossible to speak to everyone. It may be that a good match within the group is not realised because the two participants did not have the opportunity to interact. Providing profiles of mentors/mentees before the event would therefore help participants direct their attentions to those whose profiles suggest a good match and ensure preferences are better informed.

Lessons

Based on the experience thus far and the feedback from the participants, the following key lessons are evident:

- A transparent matching process is fundamental to support the credibility of the programme and provide participants with absolute clarity, addressing any concerns or questions.
- Participants need to understand the matching process. This fosters a feeling of confidence with the project team and the programme, ensuring that pairings get off on the right footing.
- Giving all participants an element of choice, surfacing both positive and negative preferences, aims to foster a sense of contribution and ownership. To some extent they may have already 'bought into' the relationship as they have had an input into who they are matched with.
- It is important to be explicit about the practical implications of participants' preferences. It is not always possible to match against all positive and negative preferences, in all cases. This is particularly in the case of mentees or mentors stating a particular preference for an individual. On one training day, a mentor was named by 12 mentees; clearly 11 of the mentees would not be allocated their first choice individual preference. Although only 17% of mentors and 25% of mentees said this was their most important criteria, a number were disappointed when they were not allocated a named individual. Highlighting this type of scenario to participants of future programmes may be one way in which the team can manage expectations and help avoid disappointment.
- It is important to be responsive to the requests of participants and perhaps adopt an 'open' element which allows the participants to express additional preferences. This should include a caveat that matching on the basis of additional commentary may not always be possible.

Source: Contributed by Dr Julie Haddock-Millar, Senior Lecturer and Teaching Fellow, Middlesex University Business School and Chris Rigby, Senior Lecturer, Middlesex University Business School.

SUMMARY

Matching mentors and mentees isn't a science but it is possible to make more effective pairings by gathering sufficient breadth of data on mentors and mentees and by involving them in making informed choices. It is remarkable how easily people in mentoring relationships develop a high level of rapport when they have a clear understanding of what they are trying to achieve together, and what behaviours they should expect of each other.

CHAPTER 7

Setting up the Mentoring Programme

Some form of spontaneous mentoring takes place in most organisations, whether acknowledged or not. A formalised programme helps harness that energy to the organisation's objectives and extend the reach of mentoring to groups who might otherwise have been overlooked, while avoiding most of the downsides of informal mentoring. Well-designed programmes greatly enhance the benefits to both participants and the organisation.

It's easy to over-bureaucratise the mentoring programme, however. Ideally, there is just enough structure and support to ensure that:

- mentors and mentees are reasonably well-matched
- they understand their roles and how the relationship evolves
- they have enough relevant skills and tools resources to start with confidence
- the progress of each relationship is monitored so the programme manager can intervene, if needed
- participants feel that there is an alignment between the organisation's aims for the programme and their own
- top management understands the programme and can give appropriate support as needed.

THE MENTORING QUADRANGLE

There are usually four people involved in a mentoring relationship. Together, they make up a mentoring quadrangle:

- the mentee
- the mentor
- the line manager
- the programme co-ordinator, who monitors the relationships and looks at resources for training opportunities.

Figure 11 The mentoring quadrangle

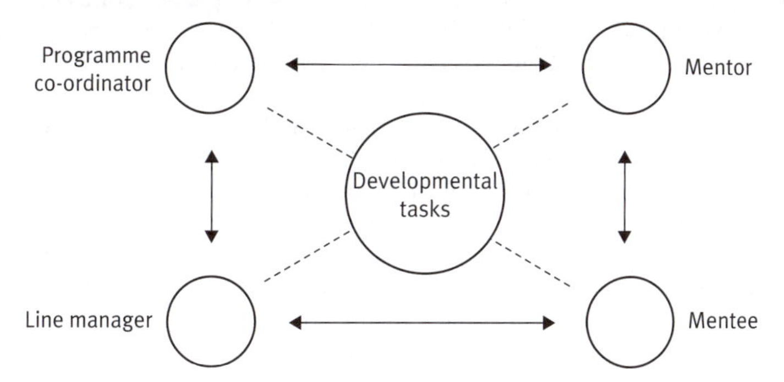

The clearer all four are about the objectives and effort required, the more successful the programme will be. All must be involved and consulted about career moves and developmental tasks that will take the mentee away from day-to-day work and responsibilities.

Each organisation has to draw up a mentoring programme that fits its particular company culture and answers the needs of its own employees. To ensure the success of the mentoring programme, a company must be prepared to be flexible in its approach and be willing to assess continuously and, if necessary, modify the programme.

SETTING PROGRAMME OBJECTIVES

As with any major corporate programme, it's important to have a clear statement of objectives against which progress may be measured. Typical objectives might be:

- to establish a cadre of broadly trained generalist managers at or just below middle management
- to speed and improve the induction of specific types of recruits and reduce wastage within the first year of their employment
- to allow top management to assess the ability of both individual young managers and the rising generation of managers as a whole
- to provide equal opportunities for disadvantaged groups of employees.

In each case, HR can establish with top management a set of assessment criteria and a timetable for achieving specific levels of results.

Putting these objectives into practice requires a great deal of preparation. Usually at least six months to a year is needed to gain acceptance of the concept from the key people in the organisation to establish objectives and measurements, to design support facilities, such as special training courses, and to begin the process of selecting participants.

PREPARING THE COMPANY FOR A MENTORING PROGRAMME

ORGANISATIONAL READINESS FOR MENTORING

An important element in designing the programme, especially in terms of the training provision and communication within the organisation, is to understand just how supportive the environment will be towards mentoring. How will mentors and mentees be perceived? Will line managers willingly let them spend time in mentoring meetings? Are there any cultural factors which might inhibit mentees from using the relationship appropriately?

In most of the programme failures I have seen, a major contributing factor has been not taking into account contextual factors that will undermine the programme.

Some examples that illustrate the point:

- A large UK-based financial services organisation found that its system of billable hours placed a major potential barrier in the way of mentors and mentees, because they would effectively be penalised for spending time on the relationship during official working hours. The solution was to produce a budget line specifically for time spent on the programme and to ensure that line managers understood the importance of making this available.
- The HR function in a UK national institution insisted that it knew exactly what the likely concerns of mentors and mentees would be and saw no need to conduct any research prior to training. Subsequently, it became very clear that the organisational culture made it difficult for the mentees – newly recruited graduates – to admit that they had any issues to deal with. They soon learned that projecting confidence and competence was essential, if their appointment was to be confirmed at the end of their two-year induction. The mentees also felt that senior managers, from whom the mentors were drawn, were remote and unapproachable, so they were reluctant to

disturb them with any problems they did have. The net result was that most relationships never really took off.

- An engineering company assumed that women managers would welcome a mentoring programme aimed specifically at them. Persuaded to do some initial research, it discovered that many of the women felt that labelling the programme as a women's initiative would devalue it, and that they would be less likely to take part.

Good practice is to carry out a 'readiness for mentoring' evaluation that examines:

- the overall developmental climate. Will mentoring fit in naturally, or will it require a lot more effort to get people to change perceptions and behaviours?
- top management commitment
- the recent history of self-development initiatives. Were they sustainable or regarded as another management fad?
- other major initiatives by HR or the business that might compete for attention and resources with a mentoring programme in the timeframe planned
- the past history (if any) of mentoring in the organisation.

ENSURE TOP MANAGEMENT COMMITMENT

Top management needs to demonstrate to the rest of the company that it considers mentoring to be a legitimate and effective method of developing staff. Top management must support the programme verbally and materially. Ideally, they should be prepared to talk about their own experiences as mentors and mentees. It must promote mentoring within the company through speeches, letters, memoranda and articles in the company newsletter. Articles in the public media can reinforce the message greatly, because employees often take greater note of information they read in independent newspapers and magazines than they do of the same information presented in official company publications. Senior management can also attend general meetings of groups of mentoring pairs. These strategies are especially necessary if general unease, confusion, or even suspicion about the programme exists in the company.

ADAPT THE PROGRAMME TO THE COMPANY'S DEVELOPMENT PRIORITIES

Try to fit the mentoring programme into the context of a wider framework of employee development and human resource management, and explain this framework to employees. Problems are more likely to arise if the programme exists in isolation. If it seems that mentoring is the only form of career development in the company, employees may easily assume that those chosen to participate are destined automatically for senior management and the morale of those not on the programme would suffer appreciably. Those individuals who are on the programme may be encouraged to believe that all their chances of promotion lie in the mentoring relationship. As a result, they may throw all their efforts into that area and neglect other equally important aspects of their work and personal development. To avoid these pitfalls, mentoring should be seen as only one dimension of career development.

The company should also make sure mentees have other opportunities to improve their skills beyond those arising within the mentoring programme. They should have access to internal or external workshops, self-development and distance-learning materials, as well as career development workshops.

ENSURE COMMITMENT AND PARTICIPATION

Ensure that participation is voluntary. Mentoring demands time and effort so commitment is essential. Inform potential mentors of potential problems and challenges and what they should expect of the relationship. Some companies give all new mentors and mentees the chance to hear from existing or recent participants about the pitfalls and pleasures mentoring can bring.

ENSURE SUPPORT SYSTEMS ARE IN PLACE

The most important of the support systems required are:

- Clear information about the purpose of the programme and who is eligible for it.
- Some basic information about mentoring and how to apply for the programme.
- A systematic, transparent system for matching mentors and mentees (see Chapter 6).
- A well-focused training programme for both mentor and mentee.
- Some form of mutual support mechanism, where mentor and mentee groups can meet from time to time to share experience and receive further advice or training.
- An intranet-based platform with lots of additional information about mentoring. (Mining company Anglo American has an extensive HR portal on its corporate intranet. Included in the resource is a database for mentors and mentees, as well as materials to support local HR professionals in being champions for mentoring in their locations around the world.)
- Supervision – more frequently associated with coaching, professional supervision is also now being used to support mentors. The London Deanery provides regular supervision for the medical professionals in its programme. Similarly, The Association of Danish Lawyers and Economists (Djøf), uses supervision in one of the largest mentoring programmes in Europe. Supervision provides an opportunity to:
  - continue to develop mentor skills
  - identify and deal with relationship problems
  - enable mentors to share concerns
  - identify common issues raised by mentees (in a number of cases, this information has led to substantial changes in HR policy or procedures)
  - ensure that the mentors understand and work within an ethical framework and respect boundaries.

Some companies have supported mentoring programmes with regular newsletters aimed at drip-feeding new concepts and tools. Where the programme has a large group of people all starting at the same time, these newsletters can be timed to coincide with likely transitions between stages in the mentoring relationship.

ENSURE ACCEPTANCE OF THE TIME INVOLVED

Make sure everyone understands the amount of time commitment involved on the part of the mentor, the mentee and the mentee's manager.

Two key questions that must be asked are:

1. How disruptive to the normal work of these people will the time commitment be?
2. How valuable will this time and effort be in achieving the objective of developing the mentee?

Two useful ground rules help to put the time issue into perspective:

1. If you meet less than once a quarter, you haven't got a relationship (it's just an acquaintance); if you meet much more than once a month, the mentor is probably doing the line manager's job.
2. Ideally, meetings should last 60–90 minutes. Below this, it's difficult to address issues in real depth. Above two hours and you are probably going round the houses. It can

be good practice to put an extra half hour into the diary to allow for those occasions when a really crucial issue comes to the surface towards the end of the scheduled time.

DEMYSTIFY THE MENTORING PROGRAMME

Demystify the mentoring programme for those who are not involved. The process and objectives of the programme should be explained clearly, setting out and emphasising the benefits to the organisation as a whole. If it is decided to establish only a small number of mentoring pairs as a pilot at the beginning of a programme, the organisation should explain to applicants not included that they will have an opportunity to reapply in the future.

ENSURE CONFIDENTIALITY

Confidentiality is essential if the mentee is to open up to the mentor to produce the kind of frank relationship necessary for success.

Confidentiality in mentoring is rarely absolute. Leaving aside the issue of legal obligations (eg becoming an accessory after the fact), different organisations have different expectations of the level of confidentiality that can apply. At a City financial services company, top management has been careful to draw the distinction between privacy (being able to talk about issues in a relationship of trust) and confidentiality (the expectation that nothing said can be discussed outside the relationship without mutual agreement).

Clearly, the less confidence the mentee (let alone the mentor) has that what he or she says will remain between them alone, the more reluctant the mentee will be in speaking openly of his or her feelings and concerns. Said one mentee:

> My line manager and my mentor play golf together every Sunday.
>
> There are things I'd like to explore with the mentor, about how to tackle some of my manager's behaviours, but I'm never sure how much I dare say. If my manager thought I was criticising him behind his back, I'd have a real problem. As it is, twice now they have both made much the same suggestion to me about an issue I've brought up, which makes me suspicious that they have been discussing me.

Although issues of broken confidentiality are remarkably rare in mentoring, concerns over confidentiality remain one of the biggest limiting factors on relationships. Making the ground rules clear and trying, wherever possible, to avoid mentor and line manager being too close operationally or personally, are obvious practical measures to take.

It's also advisable to avoid role confusion. Some of the professional institutes, for example in engineering, have used mentoring for years as a means of assisting people on their route to chartered status. Most expected the mentor to carry out some form of assessment of the mentee, but this practice has gradually been dropped, not least because it introduced a dynamic into the relationship that made it difficult for the mentee to seek anything but technical advice – much of which was more readily available from other sources. Divorcing the measurement and mentoring processes enriches the relationships and helps build more rounded professionals.

While it's not essential to spend a lot of time on confidentiality in mentor and mentee training, it is important to discuss it enough to give people a flavour of the kind of issues that may occur. Here are some of those that I use in training:

- The mentee's boss asks him to pump the mentor for information about planned structural changes that might affect both of them and to share this later.
- The mentee's boss asks the mentor for information on the mentee's intentions.

- The mentee reveals that an unethical practice is going on in his department. Should the mentor escalate this? Or intervene herself?
- The mentor knows that a major change is about to happen in the mentee's department, of which the mentee is unaware, but will open up significant opportunities for the mentee. The mentee reveals they have had an attractive approach from a headhunter. How much should the mentor say?

HOW TO PREPARE THE MENTOR AND THE MENTEE

It is essential to supply as much information as possible to the two most important participants of the programme – the mentor and the mentee – for both need to understand the purpose and objectives of the programme for the individual and for the company. Both also need to understand what is expected of them. The advantages of the relationship to both the mentor and the mentee should be particularly emphasised.

THE MENTOR

The most important aim in the preparatory stage of the programme is to motivate the mentor and help him or her see how he or she can contribute to the mentee's development. Issues to address include:

Being open about the risks

Organisations can help the mentor to examine frankly the potential risks involved in being a mentor. Programme co-ordinators should make it clear to the mentor and the company in general that the relationship is not guaranteed to be successful and that a failed pairing will not reflect badly on the mentor. Indeed, having the self-confidence to wind down a relationship that is not going anywhere should be seen as a sign of the mentor's developmental competence.

Creating a mentor support network

Introduce the mentor to other managers who have experience in mentoring and who can discuss the various stages of the relationship and the challenges and difficulties that are likely to arise. Organisations can also appoint a senior or 'super' mentor to counsel and guide the less experienced mentor. Once the programme is under way, peer support can be highly influential in maintaining the mentors' confidence and commitment.

THE MENTEE

If the mentee is to take appropriate responsibility for the relationship, he or she needs to understand:

- what the organisation expects from the programme
- what can realistically be expected of the mentor
- what the mentor should expect of him or her
- what he or she can do to make the relationship deliver positive outcomes for both parties.

GETTING STARTED ON THE MENTORING RELATIONSHIP

Although a handful of companies start the whole process with a meeting at which the line manager or the scheme co-ordinator facilitates, in general this is perceived to be unnecessarily intrusive. Instead, mentor and mentee are usually encouraged to meet at a mutually convenient and not too formal place to work out on their own how they want to run their relationship. However, the primary objective of the first meeting is to get to know each other and build the rapport they will need to make the relationship work.

At this or the next meeting, the mentee should also be prepared to share with the mentor any information he or she has that is relevant to issues he or she wants to work on – for example, performance appraisals, assessment centre results or the outcomes of psychometric tests undertaken. I often ask my mentees to record once a week or so the three things that have most pleased and most frustrated them. Then either we examine the list together to look for patterns, or the mentees extract their own meaning from the list before we meet. In this way, the dialogue becomes grounded in actual, recent experience rather than hypotheticals. Long-term developmental goals can be illuminated through examining more recent successes and failures.

THE ROLE OF THE LINE MANAGER VS THAT OF THE MENTOR

To avoid clashes between mentor and line manager, or worse, deliberate manipulation of them by the mentee, it is important that line manager and mentor are clear about where the boundaries of their responsibility towards the mentee lie. Table 5 attempts to distinguish between the responsibilities and indicate where the responsibility is shared. Some organisations may wish to move the responsibilities around to suit their specific circumstances – no problem, as long as line managers and mentors are clear where they stand.

Table 5 Development roles of line manager and mentor

Line manager	Shared	Mentor
Performance appraisal.	Encouragement, motivation to learn.	Help learner develop insights into causes of poor performance.
Agreed developmental goals within learner's current job.	Shape goals beyond current job.	Help learner manage the integration of job, career and personal goals.
Help learner build relationships within the team.	Help learner build relationships outside team.	Help learner build relationships with line manager.
Find opportunities to stretch learner's performance.	Find opportunities to stretch learner's thinking.	Challenge learner's thinking and assumptions.
Give constructive feedback through observation.	Help learner develop skills of intrinsic observation.	Help learner accept and manage feedback constructively.
Role model for task fulfilment and growth.	Role model of general behaviour.	Role model for personal and career achievement.

TESTING THE PROGRAMME

Start in a modest way to make sure that the initial effort is well designed and fulfils its objectives. Once a trial programme, involving say 5–20 mentoring pairs, has been successfully established, the company can decide to be more ambitious and expand its size and timescale. In this way the organisation can avoid most of the disillusionment and backlash that can come when a full-blown programme fails to live up to its objectives.

TRAINING

FOR THE MENTOR

An organisation can run workshops for the mentor suggesting various methods of 'helping to learn'. A workshop or series of webinars might deal with:

- the purpose of the programme
- the benefits of the mentoring relationship
- concepts and models of mentoring
- how the relationship typically evolves
- the dynamic nature of the relationship, its stages and phases
- the core qualities and skills of an effective mentor
- practical tools and techniques for helping the mentee
- anticipating and forestalling possible problems
- adapting mentoring practices to particular settings.

It would also provide opportunities to put the skills into practice. While role play can be useful, my experience is that mentors learn a lot more through real play – working on issues that are of genuine concern to them. Hence, it's important to get them to come to the workshop with one or two issues that they will be prepared to share in the role of mentee, and on which they would value some help with their thinking.

Typically, initial mentor training workshops last one to two days and focus both on building awareness of the role and on raising awareness of key mentoring skills. In practice, however, many organisations now insist that initial training be carried out in much shorter periods. This poses a real challenge for the trainer, who must not only ensure that mentors emerge from half a day's training with enough understanding and confidence to try being a mentor, but must also find innovative ways of encouraging them to come back to review their progress. The shorter the training upfront, the more time that will need to be invested in well-timed additional support, through review sessions, webinars, supervision and so on. As a broad rule, it takes a minimum of 16 hours over the first year for a mentor to acquire the skills and know-how they need.

One increasingly popular option is to deliver some training by a mixture of webinar and virtual learning, backed up with required reading, supervision and practice. The downside is that mentors don't have an opportunity to practice in the safety of the classroom, so they tend to be more cautious in how they approach their role. Also, it's very hard to produce generic demonstrations of mentoring conversations that are suitable for editing down into short learning videos.

An option for very senior people in organisations is to have personalised training. I often work with CEOs, who are too busy to attend formal training (or are concerned that their presence might alter the dynamics of a workshop), on a one-to-one basis. After a two-hour briefing, which explores their previous experience and motivations, I observe them in a mentoring session, then give feedback to both mentor and mentee. This is essentially a coaching and supervision approach to mentor training and it helps to emphasise in the content advanced developmental techniques and the role of mentoring in shaping future leaders. One of the benefits of this approach is that it provides a safe environment to challenge leaders over whether they really have the skills they think they have. For example, in general, the more senior people are, the less effective they may be at listening and the more reliant on giving advice.

FOR THE MENTEE

Mentee training tends to follow a very similar pattern to that for mentors, but places greater emphasis on:

- helping the mentee work out what they want from mentoring and from their careers more generally
- skills and attributes of an effective mentee (see Chapter 5)
- career self-management
- raising self-awareness.

It is relatively common to support mentees additionally with further learning opportunities, such as action learning sets, where they can assist with each other's development.

An additional element I have introduced into many mentee training workshops is a more intensive session on building and using networks. The more adept the mentee becomes at using networking, the more helpful the mentor can be. A good starting point for developing learning nets is the peer group, which may have all the knowledge the graduate mentee needs to gain introductions to areas of the business he or she would like to know about.

MENTORING QUALIFICATIONS

Relatively few mentoring programmes offer mentors the opportunity to acquire an accreditation in the role. This is slowly changing. Many coaching certificate and diploma courses at NVQ levels 5, 6 and 7 now also include mentoring in the title. It's wise to be sceptical about how much mentoring there will be in the content – some courses appear to simply be using coaching and mentoring as interchangeable terms. However, there are a number of certificate and diploma courses available. At a professional mentoring level, as I write a number of providers around the world are collaborating to establish an International Association of Mentoring Academies. Highly experienced mentors, who are prepared to build a portfolio of evidence about their practice, may also seek the European Individual Award of the European Mentoring and Coaching Council (EMCC).

For the ordinary manager, for whom mentoring is a small part of their activities, the effort–reward ratio of seeking an accreditation may not be worthwhile. The requirements for further reading, maintaining a learning log, reflection, and perhaps a short dissertation effectively treble the time investment, even for accreditation at foundation level. However, for anyone operating as a professional mentor – for example, working with entrepreneurs – evidence of competence in the role is at the very least desirable.

SOME BASIC GUIDELINES IN THE DESIGN OF MENTORING TRAINING

The key questions in designing the training support for a mentoring programme are:

- Who should be trained?
- How much training is needed?
- Should mentor and mentee be trained together or separately?
- What makes for quality of training?
- When and how should training be delivered?

WHO SHOULD BE TRAINED?

The basic statistics of training in mentoring appear roughly to be:

- Don't train or brief any of the participants – expect 10% of relationships to deliver significant learning for one or both parties. (That's the base line of people who have had

previous exposure to effective mentoring or who have a very strong instinctive capability.)
- Rely on a briefing only – expect 30% of relationships to succeed. (That's the proportion of mentors who will extrapolate from other situations and training, to lock into the role.)
- Train mentors but not mentees – expect up to 60% of relationships to deliver learning for mentors and perhaps half as many to deliver learning for the mentors. (Mentees will typically fail to take over the management of the relationship and will not fully appreciate their own and their mentors' roles.)
- Train both mentors and mentees – expect 90% plus of relationships to deliver significant learning for both parties, especially when line managers are also well briefed and informed in general about the programme.

It also helps if the steering group and/or scheme co-ordinator have attended a workshop aimed at broadening their understanding of mentoring concept and good practice.

HOW MUCH TRAINING IS NEEDED?

The answer here is that it depends on the level at which mentoring is to take place. If the mentor is to be a professional, working with say executives or young offenders, an extensive period of theoretical learning and practice is essential. (See Chapter 5 on competencies for a longer discussion of this issue.) For the manager in a workplace, however, the basic need is for enough understanding and skill to respond appropriately to the mentee's needs for guidance, help in thinking issues through, and general support; and to know where the boundaries of his or her competence lie (and hence to refer on to specialist support if needed).

Realistically, this can't be done in less than a day. Moreover, experience indicates time and again that a single, sheep-dip event is not enough. To sustain the programme, mentors need to come back together again at least once over the following six to eight months to review what they have learned, to identify problem areas and to be equipped with additional techniques, relevant to the situations they have encountered.

Mentee training is usually easier to arrange, especially when the mentees are relatively junior in the organisation. Some organisations have skimped here, opting instead for a briefing in the mistaken belief that the mentees' role is relatively passive. In reality, the mentees need to have as broad an understanding of the process as the mentor. They also need to acquire a portfolio of skills to manage the relationship and to help the mentor help them.

SHOULD MENTOR AND MENTEE BE TRAINED TOGETHER OR SEPARATELY?[1]

One of the most difficult and contentious questions we encounter in helping organisations design and implement mentoring schemes is whether to conduct the training for the two groups separately or together. There isn't a generic right answer and our experience covers both options. Yet getting this aspect right can make or break a programme and we have seen a number of examples of failure, where it has been badly managed.

The starting point for the scheme co-ordinator in considering this issue is that both mentors and mentees need to undergo some training if the majority of relationships are going to deliver significant benefits. The quality and quantity of mutual learning and the proportion of relationships seen by both parties as successful

[1] This section is extracted from an article by David Clutterbuck and Jenny Sweeney *Apart or together: good practice in training mentors and mentees.* Published in the Clutterbuck Associates newsletter, September 2003.

is greatly enhanced with appropriate initial training. Bringing participant groups back together again to review experience and receive additional ad hoc training as needed, also improves the success rate.

Within the initial training, the critical elements for both mentors and mentees are:

- gaining a complementary understanding of how to manage the relationship – the roles, responsibilities, and expected behaviours – and how it should evolve over time
- learning the skills of being an effective mentor/mentee. Our observation is that the mentees are best able to help the mentor help them if they understand the processes/techniques the mentor is using and can collaborate in making those processes work.

In both elements, an appreciation of the other party's perspective is going to be very helpful, if not essential, in getting the most out of the relationship. But whether that need is best addressed through joint or separate training events depends very much on circumstance.

Let's look at the arguments for each approach, with some examples of positive and negative experience.

The case for training together

Certain situations make it quite difficult to separate out mentors from mentees. For example, at a pharmaceutical company, people who came to the initial workshops did not know whether they wanted to be a mentor or a mentee. In practice, people who came with one role in mind often decided they would best adopt the other; and some opted for both.

Another situation where joint training is common is in cascade mentoring programmes, where several layers of employees are being mentored by those above; many of the participants end up playing both roles, within different relationships.

An important consideration in the success of a programme is ensuring that both mentor and mentee receive appropriate training as soon as possible after they are selected for inclusion. One programme ran into severe problems because the time gap between training of mentors and training of mentees gradually extended until many of the participants simply lost interest. Where numbers are small and/or people join the programme at irregular intervals, a combination of instruction pack and individual briefings can suffice, as long as there are regular events where the participants can meet (physically or virtually) for interactive learning about mentoring roles and skills.

A third factor in favour of training together is that it provides a valuable opportunity to experience the other side's perspective directly. An illustration of what happens when one or both parties do not understand the other's perspective comes from a large and venerable financial institution. The programme failed because mentees didn't really believe mentors were approachable and willing to discuss a wide range of developmental topics. Their observations about the organisation's culture (sort your own problems, don't complain, never admit any weaknesses) got in the way because they had never heard the mentors – either individually or as a group – commit to the different agenda.

There are other ways to share perspectives and expectations – for example, a number of companies co-opt mentors from the previous year's programme to talk to mentees about their experience and vice versa – but it is difficult to create the same level of understanding as comes from the immediate and intuitive responses of a number of mentors or mentees together. BP, which introduced an upward mentoring programme where junior people of different race and/or gender become mutual mentors to senior managers, opted to train both together because it needed to build initial confidence among mentees that senior managers were genuinely committed to open dialogue on diversity issues. In such circumstances, there is no real substitute for hearing it direct.

In another organisation – a government department – mentees use a website to select a mentor from a pool of volunteers, but not everyone is sure at the beginning which role they will take. For this reason – and to manage the numbers, so that training could be on offer as soon as possible after a pairing was made – the practical solution was to train both together. Those people who are sure they wanted to become mentees usually find particular value in skills training, because it helps them get more out of the programme and their mentor.

The case for training apart

The case for training apart is equally as strong, and equally as dependent on circumstances. Most commonly it occurs in relatively traditional programmes, where mentors and mentees have already been selected, although they may or may not have been matched.

Among the arguments for separate training are:

1. It enables mentors and mentees to be open about their hopes and fears for the programme. Typical fears among mentors relate to whether they are really capable of doing the role well. Among mentees there may be concerns about confidentiality, or about why they have been selected to take part. (Is there really a hidden remedial agenda, for example?)

   The point is illustrated by the following quote from a mentee in a major chemicals business when the mentees as a group were offered the chance to merge their training with a mentor group:

   > I've got to know one mentor very well and I'm very open with him. That doesn't mean I see all the other mentors in the same light – they are still senior managers to me. My behaviour would revert to normal in that group, which would make me feel false in the relationship with my own mentor.

   In cultures which are not very positive towards developmental behaviours and where mentoring and coaching are not seen as natural to everyday management, such concerns will be particularly influential on the success of the programme. By contrast, organisations with very positive developmental cultures may well find that people prefer to be trained together, as this is one more opportunity to learn from another group.

2. It is much easier to focus the workshops around the specific needs of each group. While much of the broad agenda for a workshop will be common, mentors need to spend more time practising skills and techniques, while mentees need more time to consider how they want to use a mentor and how they will gradually take the lead in managing the relationship.

3. The difficulty of getting senior managers to commit sufficient time to training for the role. A day is generally regarded as the minimum initial training for both mentor and mentee, but if the mentors resist then the programme co-ordinator has the choice of training separately, or trying to cram training for both into insufficient time. Training separately doesn't overcome the senior manager problem, but it does ensure the mentees are adequately prepared for their roles.

So there is no right answer, but hopefully this analysis will help you decide which approach will work best for your scheme.

WHAT MAKES FOR QUALITY OF TRAINING?

Given that quality derives from 'fitness for purpose', a lot depends on the objectives of the scheme and the context in which it takes place. In mentee terms, what will suit a group of legal analysts seeking partnership is unlikely to do the job for a bunch of young offenders; and the same would be true for their respective mentors.

Below are some of the key factors to take into account.

Composition

There should be a good mix of:

- theory (most training we have evaluated is very poor on mentoring theory, although it often includes generalised management or behavioural theory)
- discussion of scheme purpose
- discussion of roles and responsibilities
- opportunity to explore one's own motives and objectives and, if possible, those of the other party
- exploration of competencies of an effective mentor and mentee
- exposure to relevant skills of relationship management
- practice of relevant skills for learning within the mentoring dyad.

Groundedness

It makes a substantial difference to people's motivation if the training sessions are attended by top management, to outline the value of the programme to the organisation and to talk about their own experiences in the mentor and/or mentee role. It is also useful to invite participants from previous schemes to discuss their experience – warts and all.

Trainer/facilitator knowledge

It adds considerably to the credibility of the workshop if the trainer is able to refer to his or her own experience as mentor and mentee. Participants also appear to value it when the facilitator is able to provide a breadth of example of good practice from other schemes, and especially from other organisations.

MATCHING TRAINING PROVISION TO THE PHASES OF RELATIONSHIP EVOLUTION

One approach that does not work is to throw all the training for mentors and mentees at them in one go. There's simply too much to absorb and people need an opportunity to practise basic skills and techniques before they attempt more advanced ones. Broadly speaking, training interventions can best be made as they move from one phase of the relationship to the next. (See Chapter 12 for a more detailed description of the phases.)

At the initiation phase of the relationship, mentors and mentees need to understand the purpose of the programme, how to build rapport, and how to begin to set goals and boundaries for the relationship. A few months later, they need the skills to review progress and sharpen up personal goals. They also typically value an opportunity to refresh their understanding of the basics. Some months later again, by which time they should be in the progress-making phase, they will appreciate more advanced skills of drawing out and exploring issues. One very successful scheme, for example, instructs participants in emotional intelligence at this point. Finally, both mentor and mentee need to be prepared for a positive winding-up of the relationship and they usually value an opportunity to discuss how best to accomplish that.

Some organisations, especially corporations in the United States with very large mentoring programmes, have established monthly lunch or breakfast seminars, aimed at providing continuous development for mentors and mentees. Other organisations have opted for an initial intensive one-day introduction to mentoring, followed by two or three one- or two-day further development sessions. The aim, in both cases, is to maintain a steady pace of process learning for both mentor and mentee.

PUTTING TRAINING AND SCHEME MANAGEMENT TOGETHER

Table 6 is an example of how the scheme management and training processes can be integrated over a 12-month programme. This is not intended to be a fixed template – merely an illustration of what a well-planned programme might involve.

Table 6 A template for training over a 12-month programme

Training intervention	Mentor development	Mentee development
Rapport-building/direction setting **Communication with sponsors:** • Programme objectives and expected benefits. • Results of initial survey of participants. • Results of readiness for mentoring survey.	**Skills:** • Understanding of mentoring process and roles. • Introduction to reflective space. • Relationship development and management (including boundary management). • Questioning/listening techniques. • Goal setting. • Managing intrinsic feedback. • Double loop learning processes. **Measurement:** • Training effectiveness. • Survey to assess expectations of the mentoring relationship.	**Skills:** • Understanding of mentoring process and roles. • Introduction to reflective space. • Relationship development and management (including boundary management). • Goal setting. • Managing intrinsic feedback. • Double loop learning processes. **Measurement:** • Training effectiveness. • Survey to assess expectations of the mentoring relationship.
Initial review **Communication with sponsors:** • Results of survey part two. • Meet the participants session.	**Skills:** • Informal relationship review processes (how are we doing?). • Using anecdote and story. • Triple loop learning processes. • The mentor as networker/link to resources. • The mentor as career counsellor/workplace counsellor. **Sustaining interest:** • Newsletter 1. **Measurement:** • Survey to assess mentor and mentee behaviours/relationship quality.	**Skills:** • Career self-management • How to pose and pursue issues for discussion • Managing the learning net. **Sustaining interest:** • Newsletter 1. **Measurement:** • Survey to assess mentor and mentee behaviours/relationship quality.

Training intervention	Mentor development	Mentee development
Secondary review **Communication with sponsors:** • Results of dynamics survey part 3. • Developers' Council.	**Skills:** • Managing constructive challenge and confrontation. • The mentor as guardian. • The mentor as coach. • Understanding and using emotional intelligence. **Sustaining interest:** • Newsletter 3. • Developers' Council. **Measurement:** • Survey to measure outcomes.	**Skills:** • Managing constructive challenge and confrontation. **Sustaining interest:** • Newsletter 3. **Measurement:** • Survey to measure outcomes.
Wind-up review **Communication with sponsors:** • Plans for next phases of the programme/new target groups. • Report of balanced scorecard survey	**Skills:** • How to move beyond the formal relationship. • Formal learning review. • Becoming a mentee – whether, when and how. • Further (advanced) techniques and approaches. **Sustaining interest:** • Developers' Council. **Measurement:** • Balanced scorecard. • Mentoring scheme standards.	**Skills:** • How to move beyond the formal relationship. • Formal learning review. • Becoming a mentor – whether, when and how. **Sustaining interest:** • Alumni group. **Measurement:** • Balanced scorecard. • Mentoring scheme standards.

EXPLANATIONS

Newsletter – a summary of what individual pairs are doing, tips and techniques, questions asked on the hotline or to the programme co-ordinator.

Alumni group – one or two of the mentees agrees to manage a monthly chat room for their colleagues. Each new wave of mentees is invited to participate.

Developers' Council – mentors are recognised for their role as developers. They meet with top management periodically to discuss the broader issues of talent management and people development. In this way, they become part of the strategic thinking of the organisation with regard to people issues.

Balanced scorecard – a survey method that assesses the programme against four elements:

1. relationship processes
2. relationship outcomes
3. programme processes
4. programme outcomes.

ROLE OF THE MENTORING PROGRAMME MANAGER

A good mentoring programme manager is integral to programme success. It is their energy and enthusiasm for mentoring specifically and for developing others more generally that will drive the programme and keep momentum within it.

It is also worth noting that setting up, running and properly supporting a mentoring programme takes a great deal of time. For a pilot programme aimed at around 15 pairs you can expect to spend:

- 8–15 days preparing the scheme and the organisation.
- 1–2 days training and initial hand-holding for each group of mentees and mentors.
- 3–5 days of review and on-going measurement.
- 2–4 days of general troubleshooting.
- 3 days of full review and programme redesign after 12 months.

Following that, maintenance of the scheme is likely to require 2–3 days per month, with a greater load during the preparation and launch stages. For a more complex, larger programme aimed at an audience needing greater support, the time investment will be higher and more consistently spread across the programme. So it is clear that a highly skilled and enthusiastic programme manager is essential.

The role and responsibilities of the programme manager include:

1. Promote the concept of mentoring and ensure commitment from the business – making sure that senior management understands what mentoring will be and that it being supportive of mentoring is essential. They identify where mentoring will add most value to the organisation by showing how it can solve real business issues and they will bring a strong argument explaining how this will work.
2. Define and implement the process – this will include defining the objectives and success criteria for the programme; supporting the planning for recruitment, matching and training of potential participants, how the programme will be measured and maintaining the momentum in the programme.
3. Provide and maintain confidentiality – ensuring information gathered as part of the mentoring programme is secure and to provide support to participants around the issue of confidentiality.
4. Give honest and constructive feedback to mentees and mentors – this may be at the recruitment stage, during the matching or if relationships are struggling and you need to intervene.
5. Managing expectations of all stakeholders – this will involve ensuring that all participants have sufficient initial understanding of their roles and responsibilities before starting their role as a mentee/mentor, but also that line managers and any steering group are also aware of what is expected of them.
6. Provide appropriate resources for support – these will need to be identified during the programme design, but the programme manager will be the one who ensures that it is easy to get involved, that they understand any matching process, receive the training they need for their role, that pairs have access to suitable resources, further development and the opportunity to reflect with their peers.
7. Evaluate the scheme – it will be their responsibility to ensure that not only does measurement take place but that the data is analysed, shared and responded to. A great programme manager is constantly assessing the status of their programme and making adjustments to it based on both the firm and anecdotal evidence they see. This will also need to be done upon completion of the programme.

8 Keep all stakeholders well informed – this involves sharing all evaluation data and detailing any challenges that they've encountered. Keeping any steering group or senior management close to the programme will give you more scope to enhance the programme and develop it and keep them motivated to support it.

9 Maintain financial control over the programme.

10 Set up and maintain administrative records for the programme – there is a great deal of data that needs to be gathered during the course of a programme and much of it is important to log so that you can refer back to it at a later stage. For example:

   - mentee and mentor details
   - training attended
   - matching details
   - date of first meeting
   - waiting list of participants
   - relationship and programme outcomes.

A programme manger will ensure appropriate systems are put in place to track this data and will store and share this data safely.

A great programme manager will also ideally have the following skills:

- good interpersonal skills and insights
- political astuteness
- knowledge of the organisation and culture
- clarity around business priorities and politics of the organisation
- good communication skills (both verbal and written)
- access to top management
- time to listen and become involved
- facilitation skills
- project management skills
- working knowledge of mentoring theory and practice
- experience of being a mentee and/or mentor.

SOME HINTS AND TIPS FROM PREVIOUS PROGRAMME MANAGERS

- Do not take this on if you already have a heavy workload – it takes a lot of time and energy as you get constant queries.
- Do not underestimate the need for good administrative support – there is a lot of admin in getting things set up and tracking relationships without interfering in them.
- Set realistic timescales – getting stakeholders on board, recruiting participants, and getting training in place and participants booked on to that takes time.
- Manage expectations. Do not underestimate either mentee and mentor expectations of the programme. Be prepared to handle difficult conversations, such as:
  - directors or chief executives not being happy with their mentee
  - mentees who are not given the mentor they wanted
  - not everyone will get paired up, or if they do some relationships may not work out
  - some mentors or mentees may leave the organisation.
- Just because a mentor or mentee is part of the programme, it does not mean they cannot use their own initiative to find an alternative mentor or mentee.
- A guide that can go out to line managers is very helpful; lots of mentees request this.
- Giving feedback once pairings are set up is very important.
- Accept that not everyone will be happy.
- Do not rely on just one mechanism of communication to advertise the programme.

- If you use matching forms, double check what information you need in them – the more data you collect the more challenging it is to match.
- Do not miss out on chief executive and director-level mentors just because they cannot attend training; most have done mentoring already and are very good at it.
- Ensure you have support and a source of advice to keep you sane.

SUMMARY

To be really successful, a mentoring programme must obtain acceptance and commitment from participants and non-participants alike. The scheme should have empathetic, carefully selected and trained mentors and mentees who understand how to make the most of opportunities, and clear goals that are accepted by all. A great deal of effort is therefore needed to prepare employees at all levels for the introduction of the programme, ensuring that everyone knows what is happening, and why and how the scheme will work. Particular attention should be given to the mentoring pairs, the mentee's boss and the mentee's peers. Starting small with a modest experiment helps take some of the bugs out of the system before it is applied generally throughout the organisation.

EXPLORE FURTHER

CLUTTERBUCK, D. (2013) *Making the most of developmental mentoring: a practical guide for mentors and mentees*. Coaching and Mentoring International.

CRANWELL-WARD, J., BOSSONS, P. and GOVER, S. (2004) *Mentoring: a Henley review of best practice*. Basingstoke: Palgrave.

KLASEN, N. and CLUTTERBUCK, D. (2002) *Implementing mentoring schemes: a practical guide to successful programs*. Oxford: Elsevier Butterworth-Heinemann.

CHAPTER 8

Beginning the Mentoring Relationship

The relationship should develop swiftly and smoothly if both mentor and mentee have been well matched and well prepared. The phases the relationship typically goes through are examined in the next chapter. In this short section we look at how to make sure that the mentoring pair make the most of the opportunity given them.

By the time the mentor and mentee hold their first formal meeting under the mentoring programme, both should have a clear idea of the objectives of the relationship. These may be relatively vague at this stage, not least because the programme is intended to help the mentee refine and develop his or her career objectives. However, it should at least start with some form of assessment of the mentee's strengths and weaknesses, the nature of the transition he or she would like to make, and what the longer-term ambitions are. It will also, of course, take into account the general programme objectives, which both parties should understand clearly.

Typical starting objectives might include the following:

- Help the mentee develop greater self-insight and self-awareness – to become clearer about their personal values and identity.
- Introduce the mentee to other, parallel functions or departments whose work he or she will need to understand to progress, or that may open his or her eyes to potential sideways moves.
- Help the mentee develop and refine their personal sense of purpose – what is it that they want to contribute to the world?
- Help the mentee break down a seemingly impossible or far-fetched goal into a series of more tangible tasks that he or she can begin to address. Having a more or less detailed route map of the experience, skills and competencies he or she needs to gather, the mentee can enter on to a self-development or career management path with greater confidence and commitment.
- Help the mentee think through how to raise his or her visibility where it matters.
- Help the mentee establish the informal networks he or she needs to be effective in the organisation.
- Act as a sounding board in helping the mentee work out how to manage difficult relationships with working colleagues.
- Help the mentee think through how to apply in practice what he or she is learning through theoretical study.
- Gain a real understanding of the career choices that face the mentee and the implications of each choice.

Some organisations prefer to set out objectives in terms of process rather than outcomes. For example, a large UK chemical company set out the following responsibilities at the beginning of a mentoring relationship:

- Meet the mentee once a month for at least an hour by timetabling formally in advance.
- Ensure that the mentee maintains a brief diary of daily events to form the basis for the monthly discussion.
- Develop a personal relationship with the mentee.
- Maintain the relationship for two years.

The reasoning here – which is borne out by research – is that in many cases the mentee's objectives from the relationship may initially be quite vague. Part of the role of mentoring is to help them in the processes of reflection, introspection and understanding of their context and the opportunities open to them, so that they can clarify what they want. A high proportion of the time, mentees' objectives change as the relationship progresses.

It is also important that the two people start off with the same understanding of the ground rules of the relationship. In particular, there have to be clear rules of behaviour. Hence the need for an ethical code of practice and for a contracting process between mentor and mentee.

An ethical code of practice for mentoring

- The mentor's role is to respond to the mentee's developmental needs and agenda; it is not to impose his or her own agenda.
- Mentors must work within the current agreement with the mentee about confidentiality that is appropriate within the context.
- The mentor will not intrude into areas the mentee wishes to keep private until invited to do so. However, he or she should help the mentee recognise how other issues may relate to those areas.
- Mentor and mentee should aim to be open and truthful with each other and themselves about the relationship itself.
- The mentoring relationship must not be exploitative in any way, nor can it be open to misinterpretation.
- Mentors need to be aware of the limits of their own competence and operate within these limits.
- Mentors have a responsibility to develop their own competence in the practice of mentoring.
- The mentee must accept increasing responsibility for managing the relationship; the mentor should empower them to do so and must generally promote the mentee's autonomy.
- Mentor and mentee should respect each other's time and other responsibilities, ensuring that they do not impose beyond what is reasonable.
- Mentor and mentee share responsibility for the smooth winding down of the relationship when it has achieved its purpose – they must both avoid creating dependency.
- Either party may dissolve the relationship. However, both mentor and mentee have a responsibility for discussing the matter together as part of mutual learning.
- The mentee should be aware of his or her rights and any complaints procedures.
- Mentors must be aware of any current law and work within the law.
- Mentor and mentee must be aware that all records are subject to statutory regulations under the Data Protection Act 1998.

THE MENTORING CONTRACT

The notion of a mentoring contract is widespread and poses a similar conundrum to measurement. To what extent should we risk bureaucratising an essentially informal process? Some clarity is essential, but how much, and does a written document contribute greatly to clarity anyway?

There is no straightforward answer, not least because it depends on circumstance. In an experiment some years ago within the National Health Service, I provided 100 pairs of mentors and mentees with detailed discussion guides, formal contracts to sign, and extensive background notes. I then invited them to use these religiously, to scan them and put them aside, or to ignore them altogether. When we reviewed the results, it became clear that only 20% had completed the contracts, while the others had roughly half and half scanned or ditched them. The success rate of the relationships did not seem to be affected by their choice. From this, I conclude, it should be left to the mentee and mentor to decide how they approach the issue of contracting.

What does seem to be essential is that both sides discuss the relationship objectives, their expectations of each other, and how they will manage the relationship. The following checklist provides a basic set of questions most people can relate to in discussing these issues.

MENTORING GROUND RULES

1 a. Are we clear about each other's expectations of:

- each other?
- the mentoring relationship?
- what we hope to learn from each other?

b. How closely do our expectations match?
c. How directive or non-directive should the mentor be in each meeting?

2 a. What are the core topics we want to discuss?
b. What, if any, are the limits to the scope of discussion (ie what we talk about)?

3 Who will take primary responsibility – ie the mentor, the mentee or both together – for:

- deciding how often to meet?
- setting the agenda for meetings?
- ensuring that meetings take place?
- organising where to meet, and for how long?
- defining learning goals?
- initiating reviews of progress?

4 How formal or informal do we want our meetings to be?

5 To what extent is the mentor prepared to allow the mentee to:

- use his or her authority?
- use his or her networks?
- take up time between meetings?

6 Are we agreed that openness and trust are essential? How will we ensure they happen?

7 Are we *both willing* to give honest and timely feedback (eg to be a critical friend)?

8 a. What, if any, are the limits to the confidentiality of this relationship?
b. What are we prepared to tell others:

- about the relationship?
- about our discussions?

c. Who shall we tell, and how?

9 What responsibilities do we owe to others as a result of this relationship (eg to line managers, peers, the programme co-ordinator)?

10 a. How do we ensure the mentee's line manager is supportive?
b. Is there a clear distinction between the roles of mentor and line manager?
c. If there are overlaps, how will these be managed?

11 When and how shall we check this relationship is 'right' for both of us?

THE FIRST MEETING

The aim of the first meeting is to establish rapport and to gain a sense of relationship purpose. It's important to meet in a neutral space (or at least somewhere both mentor and mentee can feel comfortable and relaxed). Both mentor and mentee need to feel they can work with each other and can learn from each other. If one or both feels this isn't the case, then both have a responsibility to explore what kind of mentor the mentee needs, and to trigger the 'no fault divorce clause'.

Richard Hale's (2000) study of mentoring pairs shows that the quality of rapport is highly dependent on the participants' perception that they share common values. Mentor and mentee training should therefore incorporate some practical tools and skills practice in sharing values. Diagnostic tools, such as the Reiss Motivational Profile® (RMR), can be helpful in opening up the values conversation, but it is often sufficient to ask questions such as:

- What makes you feel good about yourself and others?
- What annoys you about yourself and others?
- What are the most important things in your life?
- What qualities do you admire in other people?
- What could you not live without?
- What stirs your emotions?

Other useful issues to explore include:

- What have been the biggest lessons you have learned in your career so far?
- What does success mean to you?
- What is your personal sense of purpose?

Starting off with this level of openness and depth of conversation establishes the tone and quality of the relationship. It also helps avoid 'relationship droop' – where the relationship runs out of steam after a few meetings because it has focused only on relatively straightforward, transactional issues and failed to achieve sufficient depth and challenge.

SUMMARY

Getting the mentoring relationship off to a good start is vital. Mutual trust, shared expectations of each other and of the relationship itself, relationship momentum and the quality of the subsequent mentoring conversations all depend on the first few meetings.

CHAPTER 9

Measuring and Monitoring the Programme

The mentoring programme needs some system of feedback and evaluation in order to know whether mentoring is functioning efficiently and successfully. For example, one large UK manufacturing company holds a graduate workshop at least once a year so graduate mentees can get together and produce a report recommending changes in the system.

There are three main reasons for measuring:

- to troubleshoot individual relationships
- to provide information for quality improvement of the mentoring programme
- to demonstrate to top management that the investment in mentoring has been worthwhile.

One of the paradoxes of formal mentoring programmes is that the essence of the relationship is its *informality* – the ability to discuss in private a wide range of issues that will help the mentee cope with and learn from issues he or she encounters, putting aside any power or status differences that might operate outside the relationship. So the idea of measurement and review is, on the face of it, to some extent at odds with the need to retain a high degree of informality and ad hoc responsiveness.

In practice, a certain amount of measurement provides the foundation on which the informal relationship can grow most healthily. It allows:

- scheme managers to recognise where additional support is needed and to improve the operation of the scheme – not least the training.
- mentors and mentees to work together to build the relationship, understanding more clearly what each can and does bring to the discussions. Programme managers frequently report that contacting participants for feedback can provide a stimulus for re-examining and revitalising the relationship.

Where attempts to measure mentoring become unacceptable, they usually involve:

- an attempt to assess and report upon mentees' performance to a third party
- a link between the mentor's opinion and a specific reward for the mentee (a promotion or a diploma, for example) – here the role has become more that of a tutor
- disclosure of the content of mentoring discussions.

In such circumstances, measurement is likely to make the mentee – and sometimes the mentor – less open, less willing to admit weaknesses and less trusting, hence limiting the potential of the relationship to deliver high quantity and quality of learning.

By contrast, effective measurement in mentoring is:

- relatively unobtrusive
- valued by all parties as helpful
- timely
- straightforward and easy to apply.

THE MEASUREMENT MATRIX

Mentoring measurements fall into four categories, illustrated in Figure 12:

- Relationship processes – what happens in the relationship; for example, how often does the pair meet? Have they developed sufficient trust? Is there a clear sense of direction to the relationship? Does the mentor or the mentee have concerns about their own or the other person's contribution to the relationship?
- Programme processes – for example, how many people attended training? How effective was the training? In some cases, programme processes will also include data derived from adding together measurements from individual relationships, to gain a broad picture of what is going well and less well.
- Relationship outcomes – have mentor and mentee met the goals they set? (Some adjustment may be needed for legitimate changes in goals as circumstances evolve.)
- Programme outcomes – have we, for example, increased retention of key staff, or raised the competence of the mentees in critical areas?

Measuring all four gives you a balanced view of the mentoring programme and allows the scheme manager to intervene, with sensitivity, where needed.

Figure 12 Categories of mentoring measurement

Programme process	Programme outcome/goals
• How often do they meet: at least five meetings? • What phase have they reached in the relationship? • Are people networking more?	• Is there clear evidence of progress towards diversity objectives? • Is retention for mentees higher than for non-mentored peers? • Do we have a clearer idea of who our emerging talent is?
Relationship process	**Relationship outcomes**
• Do they trust each other/work together well? • Are they dealing with real issues? • Are they enjoying mentoring?	• Has significant learning taken place? • Has the mentee gained in competence in an area they wanted to work on? • Does the mentee have a clearer personal development plan?

WHAT SHOULD BE REVIEWED WHEN?

AT THE PROGRAMME PLANNING STAGE

There is a need at both programme and relationship level for a clear purpose upfront and a clear idea of what behaviours are expected from both mentors and mentees. It is good practice to involve potential participants and other interested parties (eg line managers, top management) to agree measurements at the beginning. At the very least this discussion will establish the extent to which measurements can be 'soft' (qualitative) or 'hard' (quantitative).

Many organisations now begin the programme with a short research project to establish likely barriers and drivers to mentoring.

IN SELECTING/TRAINING MENTORS AND MENTEES

Mentors and mentees can benefit from greater self-awareness of their strengths and weaknesses as developers of others. Mentees often need to have some ideas about the areas of interpersonal behaviour they can work on with the mentor.

AFTER THE FIRST FEW MEETINGS

This is the opportunity for mentor and mentee to review whether the relationship is going to work. Key questions here include:

- Have we established strong rapport and trust sufficient to work together?
- Does the mentee perceive the mentor's input as relevant and stimulating?
- If not, what sort of person does the mentee need to work with?

The scheme manager will want by this point to know whether people are meeting and whether they have discussed the future of the relationship.

AS THE RELATIONSHIP PROGRESSES

The scheme manager will want as a minimum to know what further support is needed, if any, in the form of further, more focused skills training, or general encouragement to participants. Good practice typically involves a short survey of participants, followed by a review session during which some ad hoc training can be provided.

AT THE END OF THE RELATIONSHIP

Assuming the relationship achieves its objectives and winds up, it is useful for both parties to review the following:

- What did we expect to achieve?
- What did we actually achieve?
- What else did we learn on the way?
- How will we use what we have learnt in future developmental relationships?

AT THE END OF THE PROGRAMME

Assuming the programme assigns an end to the formal mentoring relationship (many relationships will, of course, continue informally thereafter), the outcomes can be measured against the original goals.

SUMMARY

It's important to establish programme measures in the early planning stages – if only so participants know what success looks like and can bear that in mind in how they conduct the relationship. Robust measurements can prove decisive in protecting the programme, too. For example, a new head of learning and development at a multinational company was determined to make his mark by clearing away all the established people development programmes and starting again. Mentoring was one of a handful of programmes that survived unscathed – the result of very clear and unambiguous data about its positive impact and representation from the mentor community.

CHAPTER 10

Standards for Mentoring Programmes

One of the clear conclusions from the experiences of hundreds of mentoring programmes is that attention to doing it well pays dividends. Failure (see Chapter 13) is almost always the result of a combination of:

- inadequate groundwork (preparing the organisation and stakeholders, having clear objectives and so on)
- inadequate training (for both mentors and mentees, and ideally also for key third parties, such as the mentees' line manager)
- insufficient continuing support to sustain the programme.

Conversely, investment in these areas typically ensures that the programme delivers very good value for money and has a significant impact on the learning and careers of the majority of both mentors and mentees.

The need for standards for mentoring programmes is based on four factors:

1. Programme managers need some kind of pragmatic benchmark of good practice to use as a guideline in both designing and assessing their mentoring programmes.
2. It is increasingly important to HR professionals to be able to demonstrate that the initiatives they have implemented on behalf of the organisation are well-designed and well-founded.
3. External endorsement of a programme, to a recognised standard, gives participants greater confidence that they will receive the quality of support they need to make the most of the mentoring opportunities.
4. They provide a broad basis for measuring improvement in the quality and effectiveness of a mentoring programme.

A wide variety of organisations, including the Institute of Leadership & Management (ILM) and the European Mentoring & Coaching Council (EMCC), offer accreditation of mentor training. However, there appear to be only three sources of accreditation for mentoring programmes. The Mentoring and Befriending Foundation (MBF) (www.mandbf.org), a UK body working in primary and secondary education, youth justice and parts of the general voluntary sector administers an Approved Provider Standard (APS). This standard addresses 12 issues:

1. Clear rationale and purpose.
2. Effective organisational and management structure.
3. Competence of staff.
4. Clear process for identifying and referring service users.
5. Service users fully briefed.
6. Rigorous recruitment and selection processes.
7. Participants' involvement safeguarded.

8. Adequate training and preparation for mentors.
9. Process for matching.
10. Supervision and support for mentors.
11. Monitoring of relationships.
12. Evidence of project effectiveness.

Note that these standards focus on the training and support for the mentor. Yet we know that training and supporting mentees is equally important.

The International Mentoring Association (IMA) launched in 2013 a set of basic standards, aimed mainly at the education – including tertiary education – and community sectors (http://mentoring-association.org/standards/). They may be used as part evidence for International Standards for Mentoring Programmes in Employment (ISMPE – www.ismpe.com). Like the ISMPE, the IMA standards have six elements, in this case:

1. Clear vision of programme scope.
2. Clear roles and responsibilities for (programme) leadership.
3. Selection and assessment.
4. Mentor professional development.
5. Formative assessment (demonstrating mentee growth and progress).
6. Programme evaluation.

Launched in 2003 after extensive consultation with programme managers and other observers of good practice in 12 countries, the ISMPE are focused very closely on mentoring in the workplace. They provide a generic platform for the design and assessment of programmes for graduate recruits, diversity programmes, technical qualification programmes and most other situations with a mixture of career and personal development objectives. They apply in a wide variety of cultures and across the worlds of commerce, manufacturing, higher education and the voluntary sector.

The ISMPE are made up of a set of six core standards. The first deals with the clarity of purpose of the programme. Do all the key stakeholders understand what it aims to achieve for the organisation and for the participants? The second covers the quantity and quality of training provided. Is it sufficient to get people started with adequate confidence and an understanding of how to learn the role by doing it?

The third area covers selection and matching processes. Do mentors and mentees have a say in how they are matched? Is there an appropriate policy and approach for rematching? The fourth deals with measurement and review. Do the measures selected establish how effective the programme has been at the levels of both organisation and individual pair? The fifth explores the existence and application of ethical codes. Finally, the sixth covers programme administration and how well participants are supported beyond the initial training and matching.

The ISMPE is a not-for-profit organisation, with an international board of academics, programme managers and providers. They are supported by experienced mentoring programme designers, who have qualified as assessors. In organisations with large numbers of mentoring programmes, in-house HR professionals can train to be assessors of programmes they do not personally manage. All assessments are reviewed and monitored by a second assessor, to assure consistent quality.

Standard number 3 from the ISMPE, 'Stakeholder Training and Briefing', is as follows:

- Participants and stakeholders understand the concept of mentoring and their respective roles.
- Participants are aware of the skills and behaviours they need to apply in their roles as mentors and mentees; and have an opportunity to identify skills gaps.

- Learning support is available throughout the first 12 months of their involvement in the programme.

Table 7 contains an extract from the ISMPE.

Table 7 The International Standards for Mentoring in Employment (ISMPE): an example

Performance criteria	Questions	Suggested evidence
2.1 Participation in a process to learn the basics of mentoring is a non-negotiable condition of taking part in the mentoring programme, for both mentors and mentees.	• Is there a policy to require all mentors and mentees to attend training? • Is this policy rigorously enforced? (ie are their some matches made with participants, who have not been trained?)	• There is a record of at least some time spent learning about mentoring and associated skills by all participants. • Documentation, manager interviews, participant verification.
2.2 There is a clear and well-founded conceptual framework to explain mentoring functions and behaviours.	• Does the training material use and explain a behavioural model? • Does it relate mentoring activity to a broader developmental context? • Is the level of explanation appropriate for the audience? • Do participants understand the model? • Are they able to use it as a practical baseline for their role as mentor or mentee?	• Training workbook/ materials include appropriate models. • Documentation, manager interviews, participant verification.
2.3 Participants obtain a clear distinction between mentoring and other forms of help and learning (eg coaching, counselling, tutoring).	• Does the training material provide succinct and easily grasped distinctions? • Do participants have an opportunity to discuss and internalise those distinctions? • Are the boundaries between the different forms of 'helping to learn' clear? • Are the commonalities between the different forms of 'helping to learn' clear?	• Training workbook/ materials clarify the distinction. • Documentation, manager interviews, participant verification.
2.4 There is a clear and well-founded framework of competencies for mentors and mentees, upon which the training is based.	• Is there a competency base at all? • Is it a proper framework, or simply a list of skills? • Is it supported by research? • Is it clear why these skills/ competencies are important for a mentor? • Do participants have an opportunity to discuss these?	• Training workbook/ materials explain competencies. • Opportunity to discuss competencies • Documentation, manager interviews, participant verification.

HOW TO GET THE BEST OUT OF PROGRAMME STANDARDS

Because they are distilled from the experiences of many organisations, with many types of programme and in many cultures, any set of standards will tend to be generic in tone. That's a two-edged sword. On the one hand, you know that the issues identified have proven to be significant for many other organisations, and therefore are likely to be important for your programme, too. On the other hand, you may have very specific contextual elements to compare, which will not be covered by the standards. For example, if you are managing a reverse mentoring programme (where one party is substantially more junior in the formal hierarchy than the other, but where both take the role of mentor), then it would be helpful to be able to benchmark against other organisations with similar programmes.

The ISMPE, at least, is developing variations of its standards to meet the specific needs of some of the most common mentoring applications. However, this can only be a partial solution.

The ideal situation appears to be one that integrates the formal assessment of a programme through the most relevant of the standards with informal benchmarking, on a programme by programme basis. Useful websites to find benchmarking partners include:

- The University of New Mexico Mentoring Institute (http://mentor.unm.edu/home/).
- Mentoring Programme Managers Network, LinkedIn group (http://www.linkedin.com/groups?home=&gid=4730278&trk=anet_ug_hm).
- Coaching at Work magazine LinkedIn group (http://www.coaching-at-work.com/).
- Mentoring special interest group of the European Mentoring & Coaching Council (www.emccouncil.org).

In the meantime, relevant questions for programme managers include:

- How important is it to demonstrate that your mentoring programme is well designed and well managed?
- How will you identify improvement goals for the management and effectiveness of the programme? (Are internal measures sufficient, or are there clear benefits from benchmarking more widely?)
- Is a national or international standard most appropriate?
- Do we 'want the badge' or can we use the standards simply as a guideline to ensure we address all the issues we need to in programme design and management?

SUMMARY

It's sensible to be at least aware of the standards available for mentoring programmes and to build programmes with good practice guidelines in mind. Actively seeking to be measured against a standard can be valuable in identifying and rectifying any weaknesses in the programme.

CHAPTER 11

Peer and Reverse Mentoring

One of the primary differences between sponsorship mentoring and developmental mentoring is that the former depends on the mentor being significantly more senior in status and influence. In developmental mentoring, where what matters is the experience gap rather than the hierarchy gap, there is a lot more room for different patterns of relationship.

Whenever any two people come together in a learning relationship, they bring a whole spectrum of different experiences, some of which may be valuable to the other person. Even in a traditional mentoring relationship, where one person is older and more senior than the other, as long as the mentor is open to learning from the more junior person, there is always substantial opportunity for exchange of knowledge, skills and insight. At the very simplest level, most of my learning about making better use of my personal computer has been gained through the patience of younger people who have grown up in an IT environment, pointing out what is obvious to them, but not to me. The exchange for them is typically induction into the wider horizons of managerial and strategic thinking.

Abandoning status and authority within a relationship not only makes for greater rapport and openness, but also influences in a very positive way the quality of learning dialogue. When one party is felt to be in some sense superior, the sense of mutual exploration and discovery is muted. To some extent, this happens in all successful mentoring relationships, both developmental and sponsorship oriented, as barriers break down. In this chapter, however, we focus on mentoring relationships that are deliberately status-free: peer mentoring and reverse mentoring.

PEER MENTORING

Mentoring between peers, though by no means as widespread in formal structures as traditional mentoring, is increasingly common. For example, one of the most successful mentoring programmes in the UK National Health Service gave newly appointed chairpersons of National Health Trusts – highly experienced, very effective people within other roles – a peer mentor while they got used to the job. Some of the mentors commented that they wished they had had similar support when they went through the same experience! Also within the health service, general practitioners working for the first time with drug addicts gained a great deal of support and practical guidance from colleagues who had worked in that field for some years. In these cases there is a very specific experience gap to address. In many other examples of peer mentoring, however, particularly where the relationship is established informally, there is no single experience gap to focus upon. Both parties simply recognise the value the other person can provide in offering support, counsel and a different perspective on the issues they face. This kind of highly accepting, 'let's-work-on-what-matters-at-the-moment' relationship usually involves a strong sense of friendship and may have very ill-defined goals.

A brief Internet search produces many examples of peer mentoring with a wide variety of purposes. For example:

- The Living Positive programme in Southern Colorado pairs people who have recently contracted AIDS with peers who have learned how to live with it.

- The Children's Society has a programme that gives immigrant schoolchildren a peer mentor to help them fit in with their new environment, in and out of school.
- Washington University in St Louis has a peer mentoring programme for doctoral students, with students in their second year and beyond supporting those just starting their doctoral studies.
- In the south-west United States, a mining company uses peer mentors to maintain its safety record. Accidents are more likely to happen among new hires, but the peer mentoring programme has reduced the volume of incidents among mentored recruits by two-thirds, compared with a control group. Attrition among mentored employees was only 25% compared with unmentored colleagues, over a two-year period.
- Leicester City Council has used peer mentoring to support resettlement of homeless people.
- Peer mentoring is well-established in the field of mental health. Here's a description from a comparison of US and UK approaches to mental health support.

> Peer mentors are mental healthcare consumers well on their way to successful recovery who have been employed by the facility they are receiving care from to help those at lower functional levels with similar diagnosis. The benefits implicit therein are that the peer mentor has first-hand knowledge of what the mentee is experiencing. They understand the withdrawal pains. They can empathise with the frustrations of self-forgiveness. And they can guide mentees to more productive paths. Furthermore, peer mentors humanise the face of mental healthcare for each individual consumer; the treatment becomes relatable and believable because it is coming from the mouth of someone with the mentee's very same diagnosis who has picked themselves up, dusted themselves off, and made a success of themselves with the prescribed treatment plan.[1]

- Diabetic patients participating in a peer-mentoring programme had lower haemoglobin A1C levels and less severe diabetes over 6–10 months in an initiative that involved more than 550 patients at a single Texas health care organisation.
- Maternity mentoring (see the case study of Asda in Chapter 17) is a practical form of peer mentoring, which improves retention of female employees and helps them readjust to working life.

I have been lucky enough to have a handful of peer mentoring relationships over the years and have found that the level of challenge I receive, from someone who knows me and cares enough about me to be a critical friend, is higher than in any of the hierarchical mentoring relationships I have experienced. No-one has ever been as tough on me as my peer mentors and I'm grateful for it.

For an organisation wishing to encourage mentoring, it seems that the best way to encourage informal, peer mentoring is to develop the habit of mentoring through more traditional programmes. The traditional mentor can also help the learner think about and develop their learning net – the web of people around them, from whom they can usefully learn. The learning net includes direct reports, people in relevant professional associations and, of course, peers either within their working area or outside.

In seeking a peer mentor, the following guidelines may be helpful:

- Look for sufficient difference in experience and personality to provide a different set of perspectives.

---

[1] DOUVASA, L. (2009) *Peer Mentoring and Health Recovery*. July. Available at: http://ezinearticles.com/?Peer-Mentoring-and-Mental-Health-Recovery&id=2620137 [Accessed 18 December 2013].

- Seek someone who will be genuine and honest with you, no matter how painful what they have to say may be.
- Be accessible to each other on a regular basis (e-mail makes this much easier than used to be the case – see Chapter 19).
- Try to articulate what you value in each other – this will encourage you both to approach the other whenever you have something to chew over.
- Don't regard this as an exclusive relationship; seek to develop a number of relationships with people whose perspective you value for different reasons.

REVERSE MENTORING

Sometimes called mutual mentoring or upward mentoring, reverse mentoring has been used successfully in a variety of companies, including GE, Procter & Gamble, BT, BP, Cisco Systems and Accenture. It differs from peer mentoring in that the partners in the relationship are from different levels in the hierarchy – sometimes several levels apart – and from traditional mentoring in that it is the hierarchically more junior person who takes the primary mentoring role, although learning is still two-way.

The stimulus for upward mentoring has arisen from two main areas of concern. In diversity programmes, one of the limiting factors on progress of women and people from minority ethnic backgrounds has been the inability of top management to understand the issues. Even though they may have attended diversity awareness training, emotional commitment often only comes from seeing the issues through the eyes of someone who experiences them on a frequent basis.

The second area of concern has been the recognition that senior managers are often heavily out of touch with key areas such as new technology or customer concerns. That knowledge is usually held by people at relatively junior levels. Reverse mentoring provides a mechanism to bypass the normal communication channels, which tend to sanitise knowledge and keep the executives insulated from the concerns of employees and customers alike.

In essence, then, reverse mentoring is an opportunity for a reality check at the top of the organisation. The more junior (usually younger) employees have an opportunity to observe and learn from management thinking, to influence organisational policy and to become more at ease dealing with people of substantially greater hierarchical authority.

The benefits from reversing the mentoring roles are summarised in Table 8.

Table 8 Benefits of reverse mentoring

Benefits to senior manager	Benefits to the more junior partner	Benefits to the organisation
• Understanding perspectives of other groups in the organisation – gender, age, culture. • A sounding board on how new policies and/or strategies may be viewed from below. • Guidance on new and emerging technology. • 'Friends in low places'. • A source of challenge to their thinking.	• Visibility. • Access to senior management thinking. • A role model for their own development. • Challenge to their thinking. • Greater comfort in speaking with people in authority.	• Increased understanding and support for diversity management. • Enhanced leadership credibility. • Knowledge management. • Improved communication between layers in the organisation. • Constructive challenge to company policy and practice.

In practice, reverse mentoring programmes tend to avoid the issue of who is mentor and who is mentee, preferring to concentrate on the mutual learning roles. However, the very strong emphasis on the learning goals of the executives indicates where the primary intention of the relationships lies.

Being the 'mentor' in a reverse mentoring relationship is not easy. In most cases, the more junior person will have little experience at leading a learning dialogue with someone so senior. An important part of the training process, therefore, is to provide skills and some frameworks to structure discussions until they flow more easily.

Where the junior mentor is giving feedback on a real-time situation, we have found that a three-stage framework helps.

1 Initially, a briefing dialogue enables the pair to look at the upcoming activity and agree the focus for feedback.
2 A feedback dialogue allows full exploration of the experience.
3 A debrief dialogue looks at how the mentoring process worked and how it could be improved for future sessions.

The framework puts the junior mentor comfortably into the questioning role, allowing him or her to take the lead.

Mentors, too, need time to think through the relationship so that they accept and enjoy this reversal of roles. Although supportive of the concept, it is all too easy in the mentoring meeting to slip back into default mode and for the senior person to take the lead. Having a discussion framework that is understood by both parties gives the senior person confidence in the process, allowing him or her to participate freely and both to feel less threatened.

The following case studies illustrate the kind of approaches to reverse mentoring adopted by three organisations. The Procter & Gamble case is particularly interesting because it occurs in a traditional sponsorship mentoring environment in which hierarchy and status might have been expected to create a barrier to the learning relationship. The interest in peer and reverse mentoring is growing rapidly and these approaches are likely to become increasingly significant in the design of broad mentoring capability within large organisations.

CASE STUDY

EXAMPLES OF REVERSE MENTORING

Reverse mentoring cases tend to divide into three overlapping categories, revolving around:

1 **Technology and knowledge transfer:** Ogilvy & Mather managing director, Spencer Osborn, told *The Wall Street Journal* (WSJ) that his junior mentors have taught him how to jazz up his Twitter posts, which had a reputation for being 'very boring'. In the same article, the WSJ reports that:

> Andrew Graff, CEO of Allen & Gerritsen, a Watertown, Mass., ad agency, says he was one of the first to volunteer when his company launched a reverse mentoring programme last year. Under the programme, mentors and mentees meet every three weeks for 90 minutes over lunch or coffee. The 47-year-old has since come to lean on his mentor, 23-year-old Eric Leist, for guidance on everything from the latest smartphone apps to the layout for a new office. Mr. Graff says the most

important lesson he has learned is how to be flexible, including allowing employees to work unconventional hours and to check in from home or a coffee shop (Kwoh 2011).

2. **Generation gaps:** Alan Webber, the co-founder of Fast Company, is quoted having said that reverse mentoring is:

   > A situation where the old fogies in an organisation realise that by the time you're in your forties and fifties, you're not in touch with the future the same way the young twenty-somethings are. They come with fresh eyes, open minds, and instant links to the technology of our future (Quast 2011).

3. **Diversity awareness:** As in the cases of Procter & Gamble and Reuters US below.

The Cabinet Office

This case was first published in *Mentoring in Action* (Clutterbuck and Megginson 1999). Leslie Martinson was at the time a civil servant in the Cabinet Office, with a role that demanded she obtain a good instinctive understanding of the world of training. As this was not her core background Leslie enrolled on a two-year advanced diploma programme for trainers, which encouraged participants to seek mentors. The mentor she chose was someone younger and in a grade below, but with very extensive training experience. Ignoring the status difference made for relaxed, often humorous but intense meetings, where Leslie was able to explore her progress towards becoming an effective trainer, plus a number of other personal development goals she had set for herself.

The relationship survived changes of jobs on both sides, including one that took Leslie into the position of supervising her mentor's boss. The relationship dissolved as she completed the programme and both of them moved on to new fields.

Procter & Gamble (P&G)

A higher turnover among women in junior and middle management posts was one of the key triggers for the Mentoring Up programme introduced in P&G's marketing division in the US some years ago. The traditional response to this kind of problem in mentoring terms is to institute a glass ceiling programme, under which senior executives (usually predominantly male) would adopt younger, more junior protégés and nurture their progress. In this case, however, the company was astute enough to recognise that this approach (which was considered) would simply reinforce the cultural aspects of the problem. These could only be addressed by creating an environment in which the male executives learned to understand the problems of diversity for themselves.

The programme that resulted provided male managers with female mentors, usually more junior than themselves, whose role was to:

- provide them with informal, non-threatening feedback on how to manage issues specific to women
- act as a sounding board.

At the same time, the programme allowed the women mentors to develop quality relationships with people at senior level and hence to become more visible within the organisation. The results of the initiative include a remarkable improvement in the retention problem.

The Hartford

The Hartford is an insurance company, based in Connecticut, US. The CEO introduced reverse mentoring to help the company 'become more fluent in social media, mobile computing, The Cloud, and other digital technologies our customers and partners are using.'[2] As well as keeping up to date with changing technology and customer buying habits, he wanted to raise the company's profile as an employer of choice and impact the bottom line.

The reverse mentoring programme started with junior employees sharing their knowledge of social media with senior executives. Most of the executives acknowledged benefits both for their personal growth and for the business. From the first 12 mentors, 11 were promoted within the first year of the programme.

Reuters US

Reuters opted for a reverse mentoring programme because it was disappointed with the impact of diversity awareness training. Mentors were chosen through an interview process that included a brief role play and exploration of their motivations, how they shared their stories, how comfortable they were with the power issues, and how well they were able to address issues relating to diversity conflict.

Matching was guided by three principles:

1. They must work in different parts of the business, to avoid any career risks for the mentor.
2. Where possible, matches were cross-gender.
3. Each pair should share a significant similarity.

Mentors were given half a day's training and each pair was expected to meet monthly for at least six months. Meetings were held in neutral territory (ie not in the senior manager's office) to avoid any power pollution of the relationship. According to CEO John Robinson, himself a mentee:

> Our Reverse Mentoring Programme has been a revelation for many people. It has opened up new perspectives and has created an interactive dialogue that puts diversity issues on the table for direct and practical discussions. It has allowed us to get engaged in the issues and learn more about ourselves and our perspectives. Often our people have found this a transforming experience, and it has brought real focus to the opportunities that individuals and our business as a whole are now benefiting from.

The reverse mentoring programme was only 10% as costly as the previous diversity awareness training.

Scottish Water and Tesco Bank are both using reverse mentoring to support senior managers in becoming comfortable with social media.

HOW TO GET THE MOST FROM A PEER LEARNING ALLIANCE

Peer learning alliances (PLAs) are one of the most powerful variations to emerge in the development of mentoring. PLAs bring together people with different experience to learn from each other. They do so by:

- sharing experience, knowledge, and good practice
- challenging each other's assumptions about issues such as leadership, management, or diversity

[2] DEANGELIS, K.L. (2013) *Reverse Mentoring at the Hartford: Cross-generational transfer of knowledge about social media*. May. Available at: http://www.bc.edu/content/dam/files/research_sites/agingandwork/pdf/publications/hartford.pdf [Accessed 18 December 2013].

- providing a sounding board – someone who isn't involved yet is sufficiently concerned to listen and, where appropriate, guide
- expanding each other's networks
- opening new horizons and perspectives for each other.

The keys to effective PLAs are:

- Both parties are genuine volunteers.
- Both see the potential to learn from someone who works in a different environment.
- Both are willing to challenge and be challenged.
- Both have a clear understanding, through appropriate training, of their roles and responsibilities, the purpose of the relationship, and the skills required to manage the relationship well.
- They both prepare for each meeting beforehand; and reflect upon it afterwards.
- They have opportunities to review the relationship together.
- There is a well-informed source of advice and co-ordination in each organisation to support the participants.
- There is an appropriate balance between formality and informality – sufficient structure and measurement to provide the support they need, but not so much that it stifles open dialogue or becomes in any way intrusive.

Some key questions participants in PLAs can usefully ask themselves before agreeing a learning partnership are:

- How would I like this relationship to change me? To contribute to changing my abilities? My circumstances?
- What experience do I have that would be a useful exchange with someone from a different kind of management structure?
- How will I make sure I understand what the other partner is looking for in this arrangement?
- How will I be able to apply what I learn in managing this relationship to how I help my direct reports and other people in my own organisation develop?
- How much time and mental energy am I prepared to invest in this process?
- How does my skill set fit that of an effective peer learning partner? (If I don't know, how am I going to find out?)
- How will I make sure this is an enjoyable experience for both of us?

The most successful PLAs are typically those where both partners are very clear about what they want to achieve through the relationship and how they are going to make that happen. Rapport is important, however. The first two meetings should be seen as a probationary period, in which each decides whether they want to continue, to change partners, or to withdraw from the programme. It can be difficult to really open with someone you don't know and who is from a very different work background, but it's important for both partners to take some early risks, in terms of personal disclosure. The more you can direct the initial discussion towards what you value and to what is important in your life, the easier it will be to establish rapid, mutual trust.

It's also important to set the tone for the relationship, in terms of constructive challenge. Establishing an *expectation* of being asked thought-provoking questions at every meeting raises the quality of the dialogue and the amount of learning that takes place. Taking time to reflect and consider issues, rather than just talking at each other, is also fundamental to good outcomes from the PLA.

There are lots of benefits from this kind of learning relationship. Organisations benefit from higher levels of talent retention. Individual participants enlarge their horizons and more often than not achieve a greater sense of security in their normal job role. There is, however, a considerable investment that needs to be made by both participants and organisations, primarily in time and energy, to obtain the full value from the arrangement.

SUMMARY

Peer mentoring and reverse mentoring are becoming increasingly popular as a form of developmental mentoring. Peer mentoring is particularly useful within formal mentoring arrangements, because it can greatly extend the number of potential mentors available. Reverse mentoring has great potential to change organisational culture, especially in the context of diversity.

CHAPTER 12

Phases of the Mentoring Relationship

Mentoring is a dynamic relationship, aimed at bringing about change: both internal (within the participant) and external (in their circumstances). When it works well, mentoring stimulates change in the mentor as well as the mentee. Because it is a dynamic relationship, it evolves as mentor and mentee come to understand each other (and themselves) better and as the mentee clarifies what they want from their life and career.

Not surprisingly, the way the relationship evolves is not the same in sponsorship and developmental mentoring, although there are many similarities. One of the influencing factors is the length of the relationship, which tends to be much longer-term in sponsorship mentoring. Also relevant is the fact that sponsorship mentoring often occurs as a result of people already working together directly or indirectly, while developmental mentoring is most often designed to place some functional distance between mentor and mentee.

HOW SPONSORSHIP MENTORING RELATIONSHIPS EVOLVE

In the sponsorship model of mentoring, the relationship with the mentor influences the career and personal development of a young employee. In the early stages of his or her career, the young employee's identity, career aspirations and business relationships are forming. The junior must learn new technical, political, and interpersonal skills. Throughout this process, the mentor relationship is often the most important vehicle for stimulating and assisting his or her development. Our understanding of how this relationship evolves is based upon a study into the nature of the mentoring process, conducted in the early 1980s by Katherine Kram (1983), then Assistant Professor of Organizational Behavior at Boston University's School of Management. Kram attempted to discover the significance of the relationship for the mentor and the mentee and how mentoring influenced each party's career and self-development. She also tried to establish whether mentoring relationships share any similar characteristics.

Kram conducted her survey in a public utility company of 15,000 employees in the north-east region of the USA. She studied 18 mentoring pairs using in-depth interviews. The young mentees' ages ranged between 26 and 34, while the mentors' ages ranged between 39 and 63. The relationships varied considerably in duration, but Kram found that they were on average about five years long. Each relationship generally progressed through four distinct stages. In the remainder of this chapter we explore each of those phases – initiation (the start), the middle period, dissolving the relationship, and restarting – alongside the slightly different evolution observed in developmental mentoring. Figure 13 outlines these differences.

Kram's study was based on sponsorship mentoring and a definition that included both off-line and boss–subordinate relationships. The relationships were all informal rather than supported, so its general applicability to mentoring may be limited. She identifies four successive stages a relationship typically goes through: initiation, cultivation (in which 'the positive expectations that emerged during the initiation phase are tested against reality'), separation and redefinition. (See Figure 13.)

HOW DEVELOPMENTAL MENTORING RELATIONSHIPS EVOLVE

Developmental mentoring relationships, at least in the context of mentoring programmes, appear to have five phases: rapport-building, setting direction, making progress, winding up and moving on. Inevitably, there is some overlap between these phases and a degree of iteration. For example, a mentee may come to the relationship with a strong sense of purpose at the beginning, only to find that this evolves into something very different as the mentoring process causes them to question their assumptions. When mentor and mentee are aware of these phase transitions, they are better able to manage them.

Figure 13 The phases of relationship development: a comparison of US and European approaches

Kram: Sponsorship mentoring	Developmental mentoring
Starting: suspicion evolves into trust and mutual respect. 0–12 months.	Rapport-building – getting to know each other. Direction-setting – developing a sense of relationship purpose. 0–6 months.
Middle period – mentor uses influence to help mentee advance. Working towards setting personal and career goals. 36 months.	Progress-making – high mutual learning. 7–24 months.
Dissolving the relationship. Indeterminate.	Winding down – celebrating success, moving on to new sources of learning. 12–30 months.
Restarting the relationship – coming to terms with a different status.	Continuing informally, infrequently as a sounding board.

THE START OF THE RELATIONSHIP

SPONSORSHIP MENTORING

During the first six months to a year of a successful mentoring relationship, says Kram, the young mentee may well hold an unrealistically ideal picture of the mentor. He or she frequently sees the mentor as an extremely competent figure, who gives support and guidance. In these circumstances the mentee identifies strongly with the mentor and draws emotional support from the relationship. The young manager feels he or she is cared for by someone of great importance within the organisation. The opposite, of course, may also occasionally be the case. A mentee may begin the relationship with a great deal of suspicion and an image of the more senior manager as a 'played-out timeserver'. How well the mentoring relationship works here will depend on whether the mentor wins the mentee's respect as the nature of the job he or she does and the difficulty of the decisions he or she takes become clearer.

For the sponsorship mentor, the relationship with the mentee can also be highly rewarding during this period. The mentor is drawn to the mentee because of his or her potential and willingness to learn, seeing in the mentee someone to whom his or her own values and perspectives can be passed. In a successful relationship, mentors also derive satisfaction from recognising how they can speed the mentee's growth by supplying advice and support. Many mentors also comment on the sense of pride they have in seeing their mentees progress. Both mentor and mentee develop positive expectations of each other. By the end of the first year they have gained sufficient confidence in each other and in the relationship to set in motion more substantial arrangements for learning.

DEVELOPMENTAL MENTORING

Observation of developmental mentoring relationships presents a somewhat different picture. For a start, the initiation phase seems to have two components – rapport-building and direction-setting. During rapport-building, the mentor and mentee test the water – can they work together easily? Deep friendship is not required, simply sufficient mutual respect, goodwill, and relevance of experience to begin the journey. Learning how to work together is a process of sharing that will gradually increase in intimacy as trust grows and positive experience of achieving useful insight accumulates. The mentor needs to exercise considerable skill at putting the mentee at ease, encouraging him or her to open up.

Direction-setting involves developing a consensus about the outcomes the mentee desires and some practical ideas about how to get there. The mentor needs considerable skills in helping the mentee clarify personal goals, build commitment to them and develop a practical and, if appropriate, opportunistic plan to achieve the relationship goals. The mentor may also be quite open about his or her own learning goals from the relationship – which in turn helps to reinforce the building of rapport.

A CHECKLIST FOR THE FIRST MEETING

1. Where shall we meet and for how long?
   PROP – (Professional, Relaxed, Open, Purposeful) for both parties.
2. What do we want/need to know about each other?

   Social

   - career history
   - formative life events
   - domestic circumstances
   - interests outside work
   - how you contribute to society.

   Career ambition

   - what you enjoy/dislike about working in this industry
   - where you want to be in five years' time
   - greatest achievements/failures
   - what your picture of success is
   - how clear your career goals are.

   Development goals

   - your learning journey up till now and into the future
   - what the mentee wants to improve in
   - for the current job in preparation for future jobs
   - where the mentee would most value guidance/advice/a sounding board
   - how will mentoring help the mentee become the person they aspire to be?
3. What will make this a satisfying and useful relationship for both of us?
4. What expectations do we have of each other (ground rules and verbal contract)?

5 What are our priorities?
6 How often and where shall we meet?
7 Do we want to set an agenda for our next meeting?
8 Are there any issues we should get to work on now?

Given the importance that research places upon achieving a strong connection at the level of personal values, mentor and mentee should spend a good part of the first meeting exploring values they hold in common – and those they don't. One of the simplest ways to do this is to talk about a range of things you feel *passionate* about.

THE MIDDLE PERIOD

SPONSORSHIP MENTORING

Kram's middle period lasts for two to five years and is regarded as the most rewarding for the two parties. The relationship is cultivated as the mentor coaches and promotes his or her mentee. The friendship between the two strengthens as a high degree of trust and intimacy builds up between the mentor and mentee.

The mentor's ability to coach the mentee and clarify his or her sense of purpose and identity helps to improve the mentee's sense of self-worth. In sponsorship mentoring, the mentor may provide the mentee with work opportunities that help to develop his or her managerial skills and confirm and reinforce the mentee's sense of competence and ability. The mentee understands the business scenario better and knows how better to control the work environment.

One mentee commented:

> I was very under-confident when I joined this company. I was newly divorced and I had not worked for quite some time. I was wholly intimidated by the business world. My mentor encouraged me to perform beyond my job description. She would criticise my performance, explain my mistakes and advise me on how to perform better. Above all she gave me confidence. She would say 'I know that you have the ability to do it, and I know that you *will* do it.' Her encouragement and faith in me was a great support and incentive.

It is at this stage that the mentor gains the most satisfaction from the knowledge that he or she has had an important effect on the mentee's development. One mentor tries to describe the pride he feels when he sees his mentee perform well and receive recognition from the company:

> The satisfaction I receive is similar to parental pride. You have put faith in that person and helped them develop. When they succeed, you feel it has all been worthwhile and you remember that you were instrumental in helping them to do so.

Mentors also receive technical and psychological help and support from their mentees. The mentee now has the skill to help his or her mentor as well as the ability to recognise the needs of the more senior manager. The mentor has a renewed sense of his or her own influence and power as he or she opens doors in the organisation for the mentee. The mentor also feels he or she is passing something to the company that will have lasting value. Through the mentee the sponsorship mentor can express his or her own perspectives and values. In Kram's scenario, it often takes until this point for the mentor and the mentee to have agreed upon a set of development goals or even a career path, involving at least one and usually several clearly defined promotional or horizontal moves. Discussions between the mentor and mentee now centre less on defining objectives than on strategies and tactics to achieve them. Project work that the line manager mentor sets his or her mentee is aimed both at developing skills and at assessing how well they have been absorbed. The two people meet regularly to review progress in each area where they have agreed improvement is necessary to qualify for the next career step. The mentor directs the mentee towards additional sources of learning and challenges him or her to prove the successes claimed.

DEVELOPMENTAL MENTORING

Again, the picture that emerges from developmental mentoring is different in a number of ways. For a start, the time horizon is often much shorter – many developmental mentoring relationships are well into the middle (or the progress-making) period after six months or so. Second, the mentor has no role in the projects or tasks the mentee undertakes, other than as a sounding board. Third, the developmental mentoring relationship at this stage is characterised by a much deeper level of challenge, probing, and analysis. Fourth, the mentee begins to rely much more on his or her own judgement, and is less likely to seek the mentor's approval.

Finally, the mentor often learns as much or more from their dialogue as does the mentee. This highly fulfilling phase of the relationship often settles down to a routine where the pair are sufficiently familiar and comfortable with the process to explore more and more 'difficult' issues. Sensitive areas, which the mentee has avoided, now become admissible and may provide the deepest and most transforming issues for discussion.

Throughout this whole progress-making phase, the effective mentor demonstrates a remarkably consistent skill set – consistent, that is, with every other effective mentor. Figure 14 is based on the observation of numerous mentors, ranging from the very effective to the very ineffective. The most effective mentors, even those who are strongly activist and/or task-oriented, always start the process by re-establishing rapport. For a few minutes they engage in the normal social trivialities that help people relax in each other's company. Then they ask the mentee to explain briefly what issues he or she would like to explore. One of my favourite questions to executive mentees is, 'What's keeping you awake at night this week?'

Ineffective mentors listen briefly to the mentee's account and immediately relate the issue to their own experience, when they perceive it to be relevant. They tell the mentee what happened to them, how they tackled the issue, and what lessons they learned. As a result, they frequently end up advising on the presented issue, missing deeper, more important issues. Effective mentors hold fire. First, they ask for more facts and feelings – what exactly happened? How did you feel about it? Is this a one-off recurrence?

Next, they challenge the assumptions behind the mentee's account – for example, what would an unbiased third party have thought if they were observing? The responses to this probing, and the different perspectives generated, allow mentor and mentee to analyse the situation in some form of conceptual framework. For example, 'Let's look at how your behaviour might be influencing your colleagues and vice versa.' Finally, in this first half of the mentoring session, the mentor may draw upon his or her own experience to introduce additional considerations.

We can summarise this part of the mentoring conversation as ensuring that both mentor and mentee understand the issue and its context sufficiently for the mentee to have a reasonably clear perspective on what is possible and what they want; and for the mentor to avoid rushing in with premature assumptions. Holding back on both drawing conclusions and giving advice is a core skill here.

Having understood the issues better, mentor and mentee can concentrate on developing pragmatic solutions. The 'Pygmalion effect' plays a powerful role here – effective mentors typically say something that reinforces the mentee's belief in their own self-efficacy. Before launching into problem-solving mode, however, the mentor ensures that the mentee is in a sufficiently positive frame of mind – that he or she has the confidence to consider alternative approaches and the commitment to making a change happen. Through a variety of techniques, the mentor helps the mentee catalogue possible ways forward and to assess them against the mentee's own values criteria. Having selected one or two to pursue, the pair agree who will do what in dealing with the issue. Ineffective mentors sometimes tend to take on extensive responsibilities; effective ones limit their role to tasks such as seeking out an article or report, or making an introduction. The effective mentor also presses the mentee to set mental deadlines by which he or she expects to have tackled at least the initial stages of the plan.

Figure 14 The mentoring meeting

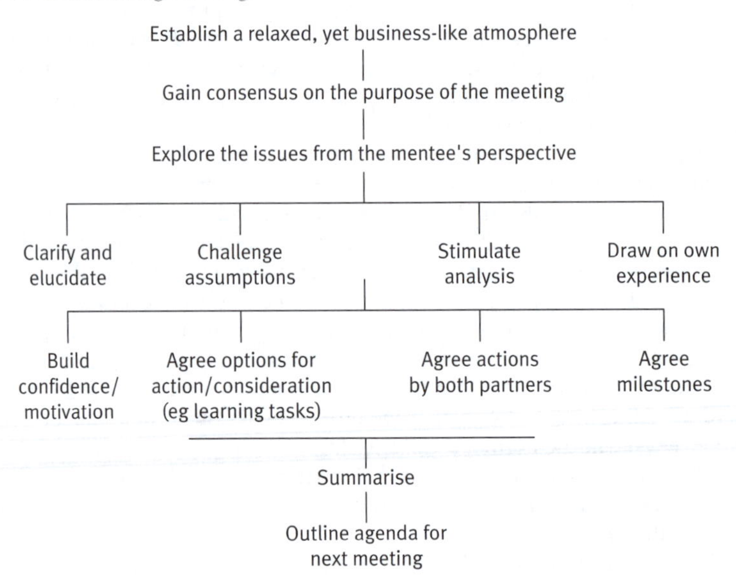

One final task remains – summarising what has been discussed. Ineffective mentors rush straight in and summarise for the mentee. In doing so, they both miss the chance to check there is a common understanding and take responsibility for the issue at least partially back on to their own shoulders. Effective mentors ensure that the mentee summarises and retains ownership of the issue throughout, including whether to bring the matter back to the agenda next time they meet.

DISSOLVING THE RELATIONSHIP

SPONSORSHIP MENTORING

In Kram's model, after two to five years the mentoring relationship begins to draw apart. The mentor and the mentee are affected by organisational changes. The mentee has advanced sufficiently to be experiencing new independence and autonomy. The mentor relationship becomes less essential as the mentee's challenges change.

Mentees may respond differently when the relationship declines according to how prepared they are for the separation. If a change in career position occurs before the mentee feels ready to operate independently of the mentor, he or she will experience a time of uncertainty and anxiety. The mentee will miss the psychological support of the mentor and be aware that he or she no longer has a 'safety net' to fall upon if he or she makes a wrong decision. The unprepared mentee can also feel abandoned and betrayed and lose confidence.

One young British mentee found her first year apart from her mentor a very difficult time emotionally. A period of redefinition was necessary as she had to demonstrate to the rest of the organisation that she was able to operate independently without her mentor:

> I had to prove to myself and the rest of the company that it was my ability which got me my new job and not my mentor's influence. I had to show I could stand alone. I think the whole process helped me to mature. Now if I have any difficulties I rely on myself.

If the mentee is fully prepared for separation from the mentor, he or she enjoys this new-found freedom and independence. It is a little like driving the car home after having passed the driving test. Most mentors accept that their mentees must move away from them and become psychologically more self-sufficient. Even after the separation has taken place, the mentor continues to encourage the mentee to move forward in his or her career. In sponsorship mentoring, the mentor will often promote the mentee at a distance and be kept informed of the mentee's progress. However, some mentors are unwilling to allow their mentees to go beyond their influence and control. This is most common in senior executives who are insecure in their own positions. The mentor tends to project his or her own negative career expectations on to the mentee. If the mentor feels he or she can go no higher in the company, he or she is unlikely to feel that a subordinate will either.

Some managers whose own careers have stagnated and offer little hope for future advancement resent a mentee who has more career opportunities. This kind of mentor does not want the mentee to outstrip him or her and as a result attempts to delay the mentee's movement by insisting the mentee stay in the same position.

Where the mentee feels ready to break the mentoring relationship but is unable to move beyond the mentor's sphere of influence, he or she may feel frustrated, restless, and ultimately hostile. This is another argument against the use of the immediate boss as a mentor. While such feelings can be absorbed across departmental boundaries, they may be explosive within the department. Some companies use the personnel department, the mentoring co-ordinator, or an arbitrator in senior management to ensure that the mentee has someone to appeal to if conflict of this kind arises. (The mentor, too, can use this formal route to express disquiet if he or she believes a mentee is being pushed too fast for his or her own good.) Such arbitration is rare, however, not least because the numbers of people involved in most companies are sufficiently small for the issues to be resolved by informal means.

For both the mentor and the mentee the period of divorce and separation is important for their reputation and career in the organisation. The mentee demonstrates his or her skills and independence while the mentor shows to colleagues and other potential mentees that he or she develops young people successfully. The progress of the mentee proves the accuracy of the mentor's insight into potential. By now, the mentee's career objectives may have changed several times as the mentor has made him or her aware of new opportunities and expected changes in the organisation. The mentee will have gradually assumed more and more of the responsibility for his or her own career objectives and will increasingly be taking the initiative in seeking out training opportunities and experience that will help him or her achieve his or her goals. In effect, the mentor has taught what he or she knows and there is little more to pass on.

DEVELOPMENTAL MENTORING

Once again, the dynamic is subtly different, not least because it is extremely rare for this kind of dependency to develop in the first place. In a relationship where the primary purpose is achieving rapid self-reliance and where the mentor is not expected to use his or her power on behalf of the mentee, winding down is a relatively straightforward affair. In many cases, where a formal time limit has been built into the scheme from the start, both parties begin to prepare for dissolution long before it starts. (In a mentoring scheme run by Shell, it was noticeable that in the relationships with the least time to run – because the mentor would be repatriated in 12–18 months – the intensity of the relationship and the learning was higher than in those where the time frame was more relaxed. The mentees knew they had to get every drop of learning they could, while they could.)

At least one meeting before the expected formal end of the relationship, mentor and mentee should begin to review:

- what the relationship has delivered in terms of expected and unexpected outcomes (changes in knowledge, behaviour, role etc.) for both parties
- what it has *not* delivered
- what they expect for the new (informal) phase of the relationship, if there is to be one
- what future mentoring needs the mentee may have that may best be met by other people.

In a study of relationship endings, David Megginson and I compared the experiences of numerous mentors and mentees. They fell into two clear categories:

- those whose formal relationship had a clear ending, in which they reviewed (and in some cases celebrated) what they had achieved together – these were almost all perceived as positive by both mentor and mentee
- those whose relationship had just drifted away over time, and which were almost always seen as negative.

Mentors and mentees whose relationship had wound down, rather than wound up, tended to feel unsure about their contribution, and sometimes betrayed. By contrast, recognising the value of the relationship enabled both parties to move on with confidence.

RESTARTING THE RELATIONSHIP

SPONSORSHIP MENTORING

In Kram's analysis both mentee and mentor continue to have some form of interaction, although it is on a more casual basis. The relationship enters a new stage where the mentee and mentor regard each other as equals. The relationship now develops into a friendship with the two maintaining contact with each other on the basis of mutual advantage rather than upon the primarily one-sided career advantage once offered. The mentee now ceases to identify with the mentor, whose weaknesses he or she now recognises alongside the strengths that had seemed so impressive in the early stages of the relationship. The bond of gratitude takes over from the bond of need. When the two become peers in the organisation, uncertainty and discomfort may occur as they adjust to the new role relationship.

This new transition can also be characterised by hostility and resentment between the mentee and the mentor. The mentee may have found it difficult to make a complete break from the mentor. When the two meet again on a more equal footing, the mentee often feels that he or she will fall into the former dependent role. To prevent this, the mentee behaves aggressively to the mentor and the former intimacy is not re-established. In developmental mentoring, a similar but gentler transition occurs. Mentor and mentee often continue to meet, but now informally, with no organisational support, no agenda, and much lower frequency. When they do meet, it is as equals, whatever their relative status in the organisation – each sees the other as a useful sounding board and a valuable person in their networks.

DEVELOPMENTAL MENTORING

Here the relationship tends to evolve naturally into a broad friendship, where mentor and mentee recognise each other as one of their learning resources and as mutual sounding boards. Meetings will be much more spontaneous and relaxed, less frequent, less focused, often based upon the fact that they both happen to be in the same place at the same time. They can, however, continue to be of significant benefit, especially if mentor and mentee now work for different organisations or widely separated parts of the same organisation. The trust accumulated within the formal mentoring programme provides the basis for being a sounding board on a wide range of often deeply personal issues. The two people often also refer on other people (sometimes their own direct reports) to each other for mentoring.

In some cases, the developmental relationship morphs into a form of sponsorship. Unlike typical sponsorship mentoring, however, this relationship is often based on a relatively deep level of appreciation of each other's strengths and weaknesses and well-founded confidence in each other's values.

USING THE PHASES IN TRAINING AND PROGRAMME MANAGEMENT

What's needed of mentor and mentee typically evolves at different stages of relationship development. The skills needed to build rapport, for example, will be subtly different to those for maintaining rapport once the relationship is well established – especially in cross-cultural relationships, for example. My current research includes trying to understand the role of humour and laughter at each stage of the relationship. It appears that the early stages are marked by very cautious, generalised and 'correct' humour. As the level of trust and intimacy grows, however, the humour becomes more personal and more natural.

An important part of mentoring programme design is to ensure that mentors and mentees are given tools and techniques appropriate to the stage of the relationship which they have (or should have) reached. Drip-feeding reminders and additional information in this way stimulates both to be aware of and reflect on how they are conducting the relationship.

SUMMARY

Clearly, every mentoring relationship is unique, just as every individual is unique. But a high proportion of relationships do seem to follow either the Kram stages of development if it is a sponsorship mentoring scheme, or the developmental mentoring model. In either case, to minimise the problems and maximise the benefits of mentoring, both the mentor and the mentee need to be well briefed on how the relationship may develop. The company, too, needs to monitor the stages of development to provide the external support that will head off serious problems before they occur.

CHAPTER 13

Problems of Mentoring Programmes and Relationships

While mentoring is a powerful human resource development tool, it is only one of many in the corporate toolbox. Badly handled, it can turn into a spanner in the works. Even well handled, it is not appropriate in all circumstances, nor is it necessarily superior to other forms of management development. Rather, it is a process to be used alongside other forms of people development and career progression, including coaching, talent management programmes and performance management. Many companies now encourage employees to have as many developmental relationships of different kinds as possible. Monica Higgins and Kathy Kram, two eminent US scholars in the field, place increasing emphasis in their studies and analysis on the role of 'developmental networks', in which people build a diverse support network that evolves with their learning needs. This network may include one or more simultaneous mentors, for different purposes (Higgins and Kram 2001).

Some companies have found the main problem is the unfamiliarity of mentoring in the business environment. Other critics say true mentor–mentee relationships are rare and should not develop at gun-point. Michael Zey, in his book *The Mentor Connection* (1984), feels that trying to formalise 'what is at best a random occurrence' can prove disastrous, if management does support the mentoring dyads.

Some formal mentoring is seen as a quick fix for companies who should really be looking at changing their whole culture. Reba Keele, Professor, Public and Community Health at Utah Valley University, feels that formal (sponsorship) mentoring, like arranged marriages, can sometimes work better in Far Eastern cultures than Western. In Japan especially, she points out, the traditional respect for age and experience provides a framework that most people can accept. She explains:

> In the Japanese organisation, the senior member of management has already accepted the fact that he is not going to become the next president. Assuming the responsibility of mentoring is considered an honour and recognition of your status. Whereas in many Western organisations, leaders attach relatively low importance to talent development. (Despite what they might say to the contrary!)

The problems presented in the following pages form some of the most common I have seen in organisational and individual mentoring around the world. Most can be forestalled by:

- clarity about what the programme is for
- recognising where the culture is and isn't supportive of mentoring
- investing upfront in preparation and obtaining commitment from leaders to be role models of mentoring good practice
- putting adequate resource behind programme management, to ensure that participants feel supported
- continuous, quality communication
- effective monitoring and troubleshooting.

We can divide the most common pitfalls into those that concern the programme and those that concern the individual mentoring relationship.

ORGANISATIONAL ISSUES

POOR PLANNING AND PREPARATION

Unclear programme objectives, failure to gain the public endorsement of senior managers, and under-resourcing the programme are all common failings. A division of a large US-based multinational insisted that its operations around the world all instituted mentoring programmes for a particular group of employees before the year end, a mere four months away. The number of relationships established would be measured and 'heads would roll' if the policy were not implemented enthusiastically. Of course, local senior management responded on the hoof, informing several hundred people in the UK alone that they would be mentor or mentee to someone else. As no-one knew what they were doing and there had been no time to gain participants' buy-in, most of the relationships got off to a rocky start. As long as it measured only the number of assigned pairings, the US head office was happy. Only when it started to look at the frequency and quality of meetings did it realise that all but a small handful of the relationships were anything more than a sham.

POOR CLARITY OF ROLE

Failure to distinguish between the roles of the line manager and the mentor leads to confusion and sometimes to conflict between mentor and line manager. Expecting the mentor to take part in appraising the mentee can also be confusing, on both sides, and lead the mentee to be very cautious about what he or she says. However, it is possible to be quite ingenious in managing this kind of potential conflict of role. At Perot Systems, where most employees work in multiple teams, there was often no single stable point of supervision to carry out an appraisal.

Instead, the individual's mentor – or in some cases, the individual – gathers appraisal feedback from a mixture of the mentee's peers, project team leaders and internal customers. This information becomes neutral information – not the mentor's opinion – which the mentor helps the mentee deal with. In this way, there is no need for the mentee to 'play up' to the mentor.

Role confusion may also occur between being a mentor and being a sponsor. While many US corporations do combine these roles, it is largely at the expense of authenticity and may not be in the long-term interests of the organisation. Indeed, there is some evidence that sponsorship mentoring contributed to the financial crisis of recent years. Sociopaths are very good at finding and manipulating sponsors – usually much better than genuinely talented people! If potential mentees see the mentoring programme as a route to sponsorship, learning objectives rapidly become subverted to career progression objectives – with resultant damage to the programme overall.

FAILURE TO SET AND MEASURE CLEAR OUTCOMES

Many schemes get introduced because someone thinks it would be generally a good thing. So it might, but in the absence of clear expected outcomes, the scheme may easily fall into disrepute as just another talking shop.

While mentoring may not involve a lot of direct cost, it does require a lot of valuable management time. Top management is justified in asking for some kind of demonstrated return on the investment. Schemes that build in relevant measurement from the start, related to clear business priorities, have arguably a better chance of securing and retaining top management support.

TOO LITTLE OR TOO MUCH FORMALITY

A mentoring scheme aimed at helping children from deprived backgrounds develop literacy and numeracy skills initially required every mentor and mentee to complete a six-page detailed report after each meeting. It hadn't occurred to the organisers that the target audience of mentees might be intimidated by all this. Getting the balance right between formality and informality isn't easy. There has to be enough formality to create a supportive framework in which relationships can flourish, but enough informality for each mentoring pair to develop its own relationship, as it feels fit. Paradoxically, the better trained the mentors and mentees are, the more confident both they and the organisation can feel in allowing relationships to develop in their own way.

By way of example of how not to do it, here is an experience recorded in a LinkedIn discussion stream.

> A few years ago I worked in an organisation that made mentoring a formal duty for employees and assigned all new employees to specific, more experienced employees for an explicit period of time. Soon, the mentoring relationship became a task defined and tracked by senior managers. There were forms to fill out to document meetings of mentors with new employees, and checklists that had to be completed listing certain topics that had to be covered in mentoring sessions, and certain questions that mentors had to ask. Inevitably, forms were also developed to track the progress of new employees being mentored. The process turned into a game from which few seemed to benefit. Mentors and new employees didn't necessarily fit each other well, and the mutual respect needed for effective mentoring often didn't exist. Forms were filled out perfunctorily so that neither mentor nor new employee would 'get into trouble'.

FAILURE TO QUALITY-CONTROL THE MENTOR POOL

It is now generally regarded as good practice to insist that mentoring relationships will only be sanctioned and supported by the organisation if the mentor and mentee have both attended at least a minimal level of training. Some companies use the mentor training sessions as subtle assessment centres for the mentors – people who demonstrate a complete unsuitability for the role can have their cards marked and, unless somebody specifically asks for them as a mentor, will never be drawn from the pool. (This doesn't meet the ISMPE standards, of course, which require that the rejected mentor is given honest feedback and supported in dealing with it!) These companies also take the view that anyone who volunteers as a mentor should be allowed to attend the training, for two reasons.

First, some of the skills and techniques may rub off on them and be used in their dealings with their direct reports; second, they may decide to become a mentee rather than a mentor. On several occasions when the latter has occurred, the person concerned has grown in the role of mentee, using his or her own mentor as a role model for his or her own attempts at acquiring better developmental skills and eventually become an effective mentor.

Where any old manager, selected by seniority rather than developmental competence, is placed into the role, it requires a strong mentee to demand and obtain the kind of deep dialogue he or she needs. The relationship may also require a considerable input of time by the programme co-ordinator, which might be better spent elsewhere. A curious logic often operates in large corporations, however: 'We are a world-class company, employing highly intelligent, world-class people. So all of our senior managers should by definition be good at developing other people. So they should all become mentors.' If all promotions were truly made because managers were good at the people skills, this logic might – just – stand up. But the reality is that managers still primarily get promoted for task achievement and organisational ability, rather than for their skills at developing others.

Once a very senior person takes on the title of mentor, there may be little appetite from the mentee, the scheme co-ordinator or anyone else to tell them that they are not doing a good job. The mentor bumbles along in blissful ignorance, the mentee feels trapped and, if there are enough people in the same situation, a deep cynicism about the whole approach establishes itself. These managers may also help to perpetuate stereotypes both in a company's management style and in its culture. Ideas and values that senior executives pass down to mentees may in reality be obsolete or irrelevant. If these values are too vigorously imposed, junior employees are discouraged from finding their own methods and instead use old solutions for new problems. As a result, the company becomes entrenched in the past and loses its ability to react quickly to the demands of the present.

BEING TOO ELITIST

Some programmes for high-flyers deliberately set out to be elitist. They want participants to recognise that being chosen as a mentee is a mark of the company's confidence in their potential. There is a downside, however – what about those left out? Since most organisations have a pyramidal structure, it follows that there will always be some junior managers who have a mentor and some who do not. There are just not enough mentors to go round, so a company faces the constant danger of alienating failed candidates.

Unfortunately, the resentment and disappointment felt by failed applicants can outweigh the benefits that successful candidates receive from the programme. A junior who does not gain entry all too often believes the selectors' decision to be based on his or her own personal limitations, rather than due to a lack of programme resources. He or she believes that it is an unspoken statement by the company indicating that he or she lacks the ability to fill important positions in the future. In short, he or she has been given a vote of 'no confidence'.

One UK company with a number of geographically spread operations invited applications for the pilot of its mentoring programme. More than 40 people applied for the 15 available places. Although the company wrote to all the unsuccessful candidates, suggesting they speak to their local employee counsellor, only one did so – and she handed in her notice. The company learned that it had to:

- make sure everyone knew the criteria for selection
- demonstrate that mentoring was just one route among many to advancement
- consider unsuccessful candidates' reactions at a much earlier stage.

Such negative experiences can be very damaging to a junior manager. His or her self-confidence and morale may be eroded to such an extent as to underrate his or her own ability and potential, and to lower his or her career aspirations accordingly. As a result, instead of having a motivated young employee who aims at promotion through a high standard of work, a company has an individual whose enthusiasm is curbed and who ceases to stretch his or her abilities because there seems to be no reward in doing so.

Alternatively, a failed candidate can feel resentment and bitterness as he or she sees peers receive treatment that seems 'preferential'. 'Favouritism' is a frequently heard complaint, as well as the accusation that peers used unfair tactics to gain a place on the programme. A mentee's friendship with a senior executive becomes 'sucking up' or 'crawling'. Envy and resentment from a mentee's peers can frequently hinder, or even destroy, a mentoring programme.

It is probably not possible to assure everyone that the selection process for high-flyer mentoring has been totally fair, and there will always be a few individuals who convince themselves that the programme caters only for those who are best at impressing the right people rather than those who are most able and deserving. However, the more open the process is – and the more people feel that they have been involved – the less of an issue this is likely to be.

BEING MENTORED BY THE CEO

Having the CEO as your mentor might sound like a career coup. However, it comes with problems, because the relationship can easily be perceived by others as one of sponsorship and it's hard for the CEO not to conflate the development needs of the mentee with his or her own needs to make strategic moves amongst executives – ie the needs of the mentee and those of the company can become entwined in ways that may not ultimately be beneficial for either. Some programmes have decided that the CEO is too powerful to be a mentor; others that it's essential they take the role of 'head mentor'. Practical guidelines seem to be:

- Keep some distance in hierarchical level between the CEO and the mentee – ideally they should be just off his or her executive chessboard, so there is no temptation to manipulate their career.
- Restrict the period of the relationship to a maximum of one year, after which mentor and mentee will move on.
- If practical, the CEO should have more than one mentee at a time – the more people he or she mentors over a three-year period, for example, the less 'special' these relationships become.
- Recognise the potential problems that come with this very visible relationship and spend time in the contracting stage clarifying how you will deal with them.

BEING TOO PROBLEM-FOCUSED

When young graduates on the Bank of England's mentoring programme (sufficiently long ago not to be the case today) failed to meet their mentors as frequently as expected and to gather much value from the relationship, investigation showed that there were two main causes. One was a reluctance to disturb someone more senior and obviously very busy with their own relatively trivial issues. The other was a perception that mentors were there to help you deal with problems, rather than to help you identify and manage opportunities. These highly intellectually capable young men and women perceived that it was not career-enhancing behaviour to admit weaknesses to anyone else in the organisation, even within a relationship of confidentiality. Greater clarity at the beginning about how mentors could add value to their personal development and career planning might have overcome some of these problems, along perhaps with a deferment of the programme until they had been with the bank long enough to develop their own ideas about how they would use a mentor and what sort of mentor would best suit them.

POWER ALIGNMENTS

Primarily a problem of sponsorship mentoring, the issue of power underlies a whole raft of common problems with mentoring schemes. For example, by assigning a mentor to a mentee in a different department or a different division, a company changes the nature of its informal structure. Close relationships that extend beyond the normal business restraints and that cut across the barrier of status and position mean that new alliances are formed between junior and senior employees. A company that has run a mentoring programme for several years may have the additional power nexus of a former mentor and a mentee, now on the same organisational rung, actively promoting and assisting each other. While this means the informal communications of a company are strengthened, it can also lead to an increase in corporate politics.

One of the objectives of the mentoring programme is at least partly to overcome the unfairness of the informal old boy networks. Unless the company is vigilant, there is a very real danger that instead of making the system more open and fair, the scheme may simply create new closed networks. If covert sources of information are available only to the chosen few within mentor–mentee relationships, only the initiated know how to gain and use company resources effectively. Through this, mentors and mentees can form a small yet powerful group capable of operating through and beyond the company's formal positions of power.

Failure to make it clear from the outset that the mentee is still primarily responsible to his or her immediate boss and not to his or her mentor can create serious power-play problems. The mentor has to guard against creating situations where the mentee uses his or her special relationship to bypass the authority of his or her boss. At the same time, the mentor must not override the mentee's boss, other than in exceptional cases. Unfortunately, obscuring the company's command structure can happen all too easily. Because the mentor and mentee are adhering to a different system of loyalty and authority, they cut across the recognised formal hierarchy. An invisible chain of command can emerge subtly to challenge the established one, resulting in confusion, conflict and bitterness.

The mentee's immediate superior can often be placed in an uncomfortable and difficult position by all this. A brittle relationship can develop between the mentee, the manager, and the mentor if the manager is completely excluded from the relationship, perhaps only learning about it by accident. The manager in this situation feels threatened and frequently resents the mentor's behaviour, interpreting it as open interference. If the mentor overrides the manager's authority, the latter will feel his or her authority is being publicly undermined. Inevitably, the manager will resort to obstructing the mentoring relationship in order to protect his or her own position. An experienced mentoring scheme administrator, quoted in a US newsletter, points out that it's only natural for the mentee's boss, who after all has a department to run, to be jealous of the mentor's influence – especially if the mentor has a powerful position in the organisation.

'Remember that the boss is the boss,' he advises would-be mentors. 'And don't let your own experiences blind you to the realities. The last thing a mentee needs is advice from the mentor that leads to conflict with the supervisor.'

Had the line manager been involved in the programme from the beginning, he might have been more co-operative. It is important that the mentor and line manager should not be seen to collude together, or even to discuss the mentee (this would make it difficult for the mentee to give full trust to the mentor). One company asks line managers to take prospective mentees to the mentor's office for the first meeting. In another, line managers and mentors are briefed together.

In companies where there are a large number of middle manager positions and few senior positions, mentors again need to conduct their mentoring relationships carefully. A manager who is unlikely to be promoted further may resent the mentee beneath him or her being groomed for advancement. The manager will realise he or she has been passed over by the company and could possibly attempt to hinder the mentee's prospects by writing unfavourable reports. In this situation the mentor and the mentee need to try to make the relationship between them as invisible as possible.

SOME SALUTARY EXAMPLES

Company A launched its mentoring scheme with a memo to its chief executives across Europe, instructing them to ensure that the top 100 women employees in the region were given mentors. The first mentors and mentees knew about it was when they also received a memo telling them that they were participants in the programme and who they had been paired up with. Mentors and mentees met up for lunch, in most cases with very little idea of what was expected of them and what outcomes should come from the mentoring process. Six months later, only three pairs were still meeting regularly. Lack of clarity of purpose, lack of skills in the role and a feeling of being press-ganged not only prevented most people establishing a positive learning relationship, but ensured that their cynicism spread to participants in other planned programmes.

Company B decided it would 'help' mentors and mentees have meaningful discussions by insisting they meet every two weeks and giving them a detailed sheet of topics to consider. It also demanded a written record of what had been discussed, in broad terms. Mentors and mentees felt they were not trusted and struggled to establish and maintain rapport. Most relationships drowned in the bureaucracy. Those that survived subverted or ignored the rules and simply concentrated on issues of concern to the mentee at the time.

Company C went for the 'sheep-dip' approach, assuming that only mentors needed training. Because the mentors were very senior, training was limited to just two hours and was mainly about explaining the role. When the relationships failed to gel, one-to-one interviews with the senior managers revealed what they would not admit in public or to their peer group: that they felt inadequate for the role, because they lacked a wide enough portfolio of skills and techniques.

RELATIONSHIP ISSUES

FAILURE TO ESTABLISH RAPPORT

In general, if two people don't 'click' within the first two meetings, the relationship is unlikely to develop the depth of trust and mutual confidence that allows mentor and mentee to address intimate issues. Having a clear developmental goal to work on (ie the mentee's learning, support or career needs) provides a significant boost to the rapport-building process – if only because it provides a clear, shared point of reference and interest. You can learn to value, like, and respect someone relatively easily if you work with him or her on something that is important to you.

The reality is, however, that some relationships are not going to work. For example, a middle-aged engineer found he simply could not develop rapport with a highly assertive young woman graduate. Part of the problem, he admitted, was that he kept slipping back into behavioural routines he had developed with his daughter, who was of a similar age and temperament. These routines typically involved a lot of telling and a fair amount of shouting. This was potentially an ideal opportunity for some reverse mentoring, in which he would have learned from the graduate how to understand his daughter's perspective, but he decided to withdraw from the programme altogether.

Rapport demands that both parties share or at least acknowledge the validity of each other's values. In the absence of this consensus, it is always better to dissolve the relationship and help the mentee find someone with whom he or she is more compatible.

LACK OF TIME

All mentoring relationships suffer from time and diary pressures – in every survey of mentoring problems I have seen, time is one of the top three issues. By definition, people who have the most wisdom to pass on are likely to be among the busiest. Mentees may also be drawn from among ambitious groups of people who are themselves working long hours. Yet both mentors and mentees typically do find the time.

In general, it seems, the people who don't make the time are those who don't have the commitment and who don't get the buzz out of reflective dialogue and increasing self-knowledge. Other people find ways around the problem, for example by developing a rolling three-meeting schedule so that a change of date one month does not lead to diary drift the next.

Sometimes what looks like a dead relationship is simply suffering from an overwhelming demand on the mentor's time. In a multinational telecom company, one of a batch of international cross-border relationships hadn't got anywhere after four months. The mentee had chased the mentor frequently, but had only received short e-mails in reply. Then, on the day of a review session, the mentee reported enthusiastically that he had at last spent some telephone time with his mentor, who apologised profusely and explained he had been moved suddenly to take up a major post in another country. Now that he was settled in, however, he was determined to make the relationship work and would fly to Europe in a week or so specifically to hold the first formal meeting.

CLARITY OF RELATIONSHIP PURPOSE

If mentor and mentee don't agree fairly quickly on some goals that the mentee would like to achieve and on which the mentor can help, the relationship will swiftly drive into the sand. It doesn't matter that the goals change over time – the sense of purpose drives the frequency of meetings and the focus on real issues.

DIFFERENCES IN MATURITY

People mature at different rates in their socio-emotional and cognitive maturity. Being older and/or more senior doesn't necessarily mean that a person is more mature (Kegan 1982). Kram and Ragins (2007, p264) point out that, if a mentor is at an earlier stage of maturity than the mentee, the relationship 'is likely to result in disillusionment and frustration'. They also suggest that a mentor, who is at a difficult stage in his or her own career cycle, may not be sufficiently responsive to the mentee's needs. To my knowledge, no matching tools address these issues at present, but it is arguable that doing so would improve the success rates of relationships.

EXPECTING TOO MUCH OF EACH OTHER

If either the mentor or mentee brings a set of unrealistic expectations to the relationship, this is unlikely to be helpful. In theory, the initial discussions and psychological contract should clarify expectations at all levels. But poor mentors often fail to carry the process through. For example, according to Katherine Kram (1983), when the mentee realises the mentor is unable to transform his or her career, the mentee may feel resentful and betrayed.

Mentees need to be realistic from the beginning, she says. They should not expect the relationship to meet every need, nor for it to continue indefinitely. 'Mentors provide different degrees of mentoring and the mentee should accept this,' she maintains.

Some mentors cross a fine line too easily between exhibiting confidence in a mentee and expecting too much. One young executive was forced to leave his job because of the unbearable pressure his mentor unknowingly placed upon him. He explains:

> He seemed to think I could do anything that he asked me to do. Eventually it got to the stage where I was terrified he would discover I was not a whiz kid and was in fact quite average. My position was made so unbearable by my mentor that I decided to quit.

Had his mentor directed him towards additional training in key areas he might well have gained the confidence to cope.

ALLOWING DEPENDENCY TO DEVELOP

Primarily an issue for sponsorship mentoring, dependency is unhealthy for both parties. Kram (1983) provides the example of a divisional manager who wished to move to headquarters and could not understand why the company was so reluctant to transfer him:

> I begged the powers that be to move me, yet they refused to alter their position. I was mystified until a colleague told me that my mentor had insisted that I was not

> ready for the move. The only thing I could do was to make it clear to him that I was grateful for all the help he had given my career, yet nevertheless I was determined to move on – or move out. He denied any involvement, but a month later I was transferred. The evidence seemed to speak for itself.

PROBLEMS WITH OTHER PEOPLE

The literature on mentoring contains a variety of references to problems with spouses, line managers, and working colleagues. Most of these can be avoided by being very open about the relationship.

Problems with spouses tend to be most common with mixed-gender mentoring relationships, for obvious reasons. These relationships can also generate malicious gossip. Experienced mentors avoid these problems by having a number of mentees of both sexes and by holding meetings relatively publicly.

Problems with line managers occur most often when the line manager feels threatened. Is the mentee bad-mouthing him or her to someone more senior? Is the mentor – perhaps from the best of motives – using his or her position of greater seniority to direct the mentee towards developmental tasks that prevent the mentee spending essential time on line responsibilities?

A lot of problems with other people can be overcome by providing clear briefings about the nature of mentoring and how it fits into the portfolio of development opportunities. A pilot programme should always be marketed as such, with a clear statement that if it is successful, it will be rolled out to as many other groups as possible. (That gives everyone who is envious a reason to help make the scheme work!)

SUMMARY

Mentoring should not be the only form of career or personal development within an organisation. Being aware of potential problems is essential for the management of both the programme and the individual relationships. All of them are avoidable, with forethought and honest conversation.

CHAPTER 14

Managing Multi-Country Mentoring Programmes

Multi-country and global mentoring programmes are becoming increasingly common in international organisations. Multi-country programmes are typically ones where each country or region is encouraged to have a mentoring programme (or several), with participants all being local. Central HR may exert more or less control over who these programmes are aimed at and how they are facilitated. Cross-border mentoring promotes more diverse mentoring conversations by linking people between national operations. And, of course, there are examples of hybrids between these two approaches.

Both kinds of programme have challenges, as indicated in Table 9, but before we explore these, let's clarify why so many multinational organisations want to use mentoring in this way, rather than leave each region or country to develop its own approaches entirely. Some of the most common reasons given are:

- Achieving a greater level of consistency in the quality and application of mentoring programmes across their international operations. I have found very few cases where this consistency was desired for its own sake. Rather, it is driven by factors such as general initiatives to raise the quality of HR, or by a wider programme of cultural change, in which the skills of coaching and mentoring are seen to be a key enabler.
- Developing a common language and set of expectations about mentoring among participants, HR and line managers throughout the organisation. One of the biggest barriers to rolling out mentoring is often a matter of different perspectives on what mentoring is and which model of mentoring the organisation espouses.
- Value for money – having a centralised resource is arguably much cheaper than developing lots of divergent local ones.
- Transfer of good practice from one location to another.
- Stimulating higher levels of international relocation among employees.
- Helping expatriates learn to work within the local culture.
- Supporting indigenisation strategies (for example, using expatriates to mentor local managers into leadership roles).

CREATING A GLOBAL MENTORING STRATEGY

Some organisations have created stand-alone global mentoring strategies, but it's more common to position them within either a wider strategy to create a coaching and mentoring culture, or a talent development (or broader employee development) strategy. As with any strategic planning process, the key questions here are:

- What are the key people issues the business needs to address?
- How specifically can mentoring assist with these?
- What applications of mentoring do we therefore want to encourage?
- How important is it to have a consistent, joined-up approach to managing these applications?

- What do we want to control centrally and locally, in terms of programme administration and design; and why?
- What do we want to support centrally and locally; and why?
- What are our key performance indicators for mentoring?

Table 9 Issues in multi-country mentoring programmes

Issues	Multiple local programmes	Cross-border mentoring
Matching	Is there a large enough pool of mentors?	How can we ensure that the distant relationship gels?
Culture	Differences between cultural assumptions of the multinational's home country and those of the host country.	Is there a need for cultural awareness training?
Power issues	Can be a big issue, if mentor and mentee work in the same location.	E-mail communication tends to produce greater psychological safety.
Initial training	Emphasis on face-to-face? How can we ensure consistency of message and quality of training?	Emphasis on webinars. How can we ensure participants have enough practice to be competent/confident?
Support and review sessions	More opportunity for face-to-face check-ins.	Check-ins normally remote.
Support platforms	How much should they be locally adapted? How do we promote their use?	How do we make them relevant to all participants and stakeholders? How do we promote their use?
Measurement	Adapting measures to the needs of the local organisation and environment.	Ensuring the language of evaluation questions is consistently understood.

ADAPTING A GLOBAL APPROACH TO LOCAL NEEDS

Many multinational mentoring programmes have failed because of perceived cultural imperialism on the part of the international headquarters. A US corporation, for example, encouraged subsidiaries around the world to set up mentoring programmes and some countries complied enthusiastically, applying models derived from within their own culture and traditions. When the company realised the diversity of approach, it tried to impose a US-centric common definition and set of processes. This killed off most of the existing programmes.

Good practice appears to involve:

- designing the programme(s) or the corporate approach to mentoring with input from a wide range of sources, and particularly from local HR and line managers
- recognising that in countries that speak the same language, the context of mentoring may be very different. (Trying to impose a US approach on the UK and Eire, or vice versa, is likely to meet resistance)
- openly acknowledging the impact of culture on the style of mentoring and including relevant cultural awareness elements in any training and supporting information resources

- designing training content and support materials with a core of common elements (definitions, skills, emphasis on learning dialogue and so on) and a more flexible approach to case studies, role plays/real plays, links with local mythology and social mores
- educating local HR professionals so that they can become champions for mentoring and identify opportunities to support regional/international programmes, and to launch local programmes aimed at specific, local issues
- clarifying other important contextual factors. For example, the qualities associated with effective leadership are not universal – there are significant differences between cultures, which may need to be taken into account
- wherever possible, rooting the mentoring 'story' in the mythology or religious beliefs of the country. Islam, Buddhism, Christianity and other religions all exemplify learning dialogue, as do many of the stories told to children in East Africa, and in Asia-Pacific cultures.

SOME SPECIFIC CULTURAL ISSUES

Several issues may be of concern. One relates to how people learn. In many cultures, the expectation of a learning relationship is one where the student listens to the teacher and absorbs information – learning by rote. Mentors and mentees need to develop a style of working together that gradually enables the mentee to challenge what the mentor says, and to bring their own thinking and ideas to the learning conversation.

The second relates to how people relate to authority (what culture researcher Gert Hofstede (Hofstede and Minkov 2010) calls power-distance). How people from different cultures react to colleagues with greater or lesser authority differs substantially. So upward mentoring is going to be more difficult in a Chinese or Malay culture, for example, than in a Scandinavian one.

A third issue concerns loss of face. Mentors in some cultures may find it difficult to share their mistakes at all, let alone with someone more junior. Yet those mistakes are an important source of co-learning. Giving feedback ranges from an almost obligatory behaviour in some cultures to anathema in others!

Sometimes difficult to understand, the fourth issue relates to how people connect to the world around them. Americans and to some extent Europeans tend to focus on the particular – for example, what specifically happened? What are you doing? Chinese people tend to see events from a wider perspective (quite literally the bigger picture) where what is happening for the individual is part of what is happening around them. This difference in perspective can lead the mentoring conversation into a tangle of cross-purposes. It's important to take this into account both in the design of the programme (how it will be presented to stakeholders) and in training participants.

Closely related, in impact at least, are the issues of family, masculinity/femininity and collectivism/individualism. In some cultures, the primary source of 'natural' mentoring is the family. It's not unusual for a Western mentor to be giving guidance that contradicts what the mentee is receiving from elders in his or her family. Mentor and mentee need to learn the skills of acknowledging and integrating these conversations.

Hofstede's individual/collective dimension of culture is relevant because people from individualist cultures are more likely to emphasise individual performance and achievement when setting relationship goals; while people from collectivist cultures tend to be more conscious of group success and well-being.

The masculine/feminine dimension explores emotional and social roles through the lens of gender. Cultures with a feminine orientation, such as in some Northern European countries, emphasise relationships, environment, co-operation and benevolence. Masculine cultures emphasise competition and achievement. This difference can lead mentor and mentee to bring quite different sets of values and assumptions to the mentoring dialogue.

Another of Hofstede's dimensions relates to uncertainty-avoidance. Cultures differ considerably in their ability to cope with ambiguity and risk. There is a stronger need in risk-avoidant cultures to emphasise rules and put greater reliance on stereotypes. It's inevitable that some mentoring relationships involving people with widely differing levels of uncertainty avoidance will encounter tensions, if the mentor takes the mentee too far out of their comfort zone.

A useful analysis of some of these issues comes from two US academics, Iris Varner and Linda Beamer (Varner and Beamer 2010). Among the issues they explore are:

- How much importance do people ascribe to verbal or nonverbal communication? In many Asian (high context) cultures nonverbal elements form a large part of the communication, whereas in many Western cultures (low context) the words have more power and it's more important to spell things out explicitly.
- How people reason. Western cultures place more emphasis on logic and cause and effect thinking. In Asian thinking everything is linked, and opposites can co-exist. The concept of Polarity Coaching (Anderson 2010) is a Western attempt to integrate these two cultural perspectives.
- Do people prefer to address issues simultaneously or sequentially?
- Do results or relationships take priority?
- How is time understood, measured and kept?
- Is change regarded as something positive or negative?

Of course, these cultural issues are very broad-brush pictures. Individual relationships are rarely so clear-cut or typical![1]

The implications for mentoring programme managers are two-fold. Firstly, training and subsequent support for participants need to take all these issues into account. Secondly, the design of programmes should also be flexible enough to accommodate some measure of acknowledgement of the validity of each of these cultural perspectives, along with guidelines on how to work within them. Some programmes deliberately match people from very different cultural backgrounds with the aim of expanding their awareness and appreciation of other cultures and ways of viewing the world. Where this works well, it is usually the case that this learning is a central part of the mentoring contract.

SUMMARY

Multi-country and international mentoring programmes require a great deal of forethought and appreciation of local and regional cultures and circumstances. It is possible to design a corporate policy and/or individual mentoring programmes centrally and ship them around the world – but engaging with cultural diversity and difference in circumstance internationally is likely to produce much better results!

[1] Recommended further reading around these issues includes: HOFSTEDE, G. and MINKOV, M. (2010); TROMPENAARS, F. and HAMPDEN-TURNER, C. (1997); ROSINSKI, P. (2003) and PLAISTER-TEN, J. (2009, 2010).

CHAPTER 15

Mentoring for Graduates and High Potentials

Mentoring is often at its most effective when people are on the brink of, or in the middle of, significant transitions. Two of the most common transitions which give rise to mentoring programmes are graduate induction, and where existing employees have been marked out as having high potential to move to the next layer of management – especially if this means going through one of the waypoints of the leadership pipeline (managing self to managing others, managing others to managing managers, and so on). These programmes are inevitably elitist, but are seen as an important investment in developing and retaining future executives and leaders.

GRADUATE MENTORING

Graduates are a costly commodity, increasingly choosy about where they work and willing to vote with their feet if they do not feel valued by the organisation they join. Mentoring is one of the fastest growing ways of supporting and developing graduates in the workplace. Organisations with long-established graduate schemes report that they:

- reduce staff turnover and recruitment costs by increasing motivation and instilling a sense of belonging
- improve internal communications including the fundamentals of the corporate vision, values and mission
- encourage employees to take responsibility more quickly for their own career development.

The transition from education to the world of work can come as a bit of a shock. The nature of learning – and the speed with which it has to take place – is considerably different. Instead of pursuing a self-focused goal (getting a degree), the graduate is expected to share team learning and team goals. Different behaviours, different thinking patterns, the need to develop some clarity of personal purpose and direction, the need to build effective networks of influence and information – these are all classic situations addressed by mentoring.

It is no coincidence, then, that formal mentoring schemes in the UK or Europe until the mid 1990s were almost all aimed at graduates. Companies could see immediate advantages in attracting and keeping this valuable asset. One large packaging company found that its graduates, teamed with mentors to address long-standing but low-priority technical problems in production, saved more through quality improvements than the entire training and recruiting budget for all the staff on site!

It did not always work out so well, however. Many schemes either collapsed as pressures of change made it more difficult for mentors to provide quality time, or simply faded away because there was no real ownership. Graduate mentoring in recent years is more often characterised by greater realism and a stronger determination to make graduate mentoring part of the organisational infrastructure.

A lot of lessons have been learned. The following represent a mixture of the most common and the most important.

MANAGING THE POWER DISTANCE

Early graduate mentoring schemes matched young people with very senior people – often at, or just below, the board. They were almost universally wasted. The executives could not empathise with the situation of someone just starting out on their career. They either preached at the graduates or tried to relive their own careers through them. They had neither time nor the inclination to act as anything but sponsors and they learned little in return.

Good practice now is to limit the size of the hierarchy and experience gap to promote empathy and mutual learning. The trick is to have enough scope for the graduate to respect and value the mentor's experience, but to be close enough to develop a genuine rapport.

TIMING THE START OF THE RELATIONSHIP

Most schemes even now assume that the mentoring relationship should begin as soon as the graduate arrives. Practical experience increasingly brings that assumption into question. It seems that a significant minority of relationships fail to gel because the graduate simply does not know enough about the organisation, nor about his or her needs, to bring real issues to the table. Both mentor and mentee rapidly become bored, and the developmental opportunity at that point is lost.

Some schemes now deliberately defer the appointment of a mentor for the first few months, preferring to give the graduate a 'buddy' from a previous intake, who can answer most of the questions about where to find things and how to behave. Mentoring relationships established after this tend to have an immediately higher sense of purpose and quality of dialogue.

LINKING TO COMPETENCIES

Early thinking on graduate mentoring was that the mentor should avoid discussion on specific competencies because it might undermine the authority of the graduate's line manager. There is, of course, still some truth in that, but the recognition is increasingly that the clarity of role between line manager (as coach), mentor, and human recourses in developing the graduate is essential. The mentor can help the graduate examine specific competency needs beyond the confines of current tasks and in the perspective of his or her career as a whole.

FOCUS ON OPPORTUNITIES, NOT PROBLEMS

Some mentoring schemes in which I have participated have struggled because the mentor has been presented as 'someone who can help you with your problems'. If the environment is such that it discourages people from discussing their problems with someone more senior (or even admitting they have problems), the pair soon run out of things to talk about. Part of the problem is that mentors often lack the career counselling skills to be of much use in helping the graduate define and seize opportunities. This argues for continued training of mentors as more all-round 'developers of people', and for the involvement of the mentor group as a whole in succession planning and development planning.

THE TWO-YEAR CLIFF EDGE

Within the typical two-year duration of the graduate mentoring scheme, the relationship generally winds down. The graduate is settled into the organisation, has become part of a normal work team, and has a reasonable idea of where he or she is headed. He or she does not really need a mentor anymore and, in that mentors are a scarce resource, the relationship is usually expected to come to an end.

What frequently happens after the two years, however, is that the graduate begins to acquire greater responsibilities which provide a whole new set of challenges, or gets bored because the challenges do not come fast enough. In either situation there is high potential for this valuable resource to be lured away.

Another common scenario is that the end of the formal programme and the sudden expansion of role come simultaneously. So just when the mentee needs mentoring most, the opportunity is taken away from them! Some programmes now postpone the formal ending of the first mentoring relationship until six months after the mentee's first supervisory role. At this point, the mentee often transitions to a secondary mentor, someone usually more senior than the first, whose role is to help the graduate – now an employee without a special label on his or her collar – to continue to develop a career within the organisation. This mentor is likely to be more challenging, better networked, and sometimes more demanding than the first. This 'layering' of levels of mentor is becoming an increasingly common characteristic of organisations which wish to maximise their use of a scarce developmental resource.

MENTORING 'HIGH POTENTIALS'

In my book, *The Talent Wave* (2012), I identify a wide range of problems with how companies identify, select, develop and promote talent. It turns out that many of the processes and procedures, such as leadership competencies, nine box grids, and succession plans result in reduced diversity and undermine organisation agility. To a large extent, this is more to do with the way they are used – as methods of making judgements about people rather than to stimulate developmental conversations. The problem with trying to tie down who is and isn't talented is that by definition, talent is unique, quirky, and unpredictable.

Nonetheless, once a talent pool has been identified, there are two immediate challenges. One is to keep and motivate them. Keep, because their 'chosen' status often makes them more mobile, especially if promotion doesn't come fast enough. Motivate, because once people are labelled as successful they are likely to slacken off, rather than devote even more effort into their development. The second problem is that people who have not been selected, but who believe themselves to be equally or more talented than peers who have, will also be dusting off their CVs.

Mentors can provide a solution to both of these problems. As role models and challengers, they can help the high potential (hypo) focus their ambition less on the extrinsic motivation of achieving the next promotion, but on the solid foundation of capability they can only acquire by continuing to be proactive in their learning. They can also help employees who have not been selected to understand what they can do to build a stronger reputation and demonstrate their potential.

In my research on talent management, I found that talented people and organisations needed to have four critical conversations. The first was the conversation the talented person has internally, about their values, strengths and weaknesses, ambitions and so on. The second was with their key stakeholders, including their boss. The third conversation was an open sharing by employees of their real intentions, their concerns and interests; with a reciprocal sharing by the organisation of how careers and job opportunities might develop in the next few years. The fourth conversation was in the virtual world, where senior and junior people come together informally to exchange ideas that lead to innovation and change.

Mentors have a role to play in all of these conversations. They can help the mentee develop self-awareness, negotiate with their boss about how they identify and seize developmental opportunities in their current job roles, and work with talented people to influence HR systems and thinking around future roles. And they can introduce mentees to virtual networks, to which then can add value and thus enhance their knowledge and reputation.

Mentors can also become 'talent spotters'. The mentoring conversation provides a very different, often much safer environment, in which to explore people's ambitions, motivations, and abilities, than in their normal working environment. For example, much talent is missed in formal HR processes because people's performance and/or visibility are negatively affected by their boss. Such people may never even appear on the talent radar, because their boss does not give them access to projects that build reputation. The mentor can help to build their self-belief and self-confidence to take part in activities outside of their immediate job role that may show them in a different light.

A common dilemma for mentors is what to do when the talent selection process has got it wrong. For example, people can often get into the talent pool on the basis of appearing to work hard and make few mistakes. But people who don't make mistakes don't learn. Because they exhibit an achievement motivation instead of a mastery motivation, their potential is limited. The mentor could be judgemental and tell the mentee 'You're not as talented as you think you are' (not likely to promote rapport!); or they could voice their concerns to the programme manager, with the result that the person might be removed from the programme (and blame the mentor!). The most frequent scenario is that they try to soldier on silently and the relationship gradually fades away. Opening up this issue in training and contracting makes it more possible to have a constructive conversation within the relationship, which can lead to appropriate conversations outside of it.

SUMMARY

From being the most common application of mentoring in employment, graduate mentoring has become just one of many. However, it is still a vital ingredient in attracting and retaining entry-level talent. Mentoring high potentials also brings many benefits, but it needs careful management to ensure that it is focused on the right people, that excluded peers are not resentful, and that it contributes to retention rather than increased turnover of talent!

CHAPTER 16

Diversity Mentoring

When I first wrote *Everyone Needs a Mentor*, the concept of using mentoring as a vehicle for promoting equal opportunity was still fairly new. The handful of diversity-related programmes there were tended to focus on high-potential women. Even the term 'diversity mentoring' – now commonly used, especially in corporate programmes – was not widely recognised. Since then, several evolutions have occurred. One is that mentoring for equal opportunity at work now addresses a wide range of target groups, from women at all levels and career stages, through ethnic minorities, to the mentally and physically disabled. The other is that the concept of equal opportunity has, to a significant extent, been overtaken firstly by diversity management, then by the concept of leveraging difference. Table 10 illustrates the difference between these three perspectives.

Table 10 From equal opportunities to leveraging difference

Equal opportunities	Diversity management	Leveraging difference
• Issue (problem) focused. • Tactical emphasis. • Focused on a small number of defined groups. • An HR issue. • 'Hard' targets (get the numbers). • About enforcing the distribution of power, privilege and advantage. • Driven by legislation.	• Opportunity focused. • Strategic emphasis. • Aimed at everyone. • Issue owned by everyone. • Changing thinking and behaviours to change the culture. • About increasing collaborative endeavour and sharing. • Driven by organisational need.	• Individual focused. • Tactical and strategic. • A wider definition of talent. • Valuing difference in all its forms. • About the quality of conversations between employees and the organisation. • Driven by alignment between individual and organisational needs.

Source: Reproduced by permission of the author and publisher. CLUTTERBUCK, D., POULSEN, K.P. and KOCHAN, F. (2012) *Developing successful diversity mentoring programmes: an international casebook*. Maidenhead: McGraw-Hill.

These different perspectives, which are not necessarily incompatible in the same organisation, tend to inform how companies design their mentoring programmes.

For many, the most practical approach is a programme aimed specifically at a clearly defined group. The problems with such an approach, however, include the following:

- There is the possibility that many potential participants don't want to be labelled in this way, as BP Engineering found when it consulted a cross-section of its female employees. Rather, they wanted to be encouraged to join a wider scheme, open to all, which would not carry the stigma of disadvantage.

- There is the difficulty of defining just who is disadvantaged (is a black female with an Oxbridge education more disadvantaged than a white male with a poor education and from a lower-class background?) and who belongs to a group. One North American company was embarrassed when homosexual employees complained that the women's leadership programme disadvantaged them, so the company formed another scheme, only to find that other groups, such as the physically disabled, also wanted the same privileges. Confused by a plethora of schemes, potential mentors backed away in droves. The company attempted to place all the disadvantaged groups into one scheme, but some groups didn't want to be categorised alongside others they considered different. The process collapsed under the weight of bureaucracy and now anyone, from any group, including the most positively advantaged, can apply for a mentor.
- How valid are the assumptions about behavioural change? For example, a gender-based glass ceiling programme defined its mentoring element in terms of helping women understand how to think and behave at a more senior level. Some of the women challenged this definition and asked for an analysis of what behaviours they needed to acquire. It soon became clear that cloning male executives might not meet the programme goal, as a high proportion of the male executives did not exemplify these behaviours either. Indeed, in many cases the female mentees were better exemplars of those behaviours than their intended mentors. Redefining the programme to legitimise building on the strengths the women had, rather than trying to change them into something else, gave a stronger sense of commitment and purpose.

Mentoring aimed to support diversity management more generally overcomes most of these problems, but it makes it much more difficult to target mentoring on people who will particularly benefit from it. Companies taking this approach tend to develop practical methods to encourage people to come forward – for example, by making mentoring an option to be considered at each performance appraisal.

Mentoring for leveraging difference goes one step further. It takes the view that all mentoring relationships are diverse; that even where people come from similar backgrounds, they will bring to the relationship many different values, skills, knowledge, experiences, and ways of thinking. Differences of gender, age, culture, discipline, education and so on are valuable contributions to organisational agility and to the multiple perspectives that underpin ethical awareness. In schemes of this type, membership is open to all, but encouragement is given to particular groups and individuals, on the grounds of the different perspectives they have to offer as much as any real or perceived disadvantages they may be under.

SAME GROUP, DIFFERENT GROUP?

One of the most controversial issues in diversity mentoring is whether the mentor should be from the same group or a different group.

A strong practical reason against same-group mentoring in many organisations is that there aren't enough people from the minority or disadvantaged group to meet the demand. Given that two, or at most three, mentees per mentor is the maximum recommended, there will frequently be a supply and demand problem. One of the major mistakes organisations make is to press into service the handful of senior managers who are black or female (or both), regardless of whether they have the aptitude and interest to be an active and effective mentor.

There seem to be five key aspects to the arguments around this issue. The first is *perspective* – whether and how the mentor can help the mentee view his or her issues in a manner useful to learning. The mentor from a different group – especially if he or she is also at a higher level in the organisation – can provide a very different set of viewpoints. If the mentor comes from the powerful majority, he or she may be better at explaining how the system functions and how to work with it, rather than against it. The mentor is able to help the mentee see barriers and opportunities in ways that make them easier to tackle. For example, a young Muslim mentee was having great difficulty adapting to working in a multinational organisation. He expected to be given frequent, clear instructions and to report back to his supervisor constantly. Instead, he found that the supervisor responded with: 'Look, you know what to do. Why don't you just get on with it?' As a result, relationships between them were very strained, especially when the mentee was passed over for a promotion.

Working with the mentor, this young man gradually came to understand what the supervisor's expectations were and the value the organisation placed upon self-reliance and demonstrating initiative. He also worked out how to fit in with the organisation's behavioural expectations, while not sacrificing any of the values important to him from his own culture. He rehearsed with the mentor how he would discuss these issues with his supervisor to build a better understanding between them.

While a difference of perspective was important here, in other cases the dominant need may be for greater empathy. The white mentor above could not easily put himself in the mentee's shoes – he had never been in such a situation. Same-group mentors can extend greater understanding. One of the classic examples is the experiment by part of the Prudential in the UK to assist returning mothers with a mentor. The mentor – a mum who had made the same transition within recent years – contacted the employee some months ahead of the return date and worked with her for several months until she had settled back in again. The mentor in this case was able to share the feelings of guilt, inadequacy and being pulled in too many directions, which so many returning mothers feel. 'Being able to talk with someone who had been there and come through it made all the difference,' said one mentee.

The second key aspect is *networking*. The mentor from the dominant group is likely to be much better connected, and even a mentor who is not in the power structure will be able to introduce the mentee to very different people. The same-group mentor is likely to have networks that largely overlap with those of the mentee.

Power is the third aspect. Minority-group mentors are less likely to be in senior positions, so they cannot provide either the depth of understanding of the organisation (another result of perspective) or – in sponsorship mentoring – the potential to exert influence on the mentee's behalf. If the mentee is ambitious, there is much to be learned from someone who has developed the skills of acquiring and using power wisely.

Being a *role model* is also an important consideration. Same-group mentors may be more likely to reinforce attitudes and behaviours that are not valued by the organisation. Different-group mentors can provide role models for behaviours that are valued. (However, it may not always be possible for the mentee to distinguish between appropriate and inappropriate role models – having a mentor from *both* groups may provide greater insight.)

In deciding whether the relationship should be constructed within the same group or across different groups, a variety of issues need to be taken into account. The most fundamental, however, is *what is the mentee's need*? If support is the most critical need, then a same-group mentor may be most appropriate. If being stretched is the goal, then a mentor from a different group may be more effective. In addition, it should be remembered that the mentor is not the only potential source of learning for the mentee – the wider the learning net the mentee can create, the more he or she can receive of both nurture and challenge.

POSITIONING DIVERSITY

The increasing numbers of women and minorities now entering careers in management suffer from a major disadvantage: by and large they are not exposed to the same range of experiences and career opportunities as men. While formal barriers have been reduced through legislation, they continue to be hindered in their careers by invisible obstacles, such as prejudice and distrust. As the demand for quality white-collar management increases, the need for organisations to question why there are so few women and minorities in management will become acute.

If these managers are accepted in the formal structure of the organisation, in the informal social structure they can still be looked on with suspicion. For example, the masculine culture of a company may mean that women are not fully integrated; in a sense they are still regarded as outsiders or interlopers.

Low expectations or stereotyped images can often mean that women and minority managers are delegated undemanding jobs, making them less visible than white male managers. Women may be expected to perform tasks that are seen as suitably 'feminine' in nature, such as personnel, rather than the more 'masculine' managerial jobs, such as financial analysis. As a result, women managers frequently lack opportunities to develop a wide range of managerial skills.

In the UK, I carried out some years ago a survey of business women, with questionnaires sent to 100 who had reached executive level inside a company, and to 100 women entrepreneurs. The response rate was a remarkable 49%. Among the key conclusions were the following:

- Successful women managers are more likely than women entrepreneurs to have had a mentor (56% compared with 43%). One reason – possibly the most important – is that the entrepreneurs quit to set up on their own precisely because their progress was blunted in large corporations, through lack of a champion at higher levels.
- 49% of the women had had a single mentor; 22% had had two; 21% had had three; and 8% had had four or five – or more – at different periods in their careers.
- 94% of the women said their relationships were beneficial to their career.
- More than half of the entrepreneurs' mentors had encouraged them to start their own businesses; 5% even helped them financially.
- The vast majority of mentoring relationships (63%) started accidentally; only 8% of the women had actually approached their mentor.
- The main benefits reported by the women were:
  - improved self-confidence and self-image
  - increased visibility to senior management (especially important to women managers)
  - focusing career aspirations
  - acting as a role model
  - help with work problems
  - improved communications and skills.
- Most mentors (79%) were male.
- More than two-fifths experienced no problems with the relationship.
- 37% had experienced problems of resentment from peers; 5% said their careers had been damaged when their mentor lost credibility in the company.
- Two-thirds had experienced some form of sexual innuendo or gossip; 19% reported that their mentor's wife felt threatened by the relationship; 11% said their own husbands resented it; 4% said their mentor became too emotionally involved with them.
- 60% of the women were acting as mentors themselves.

Dr Judi Marshall of the University of Bath found that mentoring improved the promotion prospects of women managers. Interviewing 30 women managers from middle management to director level, Marshall found that 70% either were currently or had been in a mentoring relationship. All of these women placed great value on the relationship and said it had been a very important factor in their career development, she explained. The majority of the surveyed women saw visibility as a crucial factor for success. The mentors sponsored the women and often nominated them for promotion committees when they would not have normally been considered for posts. If a mentor vouches for a woman manager, companies are more willing to promote her because they view the mentor as a 'safety net', she concludes.

POTENTIAL PROBLEMS WITH MALE–FEMALE MENTORING

BETWEEN THE MENTEE AND THE MENTOR

A female mentee often experiences disappointment with the relationship because her male mentor is unable to meet all her developmental needs. She cannot emulate him fully and in certain areas may need to find her own methods of achieving goals and resolving problems. For example, women frequently put more emphasis than men on delegating and on group discussion and often have a different style of leadership that may not be valued by a male mentor.

Pressure to adopt established sexual roles sometimes causes tension and conflict in the relationship. A male mentor may feel overly protective towards a female mentor and encourage her to be dependent. She may find it particularly difficult to terminate the relationship at the end of the mentoring programme. The same may also be true in the case of a female mentor and male mentee, especially where the age differences are similar to those in a mother–son relationship.

Says Dr Marilyn Puder-York, a clinical psychologist in New York:

> There are many very productive male–female mentoring relationships, but there must be a high sense of shared values and ethical behaviour on both sides. And you often have to counter society's perception of the relationship by having lunch instead of dinner and by including spouses in socialising. Otherwise both can pay a heavy price. In general, if a woman has a male mentor, she should seek out a woman mentor as well. Beyond the social considerations, there are politics for women that a man may not be aware of.

BETWEEN THE SPOUSES AND THE MENTORING PAIR

A mentoring relationship can seem threatening to the mentor's and mentee's partners, especially if business trips together are involved. The spouse often feels excluded by the closeness of the relationship. Mentees have found various solutions, mostly based on total openness. Social gatherings where spouses are invited make a useful opportunity to demonstrate the businesslike nature of the relationship.

BETWEEN THE COMPANY AND THE MENTORING PAIR

Sexual gossip and innuendo can kill a mentoring relationship before it gets going. Many potential male–female mentoring relationships never happen because of the fear of office gossip. In a mentoring programme it is often necessary for the two to work beyond work hours or even travel together. The two must act 'professionally', which can simply mean that behaviour has to be much more circumscribed than in a mentor relationship between two of the same sex. One mentor solved the problem of gossip: 'If you mentor one woman you are branded as a womaniser. If you mentor several, you are praised for your commitment to seeing more women in management.' The extra visibility of the relationship in the company may discourage even the highest risk-taker from being a mentor: 'A young man can have the luxury of failing quietly but a woman's mistakes are often broadcast,' explains one mentor.

MENTORING ACROSS RACIAL/CULTURAL DIVIDES

Mentoring between races requires equally sensitive handling. The potential for stereotyping to reduce the effectiveness of the relationship is high; as too is the potential to identify and overcome stereotypes. In experiments across cultures, I have found it is important to begin the relationship with an extra dose of clarity about expectations. On one occasion in Brunei, managers being trained as mentors were asked to plot the shape of the relationship in terms of where the emphasis of behaviours should rest. Figure 15 shows what the expatriate (English and Dutch) mentors concluded.

Figure 15 Mentor–mentee relationship as perceived by expatriate mentors

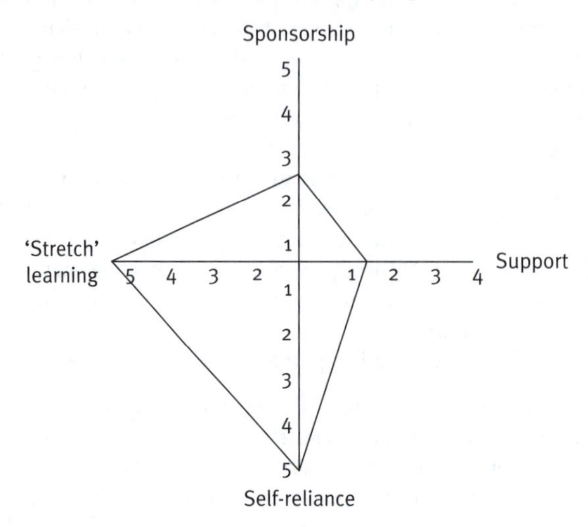

Figure 16 shows what the mentees, who were mostly local people in their mid-twenties, were expecting.

Figure 16 Mentor–mentee relationship as perceived by mentees abroad

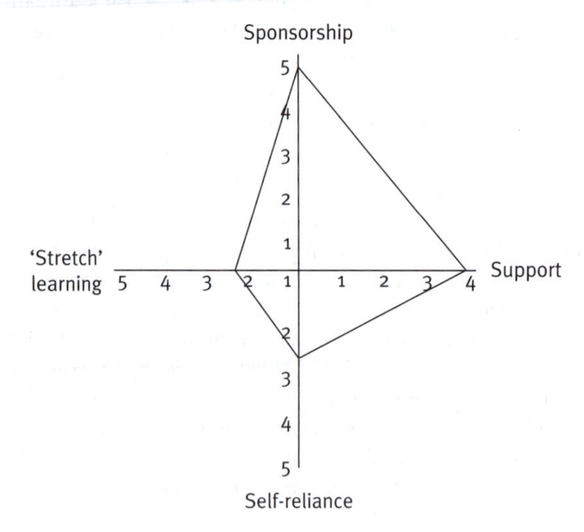

After nearly two minutes of silence one manager exclaimed, 'Now I see why I have such difficulty getting through to my direct reports!' Mentors and mentees used this information to discuss what behaviours and expectations on both sides would be appropriate, and to build a compromise acceptable to both parties.

Like mentoring across genders, mentoring across cultures is an excellent developmental experience for the mentor. Some companies now encourage such relationships as an integral part of globalising their cultures.

TRAINING MENTORS AND MENTEES TO MANAGE DIVERSITY ISSUES

When a mentoring programme has clear objectives relating to diversity (or simply involves working with people from heterogeneous backgrounds), it is beneficial to devote some training time to ensuring that both participants are aware of their own and other people's unconscious biases and stereotypes, and the power these have to limit people's performance and potential. One tool I have developed, which is now quite widely used, is the Diversity Awareness Ladder (see Table 11). This aims to make people aware of the conversations they are not having, both internal (with themselves) and external (with others), and how they can have different conversations at each stage of their awareness. The mentoring relationship also provides a safe space for people to work on their diversity awareness, and greater comfort and authenticity in the conversations they have with people they perceive as significantly different from themselves.

Table 11 The Diversity Awareness Ladder

Stage	The inner conversation	The outer conversation
1. Fear	What do I fear from this person? What do I fear learning about myself? What might I be avoiding admitting to myself?	What do we have in common? What concerns do you have about me and my intentions?
2. Wariness	What if I say the wrong thing? Is their expectation of me negative and/or stereotyped? How open and honest can I be with them?	How can we be more open with each other? How can we recognise and manage behaviours that make each other feel uncomfortable/unvalued?
3. Tolerance	What judgements am I making about this person and on what basis? What boundaries am I seeking/applying in dealing with this person?	How can we exist/work together without friction? How can we take blame out of our conversations?
4. Acceptance	Can I accept this person for who they are? Can I accept and work with the validity of their perspective, even if it's different from mine?	What values do you hold? How do you apply them? How can we make our collaboration active and purposeful?
5. Appreciation	What can I learn from this person? How could knowing them make a better/more accomplished person?	What can we learn from each other? How will we learn from each other?

Source: Reproduced by permission of the author and publisher. CLUTTERBUCK, D., POULSEN, K.P. and KOCHAN, F. (2012) *Developing successful diversity mentoring programmes: an international casebook*. Maidenhead: McGraw-Hill.

The cultural issues relating to diversity are also discussed in Chapter 14, which explores multi-country mentoring programmes.

LONDON BOROUGH OF BRENT – MENTORING FOR A DIVERSE WORKFORCE

During 2001, the London borough of Brent launched a series of initiatives under the banner of an 'Improving Brent' programme. This focused on both personal and service improvement while, at the same time, converging with the requirements of the Campaign for Racial Equality's (CRE) Equalities Action Plan.

One initiative introduced under the 'Improving Brent' umbrella was a 12-month mentoring scheme aimed initially at black and Asian staff. The stated aims of the scheme were:

- to encourage a more proactive approach to learning and move further towards becoming a learning organisation
- to enable individuals to be more self-reliant through improved career and personal/professional development that would encourage them actively to take responsibility for their actions
- to provide a development opportunity for individuals who had not been able to take part in other development initiatives
- to enable individuals to have a greater understanding of the work pressures and priorities outside their own area, providing them with a council-wide view
- to support the new council-wide appraisal process, where there was now an opportunity to discuss training and learning in general
- to ensure the management structure reflected the makeup of the whole population at the Council.

The scheme began with a manageable 25 pairs, all of whom attended a one-day formal training programme. During training, personal portfolios were filled out and then used, in conjunction with the initial application forms, to do matching.

Uniquely, the scheme was actively supported by a steering group of four people, based in different locations around the borough and, so, well-placed to help participants. Besides providing support to individuals, the role of the group was to oversee implementation of the scheme and particularly the matching and evaluation processes.

Feedback was obtained twice during the course of the year and also at the conclusion of the formal relationships. A creditable 79% of participants felt that their expectations had been met. This and other feedback was shared at an open day run by the steering group and supported by the Borough directorate. Comments made by mentees included: 'my mentor makes me think and see things through'; 'beliefs and differences were accepted and I was able to speak openly'; 'made me feel special and that someone was listening'; 'removed preconceived barriers'; 'you get what you put in'; 'my mentor's insights helped me acquire the knowledge I wanted about the unit I wanted to work in'.

For each of the three different stakeholder groups, the perceived benefits of mentoring were as follows:

Mentors

- gained insights into the work of parts of the organisation in which they did not come into direct contact – assisting in organisational integration and communication
- experienced more closely the challenges facing employees and the impact of senior management decisions on the organisation
- were able to change their own mindsets and share learning with others
- gained an opportunity to examine their own style and improve management of their own employees.

Mentees

- gained an opportunity to discuss career and development aspirations with a more senior member of staff from another service area
- had a confidant to explore current work problems and resolutions
- were able to see a range of management styles and techniques.

Brent – the organisation

- development and progression of black and Asian staff
- assisted in identifying potential, particularly for management roles
- identification and development of key competencies
- transfer of skills, leading to motivation and productivity
- source of feedback on how key organisational processes were working, such as recruitment and selection.

The steering group's purpose for holding an open day was two-fold: firstly, to share with participants and others the outcomes from the first year of mentoring; and, secondly, to provide a forum for prospective new participants to hear at first-hand what mentoring was about and how it worked in Brent.

The success of the first year's scheme was such that a second phase was launched towards the end of 2002. This was opened out to all staff, with a percentage of places being held for positive action candidates. Built into this next phase were the key learning points drawn out by the steering group from phase one:

Initial application phase

- Improve communication about the programme by using the intranet and attending team meetings; launch the next programme with an open seminar, celebrating success of this programme.
- Involve the line managers – ask them to sign mentees' application forms and arrange a briefing session specifically for them.
- Extend the opportunity to all staff, while retaining a number of positive action places.

Training

- Spend more time on clarifying roles, expectations and the level of commitment required; explain the evaluation process; emphasise that building rapport is key and can take time; focus on building/achieving medium-term objectives (vs short-term).

Matching

- It takes a lot of time; the more information you can get from participants, the better; limit the number of hierarchical levels between mentor and mentee.

Implementation

- Some people need help and support in getting started.
- Give good practice guidelines, eg on how often and how long to meet for.
- Offer occasional workshops to support mentees, such as interview skills.
- Now give more emphasis to mentor development during the year, to help them move mentees to consider medium term objectives.

Organisational learning

- To illustrate the relationship between mentoring and improved performance, change over time needs to be tracked.
- There are strong links between mentor skills and general management skills.
- Need to build on the gains for individuals.
- Need to offer more than just access to mentoring to help black and minority ethnic (BME) staff progress – need practical management experience to make them credible candidates for their first management posts – looking now to provide shadowing and other tools to facilitate this.

Mentoring is now seen as an important building block in the 'Improving Brent' programme and it continues to thrive and be supported by the steering group.

SUMMARY

Mentoring in support of diversity is one of the most positive developments in organisational learning in recent years. It benefits the disadvantaged employee, for whom doors begin to open up; it benefits the mentor, who learns how to interact with and get the most from employees of widely differing backgrounds; and it benefits the company by making much more effective use of the talent available.

CHAPTER 17

Maternity Mentoring

Maternity mentoring has its origins in the early 1990s, when it was pioneered (in the UK at least) by the Prudential. It is now used by a variety of employers, for three main reasons:

- to increase the proportion of women coming back to their previous jobs after maternity leave
- to make the transition back into work less stressful
- to reduce the time between return and contributing fully once more.

Some providers offer externally resourced maternity coaching. This differs from maternity mentoring mainly in that, while the coaches may share the experience of return to work generally, do not necessarily have an understanding of the culture and politics of the organisation. Effective maternity mentoring:

- starts well before the return date. (Ideally, it starts before the mother begins maternity leave, helping her to establish shared expectations with colleagues and bosses about when and how she will return. The mentor ensures that the employee does not become completely out of touch with events and changes in the organisation)
- trains mentors to address key issues for the mentee, including:
  - managing the emotional transition back to work (worry or even guilt)
  - managing the dual foci of attention (job and family)
  - reconnecting to the organisation (increasingly important the more senior the role, because the more senior you are, the more you need functioning networks, which are likely to have dissipated in your absence)
  - re-establishing self-confidence and career purposefulness.

A survey of 500 women about their experiences of how they and their employers react to pregnancy, identifies a range of other issues. According to the study by Nirmala Menon:

- The main reason women returned to work was for career or personal growth – only 11% said the main reason was money.
- Two-thirds identified job flexibility as the most useful thing employers could do to assist their return to work.
- 60% felt managers inadvertently sabotaged the careers of returning mothers, and almost the same number considered that organisations viewed pregnancy and motherhood as dilution of commitment to work. As a result, most of the women felt they had to constantly reconfirm their commitment to work and career. Even so, more than 70% felt their job roles had been unnecessarily diluted.
- Three-quarters believed their career aspirations and prospects were compromised by motherhood.
- Many were remarkably accepting of both insensitive behaviour by bosses, with two-fifths believing that the organisation was doing them a favour by making work adjustments to fit around their pregnancy.

The maternity mentor can help the returning mother prepare for dealing with these and other issues, rehearsing both the inner conversations that will smooth the transition, and the conversations that will be needed with other people to establish reasonable expectations on both sides, and challenge assumptions and behaviours that might limit her potential to contribute fully.

As yet, I have been unable to find any paternity mentoring programmes … but that's probably only a matter of time.

CASE STUDY

ASDA

In this case study, we share insights from the MumtoMum (M2M) maternity mentoring programme launched in the Asda Home Offices in 2012.

Background

A review of maternity returners revealed increasing numbers of colleagues taking maternity leave at the Home Offices in Asda. It was also apparent that the incidence of maternity occurred most frequently at junior to middle management level. The volume of maternity at these levels, combined with a low-cost culture, had ruled out any appetite for external investment in maternity coaching programmes. Women were returning to work post-maternity, but anecdotal evidence suggested it was frequently an isolated and isolating experience, with pre-maternity optimism often at odds with the actual experience of return. There was a belief that mentoring – helping conversations with colleagues who had currency of experience and context – had much to contribute.

Aims of the programme

Open to all and operating on a peer-to-peer basis, the M2M scheme offers support for colleagues in transition to working parenthood. The mentors are all working mothers from across the spectrum of seniority levels, who have returned to work within a two to three year period, are successfully delivering in role post-maternity leave, and have both the desire and capacity to mentor.

The scheme has a number of aims and objectives, which are to

- provide 'current' support for the colleague in transition to working parenthood
- be a sounding board and offer appropriate support through the different phases of maternity (pre-maternity leave, maternity leave and return to work)
- provide an independent connection with the business
- support smoother returns and re-engagement with work
- keep talented individuals on the road to success – whatever that means to them
- be self-sustaining – the mentees are potentially our next generation of mentors.

M2M structure

The mentoring flexes across a number of distinct phases and critical support points, respecting that each maternity leave is different, and agendas and priorities are often subject to change. M2M mentors are upskilled through an initial mentoring workshop and there is a framework for ongoing supervision and development using M2M lead mentors.

Some lessons learned

Proactive mentors

From the mentees perspective – particularly in the case of first-time mums – we find often there is a reluctance to seek mentoring support on the assumption it won't be needed! This requires mentors to take a more pro-active role in the early stages of the mentoring relationship.

Communication modes

We prepare mentors for different modes of mentoring, from face-to-face, phone and e-mentoring. The start of maternity leave typically results in a period of 'radio-silence' for up to four months as the new mum engages with a whole new way of life.

Mentor development

We have seen real benefit from investing in supervision and mentor workshops on maternity-related topics, such as confidence building, coping with tiredness, and how to recognise post-natal depression.

Ongoing evaluation and improvements to the programme

With UK statutory maternity leave at 52 weeks, summative evaluation takes considerable time. We continue to use the development and review/supervision touch points with mentors and stakeholders to make adjustments and support formative evaluation as the scheme progresses.

M2M insights

Early mentoring conversations

'The topic of discussion with my mentor at the time was; how am I going to cope with not working? I wasn't thinking about the birth. I never read that chapter. It was all about giving up work.'

The relationship

'I trusted her. I knew I could raise fears and concerns in a really safe environment.'

The mentor

'I see her as a fantastic role model as a working mum. Someone who gets the right balance at work and challenges you to really think. She asked me powerful questions to help prepare for that journey and what I might want, respecting my opinion and thoughts.'

The advice

'It was the absolute practicality and logistics of how you come back to work. Should I feed her before she goes to nursery? Give her toast in the car? It was literally down to that.'

Looking back

'I don't know if I realised how much support I would need before I went off. I was open to advice, but I don't think you realise how important that is until you're in the position.'

A metaphor for M2M

'A lifeline. It might be a bit dramatic, but the way I was feeling was dramatic. It was a massive shift.'

Source: Contributed by Nicki Seignot. Nicki is a coach/mentor and final year MSc student in Coaching and Mentoring at Sheffield Hallam Business School. She is the founder and lead mentor for M2M maternity mentoring at Asda.

SUMMARY

Not really a new kid on the block, maternity mentoring is one of the most effective ways to improve return-to-work rates and to ease returning mums back into contributing at their fullest.

CHAPTER 18

Professional and Executive Mentoring

An emerging phenomenon in the world of mentoring is the gradual professionalisation of executive mentoring, along lines similar to professional coaching. The European Mentoring and Coaching Council (EMCC) created competency frameworks for both professional coaches and professional mentors early in its history, and these provide a practical basis for self-development of people who undertake mentoring as a vocation, rather than an occasional undertaking.

The distinction between executive mentoring generally and professional mentoring is significant. Anyone who has held a leadership position in a large company or public sector organisation can set up as an executive mentor without any training or qualification for the role, other than their personal experience.

Professional mentors, by contrast, are expected to have most of the same basic competences as a developmental coach (client-centredness, a reasonable level of understanding of human behaviour and psychology, awareness of ethics and boundaries, and the skills to maintain a non-directive, inquiring and supportive conversation). Like professional coaches, they should also have regular supervision. They also typically require in addition a deep empathy with the leadership role (coming in most cases from personal experience in senior roles themselves). This empathy helps them intuit what is going on for their client and either raise the questions the client needs to understand their context, or paint the backcloth of wider context so the client can pose insightful questions for themselves.

While it might seem that there is a lot of professional mentoring going on, particularly in the area of small business support, in practice most of this is just misnamed, generally low-level consultancy. 'Mentoring sounds both more upmarket and less expensive than consultancy', one such 'mentor' told me over a glass of ale. There are numerous differences between the two roles, but the most significant are that:

- Consultancy requires much more specific expertise about specific systems and processes (it is essentially about finding answers, whereas mentoring is more about finding the right questions).
- Consultancy is aimed mostly at growing the business; mentoring at growing the owner-entrepreneur.

Executive mentoring is often also confused with being a non-executive director. Again, there are fundamental differences in the two roles, one of these being that the non-executive director is responsible to the board and the shareholders, not to an individual. In many cases, the non-executive director may adopt some of the behaviours of a mentor, but they must be careful not to compromise either or both roles.

As I write, a variety of organisations, including providers and professional associations around the world, are exploring together setting up an accreditation and good practice body for professional mentors.

THE RATIONALE FOR EXECUTIVE MENTORING

There have been both positive and negative reasons for the growth of executive mentoring. Among the common negative reasons are:

- 'Gucci mentoring' – having a mentor as a status symbol, rather like having a personal trainer
- abdication of responsibility for personal development (having a mentor means you can tick the box, even though you have done nothing proactive about your development).

Positive reasons include:

- The increasing need for leaders to take more time to reflect and to be challenged – which can often only come from someone they regard as a peer.
- The need to explore complex issues with a sounding board who understands the context, but is not involved, and so can be impartial. It's harder to do this with a colleague in the same organisation, because politics and confidentiality issues reduce the level of openness.
- Making the transition into the boardroom – learning to think like a director doesn't always come easily.
- Developing career direction. The closer people get to the top, the fewer opportunities for advancement in their own organisation. Mentoring helps the executive take a realistic view of their talents, experience and potential. The mentor may also be a useful resource in building networks that will lead to career opportunities the mentee may not have been aware of.

Underlying these reasons is a substantial change in the nature of executive roles, which have become more complex, more demanding, and more stressful. While a few decades ago people did most of their learning early in their careers, now the requirement for learning is continuous. At early career stages, the learning tends to be around task skills and socialisation. At more senior levels, the requirement shifts more towards behavioural competences and complex thinking and decision-making – which can be a lot more difficult! Power structures often prevent people being exposed to different perspectives. Flatter organisational hierarchies and matrix organisations also make the transition into executive roles more complex.

SMALL BUSINESS MENTORING

In smaller businesses, a major cause of failure is that the business grows faster than the capabilities of the owner-entrepreneur to manage it. This can be avoided, if they have a mentor to help focus attention on building their own competence in line with the evolving needs of the business.

It is unfortunate that the term mentor has been co-opted by a wide range of support and consultancy services. In the UK especially, government support schemes for small businesses use the term to describe almost any kind of help or intervention, with an emphasis on technical interventions. Or they may help with recruiting staff or writing the business plan. Genuine mentors rarely get involved at this level, because their focus is on the entrepreneur and the interface between and the entrepreneur and their business – not on the business itself.

Mentors do this by:

- helping the mentee identify issues, which need their attention
- challenging their assumptions, behaviours and practices
- acting as a sounding board, by helping the mentee with the quality of their thinking.

Core skills include:

- knowing when *not* to advise
- asking difficult questions that force insight
- working with the mentee as a key component of a complex system, with multiple layers (the leadership role, the management team, the business and the environment, in which the business operates).

Some examples of successful small business mentoring include:

- An intensive, two-year programme for businesses in mid-UK, which had high potential for growth and development through export. This involved psychological assessment of all potential mentors and was one of the initial sources of industry good practice. Lessons that emerged strongly from this project included:
  - the importance of educating mentees in how to use the volunteer business mentors
  - the value of continuing to support mentors and bringing them back together to identify common themes and to share experiences.
- A large-scale e-mail and telephone-based programme for small businesses in southern UK. Training was delivered online and detailed evaluation was carried out by Sheffield Hallam University.
- The South-East Women's Mentoring Network was established to meet the development needs of senior women in business, with the objective of helping them become leaders in existing firms or to launch their own.
- Youth Business International is a programme, now operational in more than 30 countries, aimed at helping young people create and grow businesses. Part of The Prince's Trust, the programme trains mentors, using materials developed for the purpose by David Clutterbuck.
- Mowgli is an international mentoring programme aimed at supporting people in developing countries to create and sustain businesses. The Cherie Blair Foundation for Women similarly aims to help women entrepreneurs through mentoring.

WHAT PROFESSIONAL MENTORS DO

Professional mentors help executives get at their own issues, build their own insights and self-awareness, develop their own, unique ways of handling how they interact with key colleagues and with the business. The professional mentor uses current issues to explore patterns of thinking and behaviour, often starting with the executive's values. They ask penetrating questions that stimulate thinking, challenge the executive to take control of issues avoided, help the executive put his or her own learning in context, and raise his or her ability to cope with new issues, through greater self-understanding and confidence.

To be effective, professional mentors have to have a broad knowledge and exposure to business direction, and to the patterns of senior management thinking and behaviour. They must have a store of relevant business, strategic and behavioural models – and the capacity to generate bespoke models on the spot – which can help executives explore the context of issues under discussion. They need exceptional interpersonal skills of their own, together with a more than passing competence in what can broadly be called counselling skills. Not surprisingly, these are relatively rare creatures.

One reason why professional mentoring is so much more demanding – on the executive as well as the mentor – is that it is so holistic. It seeks and deals with issues wherever they are. It requires the mentor to recognise and adapt roles according to the executive's needs at the time. So the mentor may need to be coach, counsellor, sounding board, critical friend, networker or any of a number of roles, sometimes within the same two-hour session. This constant reassessing and refocusing is helped by addressing the executive's issues from at least three viewpoints – the values and emotions that drive their behaviour and decision-making, the leader–manager style they adopt, and the needs of the business. Also frequently on the agenda are issues relating to work–life balance – an inevitable consequence of the demands of executive roles.

IN-HOUSE OR EXTERNAL MENTOR?

The cost of professional external mentors is enough to make most companies think twice about large-scale provision. In general, an external mentor will be most appropriate when:

- the executive would find it difficult to be sufficiently open to an insider
- he or she is looking to tap into specific expertise or experience not available within the company.

Internal mentors will be most appropriate when:

- there is a strong culture of peer dialogue and open learning
- the top team contains good role models for mentoring behaviours
- a knowledge of the internal politics and the organisation will be important to the relationship.

In general, it pays to take the view that a good case needs to be made for external provision and to make it clear that having an external mentor is not a status symbol, or a reward for good service, but a response to a specifically defined need. It's also important to be sure that a mentor is what is needed, rather than an executive coach or specialist counselling. A coach will be most appropriate if:

- the need is remedial or to do with a specific skill set (eg delegation rather than leadership in general)
- the relationship is intended to be a short term intervention (ie six months or less)
- achieving the developmental objective is likely to require direct observation and feedback by the external resource.

Counselling will normally be an option when the executive's performance issues are related to deeper psychological issues, rather than to technique.

CASE STUDY

DISCOVERY – AN EXECUTIVE MENTORING PROGRAMME IN NORWAY

> A society which does not educate and train its women is like a person who just trains the right arm. (Plato, 427–347 BC)

Discovery is a mentoring programme aimed at increasing the number of women in high-level executive positions in Norway. The NHO (Norwegian Federation for Business and Industry) started the programme in 1996; then in 1999 the Administrative Research Institute (AFF) at the Norwegian School of Economics and Business Administration took over the programme. Since then 760 people, 380 mentees and the same number of mentors, have participated in the programme.

The mentees come from large Norwegian organisations, mostly from finance, media, IT and manufacturing. The age of the mentees ranges from 28 to 57. They all have experience as managers, some at a very high executive level. In recent years, the programme opened to men as well, but few have taken the opportunity.

The mentors are top-level senior executives. Most of them are men, but the proportion of women is increasing. In the beginning of the programme each company selected both mentor and mentees to the programme. Since the quality of the mentoring relationship highly depends on the capability of the mentor, AFF has changed this procedure.

Today all the mentors are handpicked to meet the developing needs of the mentees.

AFF finds the mentors from its network of senior executives who have attended leadership programmes over the years since 1952. These people see the role as continuing their own leadership development as mentors. The mentors are not paid for the work – this is a Norwegian mentoring tradition!

After the companies have selected mentees, the project co-ordinators conduct comprehensive interviews in order to couple mentor and mentees.

Discovery is a one-year programme. During this year there are four kinds of formal meeting or seminar:

- *One and a half day seminar at the start.* All the mentors and mentees meet together. The purpose is to establish a good working environment for the mentoring process. We focus on what mentoring is and the role of the mentor and mentee. There is also some training in mentoring skills.
- *Meetings for the mentees.* One month after the start the mentees meet for networking and to clarify their roles.
- After four and eight months there is a *one day meeting* of both mentors and mentees for networking and sharing of experience. Some additional training in mentoring skills is also included.
- When the year is over, they all meet for *a half day seminar with a dinner*, for summarising the learning and for celebrating what is received!

During the year each mentor and mentee has at least 10 to 12 meetings of one-and-a-half to two hours. Both mentee and mentor must be committed to the programme and its goals, and make active participation a priority.

The mentors and mentees are also invited into AFF's network arrangements. They get an invitation to five half-day management seminars during each year. They also receive AFF's newsletter which contains updated articles about leadership and organisational development.

In recent years the programme co-ordinator has co-operated with Clutterbuck Associates in developing the programme and in using the The Mentoring Dynamics Survey (a diagnostic of relationship quality, which also acts as a stimulus for reflection on the progress of the relationship).

Each wave of the programme is evaluated to assess both processes and outcomes. Among the data from the evaluation:

- Both mentors and mentees are learning!
- Both report:
  - increased self-insight
  - increased self-confidence
  - better understanding and consciousness about the leadership role
  - more consciousness regarding values and attitudes
  - increased work satisfaction.

One of the aims of the programme is to help develop stronger networks and this is the one disappointing area in our evaluations, as relatively few participants make significant use of this opportunity. Participants seem to put all their efforts into the mentor–mentee relationship itself. We suspect this is in part an issue of the Norwegian culture – other research done by AFF shows that Norwegians often underestimate the importance of networking.

Source: Contributed by Jennybeth Ekeland.

SUMMARY

Professional and executive mentoring are rapidly expanding areas of practice. Most activity occurs through external provision, not least because senior managers find it hard to open out to peers, who may also be rivals for the top jobs. It's quite difficult for many executives to admit their fears and weaknesses to colleagues. However, there are no barriers to entry into the world of executive mentoring and many mentors have little or no relevant training in the role. Caveat emptor!

CHAPTER 19

Virtual Mentoring

An increasing amount of mentoring now takes place using virtual media: telephone, Skype, e-mail and even (in the case of inner-city teenagers at risk) by text. In our book *Virtual Coach, Virtual Mentor* (2009) Zulfi Hussain and I explored what research tells us about the efficacy of all these media in the context of a learning relationship. What we found was that all media, including face-to-face, have plusses and minuses. One of the surprises was that telephone, while it gives the benefit of relative immediacy of contact, was relatively ineffective for deep, reflective conversations, except when used by an exceptional listener. It seems that the need to fill silences is much greater when you can't see the other person.

In this chapter, I focus mainly on e-mentoring, as the greatest extreme to face-to-face mentoring. However, all the virtual media have a role to play in mentoring and the concept of 'multi-media mentoring' is gaining traction, because it offers such a high degree of flexibility. In training programmes for mentors and mentees, it is now increasingly common to devote some time and resource to educating participants in how to use different media in their relationship.

E-MENTORING

E-mentoring: mentoring relationships conducted primarily or entirely via e-mail.

I am, I have to admit, a converted sceptic about mentoring at a distance. Having invested so much time and research into the virtues of face-to-face developmental dialogue, I could not see how the mentoring relationship could possibly be as meaningful when the primary form of communication was e-mail. Experience as an e-mentor and interviews with participants in successful e-mentoring relationships have convinced me that e-mentoring is not an inferior substitute for 'real' mentoring. Rather, it is simply a different approach to mentoring and can be as effective – and in some cases, potentially more effective – than traditional approaches.

The arguments against e-mentoring can be summarised as follows:

- Even with teleconferencing, it is much more difficult to recognise the undertones in what someone is saying. With e-mail, you miss hesitations, prevarications and revealing facial expressions.
- Face-to-face dialogue has an immediacy that allows the two people to bounce ideas off each other creatively – it is easier to get into 'flow' when interaction is supported by non-verbal communication.
- Close visual contact allows mentors to use techniques of mirroring to build rapport.
- Words on paper can often be misleading – face-to-face, it is easier to explore what each party understands by a word or phrase.
- Distant communication often leads to a heavy focus on transactional exchanges rather than on relationship-building. This tends to make the relationship shallower. (We have no objective evidence one way or another on this, and not a great deal of anecdotal evidence either, but it is a view strongly held in some quarters.)

- It is more difficult to use techniques such as transactional analysis or neurolinguistic programming (NLP), which rely on a range of visual and auditory clues, to help the mentee explore his or her drives, motivations and fears.

However, the contra-arguments are equally convincing:

- Given an issue in writing, mentors are able to spend more time thinking about the advice they give and the questions they will ask. The quality of BDQs ('bloody difficult questions') often improves with e-mentoring. In effect, mentors ask fewer but more succinct and more insight-provoking questions than in the heat of a face-to-face dialogue.
- Equally, mentees have more time to consider their responses. Strong reflectors (in learning style jargon) particularly appreciate this space. For strong activists it provides a useful discipline to stop and think an issue through.
- Nuances that may be missed in the heat of face-to-face dialogue often become more obvious in text.
- Textual dialogue is easier to review – it is like having a transcript – and mentors report that they often spot patterns or repetitions that they would not otherwise have noticed.
- E-mentoring often allows for much more rapid responses by the mentor to the mentee's urgent enquiries. While it may take several weeks to fix up a suitable time to meet face-to-face, an e-mail exchange can take place the same day or at worst within a few days.
- Whereas a face-to-face mentoring sessions may take a focused period of a couple of hours, e-mentoring dialogue can be broken down into shorter, progressive exchanges spread over several days or more.

As Facebook and other social media have demonstrated, people are apt to be remarkably open in their self-disclosures online. It seems that online mentoring reduces the power distance between people, so they tend to have more open, more challenging conversations with someone more senior than themselves.

Like most other approaches within mentoring, e-mentoring clearly has more useful applications in some circumstances than others. Where mentor and mentee are geographically separated, especially if they are in different countries or even different time zones, it provides a practical way of ensuring frequency of interaction between mentor and mentee.

Relatively little e-mentoring is carried out in real time, involving mentor and mentee both seated at the computer at the same time. Most people find that it is more practical, in such circumstances, to use the telephone or video-conferencing.

In practice, most use of e-mentoring is hybrid. Mentoring pairs may meet perhaps once a quarter face-to-face and several times in between by e-mail. Distant pairs may communicate some of the time by e-mail, but at other times by telephone or video-conferencing, to maintain the emotional rapport.

In order to make the best of e-mentoring, it makes sense to consider what the co-ordinator and the participants should do at each stage of the relationship. At the *rapport-building* stage the difficulty is to create the relationship in the first place. Says Kevin Hunt, who organised a large-scale e-mentoring project for a small businesses (see case study at the end of this chapter):

> Within the context of mentoring, the relationship is normally one that forms naturally. However, within e-mentoring, creating the relationship early on is absolutely critical. So for large scale e-mentoring projects the ability to match individuals electronically, when they have never met, and to ensure that they establish a positive relationship, is by far the biggest challenge.

Whether the relationship is face-to-face or e-mentoring, it is normally enhanced if both parties have a measure of the other in terms of:

- general world view (ie what they feel is important in their lives)
- sense of humour (eg whether/when it is acceptable to be flippant at times)
- how strictly they will adhere to the rules on confidentiality
- what they want from the relationship
- what each can additionally offer the other
- how empathetic they will be
- what they have generally in common.

All of this *can* be established using distance media such as telephone and e-mail. However, the quality of such exchanges is subtly different from that in face-to-face meetings. (Experience from some e-learning research in the United States found that several learning pairs got along fine – until they eventually met in person. Then the relationship collapsed!) A broad ground rule for scheme co-ordinators is that they should ensure that participants who do not meet in person have a much deeper exchange of information about each other. In addition to the factual data of CVs and learning needs, it is important to tap into the emotional personality. I find the following questions to be particularly useful:

- What do you care passionately about?
- What are you most proud about in your career?
- What is your biggest fear in managing a relationship like this?
- What do you enjoy most about your work?
- How would other people describe you?
- What do you enjoy most about being a mentor?
- What is your biggest ambition at work? Outside of work?
- Who do you admire, and why?

Barraging someone with such questions is not necessarily a good idea, but selecting appropriately begins the process of establishing an understanding of and respect for the other person – and this in turn reinforces rapport.

Because rapport must be maintained throughout the relationship, it is helpful for the distant mentor and mentee to get into the habit – as would be the case in a traditional face-to-face meeting – of exchanging social information about families, children, holidays, and so on, before getting down to the nitty-gritty of the focused mentoring dialogue. Some mentoring pairs prefer to separate out these two aspects of the relationship, but most prefer to mix them.

The value of an initial face-to-face meeting before the e-mentoring relationship gets under way is illustrated by a mentoring pair of which the mentee was in Italy and the mentor in Finland. Several months after the relationship was supposed to have started, nothing had happened, other than the exchange of a few e-mails that dealt with nothing substantive. Part of the problem lay in the fact that the mentor had just been promoted to an intensive new job in the United States and had many problems of his own to deal with. In the end he flew to Italy, with the prime objective of meeting up with his mentee. From this initial meeting emerged very clear objectives and routines about how they were going to work together. This relationship, which was henceforth conducted mainly through e-mails and telephone, proved to be one of the strongest and most beneficial in the programme.

In many cases (perhaps most) however, there will be no opportunity to meet beforehand. This puts a great deal of initial pressure on the programme co-ordinator to make a success of the matching and to follow up each relationship closely for at least the first few weeks, to ensure that it is functioning effectively. Specific questions to both mentee and mentor about the potential, quality, and tone of the relationship are important, and about the relevance of the mentor's knowledge, experience and approach. The co-ordinator may well need to intervene to ensure that one or both parties have appropriate expectations of the relationship.

In the direction-setting phase, clear goals for the relationship are at least as important as in a face-to-face relationship. In practice, many people find that clarity is aided by having the goals – for both parties – written down. It sometimes becomes possible to analyse what each aspect or word of a goal means in a much more systematic way than in a normal face-to-face discussion.

During the progress-making stage, mentors and mentees have found that it helps to establish a routine of say, monthly semi-formal exchanges in which the mentee describes his or her progress, outlines current and/or ongoing issues, and is as specific as possible about the kind of help he or she would like. The mentor agrees to respond within a set time frame, and both make sure they exchange dates of holidays or business trips of more than a few days so that the expectation of contact is not broken. Attention to netiquette (considerate conventions for e-communication) is an important element of training for both parties. Some companies have produced guidelines on netiquette as a checklist for participants.

Other issues to consider in managing this phase of the e-mentoring relationship include:

- An agreed style of communication must be established – both mentors and mentees may need to learn how to 'muse' in text without rambling.
- As in a face-to-face meeting, it helps to establish at each interaction what the issues for discussion are, what outcomes are looked for, and what kind of response the mentee is looking to the mentor to make.
- Mentees have to develop the skills of explaining issues very clearly in writing – sometimes it can be difficult to balance giving enough information for the mentor to ask appropriate questions and give relevant advice, without drowning them in detail.
- The mentor should ask the mentee to summarise (just as in face-to-face mentoring) from time to time, to ensure that they are both on the same wavelength – this is often forgotten when communicating in text.
- Mentors sometimes find that the natural instinct to give advice, rather than help the mentee to come to his or her own conclusions, is stronger when they see an issue in text. Fortunately, the extra thinking time allowed by the medium provides space to overcome this instinct.

When it comes to winding up, in particular, the importance of an open review of what has been learned and achieved by both mentor and mentee, and what they have appreciated about each other's contribution to the relationship, is important in sustaining the sense of positive value and mutual respect.

At all stages in the relationship, experience by companies such as British Telecom (see following case study) suggests that using a wide range of media can enrich the relationship considerably. In addition to e-mail and telephone, there is a considerable potential for fax and document exchange, for example. It can be very satisfying for a mentor to receive a text message on his or her mobile phone, such as 'Thanks for your help. I tried the solution we discussed, and it worked!'

CASE STUDY

E-MENTORING AT BRITISH TELECOM

In 2001 Zulfi Hussain designed, developed and launched an e-mentoring programme under the auspices of BT's Ethnic Minority Network (EMN). The e-mentoring programme is designed to enhance the capabilities of a conventional mentoring programme, which has now been in existence for over seven years and is recognised as the largest of its kind in Europe.

BT EMN e-mentoring began as a pilot in June 2001, with four matched pairs of mentors and mentees, Belfast–Leicester, Leeds–Cardiff, Leeds–Glasgow and Luton–Bristol, to enable good coverage of the UK.

The e-mentoring scheme was formally launched at the BT EMN annual conference of October 2001. Since then the programme has grown steadily and is currently seen as one of the most pioneering programmes of its kind, which makes full use of all the different types of technologies available such as e-mail, audio and video conferences, net meeting and even text messaging.

The aim of both the conventional and the e-mentoring programmes, explains Zulfi Hussain, is to:

> Develop individuals and help them discover their capabilities, understand the culture of the organisation, remove barriers, break the glass ceiling, enhance their careers and achieve their full potential. However, the e-mentoring programme provides 'global reach with a local touch' by overcoming time and distance barriers, and adding a truly cross-cultural dimension.

Programme management

A small team of volunteers manages the e-mentoring programme. Each owns and manages one of the key activities, such as managing the database of participants, promoting the programme, the recruitment of the mentors and mentees, and the all-important matching process.

Because the team members are spread across the UK, their meetings are generally held by regular audio conferences, but they do meet face-to-face, if and when required – for example, to resolve any issues and make improvements to the programmes.

The recruitment of mentors and mentees is done in various ways, including face-to-face discussions, adverts in internal publications, via BT's intranet and through campaigns organised by EMN and the various BT business units.

Mentors and mentees who wish to join the programme are asked to complete an online application form on the EMN website. They are asked to provide their contact details, business unit, grade, training and qualifications, achievements in the last two years, hobbies and interests, and the characteristics of the mentor/mentee with whom they wish to be matched.

Matching and support

Mentors and mentees are matched on a regular basis to achieve best results, taking into account grade, location (where appropriate), shared interests, career aspirations and development needs.

Zulfi stresses that: 'Matches are never made merely to get people off the waiting list. The policy is to wait until a good match can be found to avoid premature failure of the mentoring relationship and any disappointment.'

A letter of introduction is sent by e-mail to the mentor and mentee, asking them to make contact with each other. They are also encouraged to prepare for the first meeting to establish the ground rules of the relationship, and to agree joint aims and objectives.

The programme management team provides ongoing support for mentors and mentees via the telephone, e-mail and, if required, face-to-face meetings. Formal training workshops are also run on a regular basis.

Conventional vs e-mentoring

The fundamental strategy and procedures for conventional and e-mentoring are pretty much the same, according to Zulfi, but the BT experience has shown that e-mentoring offers opportunities for mentors and mentees that would not otherwise be possible. These include:

- A global reach, which provides a greater range of cross-cultural and multinational exchange, enriching the experience of mentor, mentees and BT.
- Flexibility and no restrictions on time and location as a limiting factor in the matching process.
- The participation of a much wider talent pool from around the world.

Monitoring and lessons learned

The e-mentoring programme is monitored using anecdotal feedback, and verbal and written reports. Lessons learned to date include:

- The expectations of both the mentor and the mentee must be managed carefully, to avoid disappointment.
- The roles and responsibilities of the people managing the programme must be clearly defined.
- All procedures must be robust and slot in end-to-end; and the matching process must be as efficient and as swift as possible.
- The continual 'cleansing' of the database is an absolute must.
- The programme must be promoted at every opportunity, particularly to recruit new participants.
- Ongoing monitoring and regular review is essential to evaluate the effectiveness of the programme, make improvements, and measure the benefits.

Benefits

The programme has provided considerable benefits for the mentees, mentors and BT:

- The benefits to the mentees have included improved self-confidence, learning to cope with the formal and informal structure of the company, the receipt of career advice, extensive networking opportunities, and of course managerial tutelage.
- The mentors have also gained from the mentoring relationship. Benefits have included improved job satisfaction, a greater insight into their own level of knowledge, and a new perspective on BT and on the business case for diversity (as provided by the mentee).
- There is no doubt that BT has gained by having a workforce with improved motivation, improved communications, and a leadership development programme that not only develops participants, but also ensures that key cultural values are passed on.

Source: Contributed by Zulfigar Hussain.

E-MENTORING FOR SMALL BUSINESSES

The Small Business Service (SBS) and the South East England Development Agency (SEEDA) provided funding for Business Link Surrey to pilot an e-mentoring scheme for small businesses in 2002–2003. Designed and developed by Kevin Hunt, the South-East Regional Director for SBS, following research and evidence from the small business community, the project was evaluated by the Mentoring and Coaching Research Group at Sheffield Hallam University.

The aim of this project was to equip small-business owners with a short-term (three months) burst of mentoring support on which they could subsequently build, should they so wish. The mentors were experienced business people drawn from the business community and the Business Volunteers Mentor Association. The programme offered mentors and mentees training in the form of a CD-ROM that introduced them to the aims of the scheme, the roles and responsibilities, and how to get the best from the relationship. More than 40 pairs took part in the pilot, and more than half of all participants responded to the evaluation survey.

Among the key results of the survey were that:

- 96% of the mentees and 80% of the mentors described the experience as positive.
- 91% of mentees and 84% of mentors said they would like to participate in a future programme.
- 60% of mentees and 70% of mentors cited convenience, flexibility and ease as the major benefits of e-mentoring.
- 30% said they felt there was an element of impersonality about this type of mentoring.
- 50% were considering continuing the relationship after the pilot period.

Quotes from participants included:

> What the mentoring programme has done is 'enforced' delivery of a business plan, enabled prioritisation of different business opportunities, given me a clearer focus on what resources I need, and given me more confidence in my own business abilities.

> I had been sceptical about whether I would be comfortable discussing business issues/concerns with a 'stranger' by e-mail – thinking it would be too impersonal – but I was surprised by how quickly it was possible to build a relationship of trust in this way. I believe, however, that some form of meeting would have instantly strengthened the relationship.

Among key lessons from the pilot programme was the importance of:

- appropriate matching
- goal clarity on the part of the mentee
- training for both mentors and mentees
- setting a communication plan from the beginning
- supplementing e-mail with other forms of communication
- encouragement from the mentor, to sustain the mentee's motivation.

Source: Contributed by Kevin Hunt.

SUMMARY

The volume of mentoring conducted using virtual media will continue to grow. It's therefore important for programme managers to understand the pluses and minuses of different media and mixtures of media; and to ensure that participants have appropriate skills to nurture developmental conversations virtually.

CHAPTER 20

Cross-Organisational Mentoring

There are only a relatively small number of mentoring programmes which have been designed from the start to facilitate mentoring between employees of a consortium of organisations. Some examples of where this has happened include:

- A programme to support career development of women in junior and middle management at An Post, the Irish Post Office. Mentors were drawn from a variety of companies in the supply chain – both suppliers and customers.
- A large bank looked beyond its own walls for mentors to its regional directors. Building the mentees' commercial awareness was one of the principal aims, but mentors were drawn from leaders in both public and private sector organisations.
- Senior managers from a dozen companies were recruited as peer mentors for prison governors. In this case, the companies played an active role in building relationships both with the governors and, in some cases, more widely with the prisons.
- Large holding companies sometimes encourage mentoring relationships between companies and divisions. For example, Petronas, the Malaysian oil company, offers mentees two mentors – one within their own company or division and one in another company within the group. Most mentees report they gain greatest value from the mentor outside their immediate organisational boundaries.
- Public sector organisations in the same general location have formed mentoring (and in some cases, coaching) consortia to share resources. Local authorities, higher education and public services, such as health trusts, police and fire services have collaborated to share the costs of training and administration and to create a wider pool of mentors for mentees to choose from.

The benefits of this kind of mentoring can be considerable. Among them:

- A very different perspective on issues from someone not involved in the corporate politics or acclimatised to the organisational culture.
- Shared costs – particularly for training, administration, support for mentoring pairs, and evaluation.
- Potential for greater openness between mentor and mentee, because there are fewer issues of confidentiality.
- Mutual support and learning for programme facilitators (it can sometimes feel like a lonely role if you are running a programme by yourself!).

But there are disadvantages, too. In particular:

- It takes more organisation and co-ordination to make the process work, especially at the recruitment stage. For example, there are a lot more people to convince that this is a good idea!
- Employers may have greater concerns about 'poaching' of talent (although the more different the organisations are in sector, size and culture, the less likely such issues are to arise) or about commercial confidentiality.
- Participating organisations may not be ready for the programme at the same time, so launching can be delayed.

WHAT SHOULD YOU LOOK FOR IN CONSORTIUM PARTNERS?

While some difference in corporate values is desirable, a common set of broad values around talent management, respecting employees and openness to constructive challenge, create a strong foundation for success. Ideally, there should be few, if any, areas of direct competition between the organisations – if only because of the inevitability of privileged information being part of mentoring conversations. Important questions include:

- Is mentoring on this organisation's agenda right now? (If not, by the time they are ready to commit, other potential partners, who are ready now, may have lost interest or found other solutions.)
- Are there obvious champions in HR and in senior management?
- How compatible will the partner organisations be?
- Do they have potential sources of funding?
- Will they be active or passive partners?
- What is the minimum number of partner organisations we need?
- What is the maximum number of partner organisations we need?

KEY ROLES

A lead facilitator, who takes responsibility for general programme management and chairing the steering group, is essential. This person can come from outside the consortium (it helps avoid accusations of partisanship), but an internal HR professional who is able to gain the trust of participants, sponsors, and the programme lead in each of the other organisations, can be equally effective. A degree of passion about mentoring in general and the programme in particular seems to be a requisite characteristic. Some administrative support is also desirable.

KEY PROGRAMME STAGES

The key stages are:

1. Definition – what is this programme all about? What will be the benefits for the employer organisations and the participants? What is the vision of success? How many organisational partners do we need?
2. Organisational recruitment – putting together the champions and helping them. Remember in communications that each organisation may need a different message to sell the concept in to its HR and line management infrastructure. Setting up the cross-organisation steering committee and establishing how it will move from storming to performing.
3. Programme design – recruitment, training, matching, ongoing support, review and evaluation. Research among potential participants is recommended.
4. Launch – ideally one event for senior managers of all consortium organisations and key influencers, and a series of mini events in each member organisation.
5. Recruitment and matching.
6. Training.
7. General programme management and support, including monitoring and reviewing.
8. End of phase one evaluation and celebration of achievements.

SOME FAQS

Should we train people from the same organisation together, or have a mixture of participants from across the organisations? Given that the intention is to benefit from different perspectives, it generally makes more sense to mix participants.

What other support/learning could we provide for participants? One useful idea, originating from diversity mentoring, is to engage mentees in collective projects, with a representative from each company in each project group. This provides additional opportunities for cross-organisational learning. What do participants need to know about the other organisations? Learning between the mentees is enhanced when they have opportunities to get to know something of all the organisations. In both mentor and mentee training, it is useful to have presentations by participants from each company about their organisation's culture, scope, products, approach to leadership, and so on.

What if mentor and mentee live and work in widely separate locations? Distance mentoring is an increasingly common phenomenon. Training for mentors and mentees can include skills of mentoring by telephone or e-mail.

What if relationships don't work out? It's actually easier to rematch people when they are from different organisations – there are fewer consequences and less embarrassment. More difficult is gathering the informal feedback – the organisational chatter – that alerts the programme facilitators to problems with individual relationships.

SUMMARY

Cross-organisational mentoring opens up opportunities to enlarge the pool of mentors available, but it presents organisational challenges that mean it usually takes longer and more effort to launch and manage them.

CHAPTER 21

Final Issues

In this relatively brief account of mentoring and how to implement a mentoring programme, we have inevitably raised a number of issues that warrant further discussion. Below we take up some of these in more detail.

ALL GOOD MENTORING RELATIONSHIPS COME TO AN END

Although one person many have several mentors, each mentoring relationship must reach the stage where it is either not needed or not wanted any longer. For this reason it is essential that every such relationship is seen from the start as a temporary alignment. Elements of it may persist, in the form of mutual aid and friendship, for many years after, but there must be clear starting and finishing points.

Probably the best signpost of the finishing point is when the mentee has achieved the medium-term objectives established early on in the relationship. A spokesperson for Jewel Companies comments:

> We feel that after a couple of years the role loses its importance and may become a more negative element than a positive one. That is, after a few years in the business it is more important that an individual be achieving on his own rather than with special help from a senior management level mentor.

However it is done, the two parties must be able to back out of the arrangement without recrimination when one or both feel it is no longer beneficial.

GOOD MENTEES OFTEN MAKE GOOD MENTORS

Many of the most successful mentors are people who have experienced mentoring from the other side. Indeed, it is possible for a manager to be simultaneously mentored from above while he or she mentors someone yet more junior. One of the major difficulties in getting a mentoring programme off the ground is finding an adequate supply of mentors. Once the scheme has been going for many years, however, it automatically generates potential mentors from the ranks of former mentees. This is actually one of the litmus tests for the success of a programme – what proportion of mentees want to go on to become mentors?

OLD-STAGERS CAN BENEFIT FROM MENTORS TOO

Mentoring should not be regarded as solely for young, relatively new recruits. There are frequently people in the organisation whose development has been held back by circumstances other than ability. They may, for example, have had domestic ties that prevented them from demonstrating career ambition, particularly if they are married women. Or they may be in a cultural backwater in the company, out of the mainstream and in a staff position that has little interaction with key corporate functions. Equally, mentoring relationships can be effective between peers, or between a junior person and someone more senior.

FINDING A MENTOR WHEN THERE IS NO FORMAL MENTORING PROGRAMME

Many people progress in their companies by seeking their own mentors. By and large, senior managers are apt to be flattered if they are convinced the approach comes from someone who is capable of going a long way. The following ground rules may be useful within the corporate context:

TARGET ONE OR TWO PEOPLE AS POTENTIAL MENTORS

Talk to other people to discover their reputation within the firm. Is this person going places? Is he or she interested in developing other people? Is he or she known for teamwork? Will he or she have time for a mentoring relationship, or has he or she just been given a major project that will keep him or her out of the country for six months a year? Build up as accurate a picture as possible of each mentor candidate to establish who could be of most help to you in your career and/or personal development.

MAKE YOURSELF VISIBLE

It is not who you know that counts, but who knows you. You have to make potential mentors aware of your existence. Use friends, colleagues and acquaintances to identify useful networks to join. Make a point of attending social functions, 'learning breakfasts' and other developmental events.

SHOW YOU HAVE AMBITION AND WANT TO IMPROVE YOUR ABILITIES

Establishing the seriousness of your ambition to advance is essential. If the opportunity presents itself, get the senior manager involved in recommending training or reading that will help you expand your experience and knowledge.

ASK THE POTENTIAL MANAGER FORMALLY, IN PERSON, TO BE YOUR MENTOR

Most managers will be flattered and respond positively to an approach in person, either agreeing or making helpful suggestions on who else in the company might be more suitable.

In the latter case they will often make introductions or recommendations on your behalf. Even if you simply receive a blunt refusal, you have at least established your credentials as an ambitious employee, willing to learn.

INITIAL CHECKLIST

More generally, especially if you seek a mentor from the wider community, the following checklist may provide some useful starting points.

1. **What do you need a mentor for?**
   Try to clarify what kind of transition you want to make. Is it a different job? A different level of competence? A different situation in life?

2. **What kind of relationship do you want?**
   Do you want someone to be a sounding board for you, to give encouragement, to provide you with a constructive challenge and expand your horizons, or to 'look out' for you, identifying opportunities and putting you forward for them? You are less likely to find someone if you are looking for a sponsor or someone to do things for you. People are much more likely to respond to a request for sharing their experience.

3 **What sort of person would be best to be able to help you by giving advice and guidance?**
Think about the personality, age, experience. Think also about geography – how difficult would it be for the two of you to meet?

4 **What could you bring to the relationship?**
Is there any area of knowledge or experience you might usefully offer to share with a mentor?

5 **Who do you already know?**
Is there someone in your workplace, your local community, the church, local clubs, who you admire and feel you could learn from?

6 **What networks do you belong to?**
Are you a member of a professional association, an alumni club, a chamber of commerce, a sports association or similar organisation? They may already have a mentoring scheme, or be willing to put you in touch with potential mentors on an ad hoc basis.

7 **Are there mentor registers you can sign on to?**
A variety of organisations, including some charities and community organisations, provide a matching service for specific categories of people.

8 **Can you identify someone you could approach who is very well networked and could refer you either directly to potential mentors or to organisations that can help?**
Someone in any of the organisations above might be able to help you in this way. Other useful people to consider approaching include personnel professionals, senior managers, academic tutors, pastors, and career consultants.

9 **How will you make the approach?**
It is often easier when someone else makes the introduction. If you have to take the first steps yourself, however, spend some time rehearsing what you have to say. Be confident; the worse that can happen is that the person says no. In practice, most people are sufficiently flattered and respond very positively to requests that they should become a mentor.

10 **How will you translate good intentions into deeds?**
Aim to put the date for the first formal mentoring meeting into the diary as soon as he or she agrees to consider the relationship. Do not be the one to postpone the meeting – that may undo all of your good work. Above all, be considerate of the mentor's time and goodwill; make it clear how pleased you are that he or she has accepted.

Appendix

The case studies in this section have been chosen to provide a wide spectrum of applications of mentoring. Where appropriate, contact information is provided for you to obtain more detailed information.

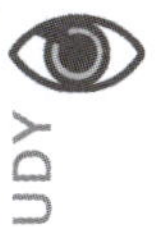

CASE STUDY

THE MENTORING DEVELOPMENT OF A FOOTBALL ASSOCIATION REFEREE

Football is one of the biggest spectator sports in the world, as well as being one of the most physical and demanding. In this often highly charged and passionate environment, the role of arbitrator sits with the 'referee', regardless of whether the game is being played out on a local park or in front of 90,000 spectators at Wembley Stadium. Consequently, these men and women often operate under immense pressure, as they strive to get their decisions right and control the game in a safe and professional manner for the enjoyment of everyone involved.

The Football Association (FA), the governing body of the game in England, provides a structured career path for their referees to progress, with in-depth development appropriate to each level along the way. As officials reach the semi-professional level of football, they have historically been assigned a coach to assist them with their transition and integration into a more challenging environment.

The reality is that not all referees, for a variety of reasons, are successful in operating at this new level, even after a reasonable period of time that stretches over two seasons. Approximately 5% are reclassified back to the lower grade each year. It has therefore always been an aim of The FA Referees' Department to enhance the developmental opportunities offered to referees at this level in order to ensure that they are better prepared and supported, in the hope that more referees can be retained.

In the summer of 2012, after a detailed development plan, researched and constructed by Rob McCarthy (FA Mentoring Scheme Leader) with expert input and advice from Professor Clutterbuck; Neale Barry (FA Head of Senior Referee Development) and David Elleray (Chairman, FA Referees' Committee) launched a pilot of a new mentoring scheme, that could both complement and work alongside the existing coaching scheme. This mentor scheme assumed responsibility for supporting and developing the newly promoted referees in their first two seasons at semi-professional level, thereby enabling the coaches to now focus on developing the talent group of referees instead.

Each referee involved in the scheme has been assigned a mentor, a highly experienced current or retired referee who operates under the leadership of the scheme leader, who is responsible for the management of both the day-to-day running of the scheme and the mentors' continuous professional development (CPD).

The mentor's role is varied. One day he may be advising on administrative queries, eg the appointing system, football-law-based issues and the appeals/moderation processes; the next he could be offering ideas for self-improvement; acting as a sounding board; reviewing assessments with his referees to identify trends; having one-to-one meetings; and supporting the referees in identifying and overcoming development areas.

The mentors conduct their duties via phone, Skype, e-mail etc. Attending games is not a prerequisite, but they will do so when a major development area is identified and where they can then offer more comprehensive hands-on advice.

Mentors have also gone through a structured and comprehensive development programme during the pilot year to help enhance their skills and confidence in the specialism.

Feedback on the new scheme has been excellent. In the recent survey, the referees rated the quality of the mentoring conversations at 84%, with the quality of advice offered to them as 86% and the overall effectiveness of the scheme to help them develop as 78%. Couple this with the mentors themselves rating the scheme as 75% effective for their referees and their belief that 78% of them show a positive attitude to mentoring; then the pilot has been a real success story.

On the back of the feedback and the impact the scheme has had to the overall performances of the officials, the pilot has now been finalised and for season 2013–14. The mentoring scheme is an important development tool in the journey of the football referee.

Source: Contributed by Rob McCarthy, Scheme Leader – FA Level 3 Referee Mentoring Scheme, Football Services Division.

CASE STUDY

MENTORING AGAINST DOMESTIC VIOLENCE

Mentors in Violence Prevention (MVP) Scotland is an adaptation of a US programme that aims to prevent domestic violence by encouraging young people to speak out. Teachers and community workers at two schools in Scotland trained 34 pupils in the fourth, fifth and sixth forms to become peer mentors to classmates and more junior pupils. The young mentors have been trained in strategies to challenge abusive behaviour in a wide variety of situations, including sexting and domestic abuse. According to MVP's US parent website:

The most important role they play is to provide younger students – and their peers – with the space to talk about important day-to-day issues like how to be supportive friends, how to respond to incidents of actual or potential abuse or harassment, what to do about threats or rumours about school violence, and how to create a student-powered, positive and harassment-free school climate. http://www.mvpnational.org

CASE STUDY

MENTORING TO ADDRESS GENDER IMBALANCE AT UNILEVER

Purpose and participants

In March 2009 Unilever launched the global mentoring programme to address the gender in-balance at director and vice president levels within the organisation. The issue was simple – we weren't promoting enough women from director to vice president and vice president to senior vice president levels, therefore this population became our target audience. The aim of the programme was that a relationship of guidance and support would grow and aid the mentee's development and accelerate the mentee's readiness for their next appointment within Unilever.

Design

We chose a senior sponsor and role model for the programme, Doug Baillie – who was then the President of Western Europe (and now our Chief HR Officer) – as he was renowned in the business for being a great mentor and someone who was passionate about the power of mentoring and the difference it could make.

We set out some key criteria for the programme that:

- All mentoring relationships would be for a duration of approximately 12–18 months.
- All mentors were either a senior vice president, a Unilever executive or a high-potential vice president. The reason for choosing such senior mentors was that they could act as advocates/sponsors to the women they were mentoring.
- Mentees had to complete an individual development plan before they started their mentoring sessions to form the basis of those sessions.
- The mentor–mentee pairings were proposed on the basis of matching the mentee's current role and experience with the mentor's current role, experience and skills.
- Line managers and HR business partners of the mentees were consulted to verify the pairings and get their inputs into the suitability of the proposed mentor.

All mentees and mentors were formally invited in writing by the sponsor to participate in the programme. They were also given the supporting documentation that they needed to read through with their letter.

Mentors were provided with a mentor guide to provide them with the key information, guidelines, suggestions and ideas to get the most out of the mentoring sessions. Mentees were provided with a mentee guide to provide them with key information, preparation work, guidelines, suggestions and ideas to enable them to get to get the most out of their mentoring sessions.

For each wave all mentors and mentees were invited to attend the virtual launch event hosted by the sponsor, which was a briefing and overview of the programme and that lasted an hour.

We also provided mentors and mentees with some webinar mentoring training in two parts: one soon after the launch event and the second a few months later to provide them with additional support and information they may need to get the most out of their mentoring sessions. It also provided a forum for mentors and mentees to share their questions and experiences. This also created a network amongst mentees and mentors.

For each wave of the programme we had regular feedback checkpoints at three months, six months and 12 months to understand how the mentoring relationships were going, identify any problems, and get feedback on how to improve the programme.

Issues with implementation

The key issues we had were that not all mentees and mentors attended the launch event at the beginning of each wave we organised, resulting in them not getting briefed on what they had to do and why they had been asked to participate.

Due to the seniority of all the mentors, many mentees struggled to find time in their diaries for their mentoring sessions and in some cases this resulted in less frequent mentoring sessions, especially if a mentee and mentor weren't in the same location.

Lessons learned

- Keep checking in with your mentees and mentors – regular contact is crucial to understand if there are any issues.
- If the mentoring relationship isn't working, admit it and move on.
- Create a mentee network so mentees can talk to fellow mentees to share their issues
- Have a clear objective for the programme – this really is important as if you're not clear from the outset of what it is you are trying to achieve then you won't know when you've achieved it.
- Link it to your business agenda – it's really powerful to do this. It gives it purpose and gets buy-in from senior leaders. It isn't then just another HR initiative!
- Don't underestimate the need for training – even though our mentors were very senior employees we still offered them training and those that attended found it really useful, especially to share experiences with other mentors and to be clear about their roles.

Outcomes

Since March 2009 seven waves of the global mentoring programme have been launched, with 164 females having been mentored over this period.

The first five waves have completed the formal part of the programme and the majority of these mentees have continued to be mentored over the past 12 months. Out of the mentees who participated in waves one to five, 30% (34) have been promoted to the next work level since the mentoring programme started.

Source: Contributed by Katherine Ray, Global Talent Capability Manager, Unilever, London.

CASE STUDY

E-MENTORING FOR HR PROFESSIONALS IN INDIA

This case study describes a unique learning opportunity for postgraduate UK students as mentees who are matched to overseas professionals as mentors to learn about international work practices and enhance their employability. The scheme specifically aimed to engage postgraduate students from Middlesex Business School as mentees to learn about diverse HR practices, using the Indian context. The composition of the mentee participants (by programme) was: MA Human Resource Management (HRM) (17), MA International HRM (2) and MBA (4).

Mentors are senior HR practitioners in multinational organisations in India, across a wide spread of sectors. They each committed to providing up to ten hours of mentoring to one student over a period of three to four months mainly by telephone, Skype or e-mail and, if and where possible, by face-to-face communication.

Between August 2011 and April 2013 the project team recruited, trained, and facilitated 23 mentor–mentee relationships. Within the framework of the scheme, the mentor–mentee matching was based on personal preferences of industry, sector or previous educational background. To involve the mentors in the matching process, where possible, mentors were offered two profiles of mentees to make their choice. Opportunity for discussion with project co-ordinators was offered at this time to the mentors. One-to-one interviews were conducted with mentees as a part of the matching process. Both mentors and mentees received brief pen portraits of each other from the project co-ordinators and from there on the mentees and mentors were encouraged to develop their relationships with the co-ordinators being available if their help was required. Within this formal structure, the individual mentoring pairs were given the freedom to build and develop their relationships (Klasen and Clutterbuck 2002). Monthly support sessions were held for mentees to help them to plan and structure their sessions to maximise their mentor–mentee conversations.

Evaluation of the scheme

The evaluation was conducted through base-line interviews with mentors and mentees, reviews of mentee progress via update meetings, and a summative questionnaire. The voices of other stakeholders, such as the project team and module tutors of mentees were heard through semi-structured interviews. The key factors which influence or appear to influence the e-mentoring conversations are as follows:

The *main* method of communication used by mentees and mentors was e-mail and telephone. However, 77% of the participants experienced some barriers and difficulty in their chosen method of communication. The main constraint was arranging mutually convenient time for telephone and Skype conversations, due to difference in time zone.

Overall, a clear message was that at least one face-to-face conversation can go a long way to building rapport and trust. The absence of the power of body language in the e-mail and telephone based mentoring (Zey 2011) can indeed hinder some mentor–mentee activities, such as in-person training. Those who used Skype confirmed that this aided in their relationship building.

e-mentoring relationship development

The evaluation applied the Clutterbuck model (1998c) of life cycle of a mentor–mentee relationship (see Figure 17) to analyse the stages of relationship of individual pairs. Following the introductory e-mails between mentees and mentors, the rapport building stage progressed at a different pace for each pair. Of the 23 matches, eight reached maturity (seven to ten hours of communication), six relationships moved between rapport building and direction and did not move to ‘progress’ stage (three to six hours of communication) and seven relationships struggled at the rapport-building stage (30 to 45 minutes) with one or two conversations either by e-mail or on the phone, and two relationships did not progress beyond the introductory e-mail exchange.

Figure 17 The dimensions of mentoring

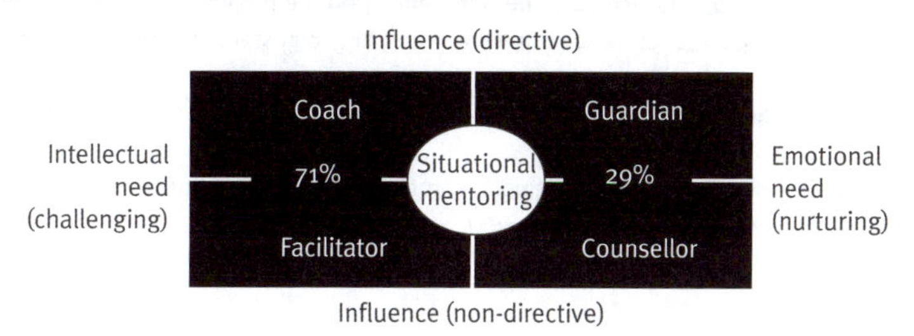

Again, using Clutterbuck's Situational Mentoring Model, which was introduced to both mentors and mentee through their development toolkit and support sessions, the most frequently adopted mentoring style of this group of mentors was analysed. Almost three-quarters (71%) of the mentors adopted either the coaching or the facilitator style, which demonstrates that the mentor conversations were non-directive, supporting the intellectual need of the mentees. As one mentor commented, 'the aim was to make them think for themselves'. The 29% of the mentors who identified with the counsellor and/or guardian style focused their conversations on sharing their expertise and offering career counselling.

Lessons learned

A key learning for the project team is acknowledging the peculiar character of this mentoring project and its participants. Firstly, this is not an in-house, intra-organisational programme; rather, it involves participants from a range of disparate organisations, geographies, cultures and time zones. Secondly, the programme does not feature employee-to-employee relationships, meaning that the partnerships are not aligned and directed to a common organisational goal or performance criteria. Thirdly, unlike in-house programmes, this project is not about organisational knowledge sharing and organisational learning; it has individual mentee employability as its goal. This means that the mentor must have a particular level of skill to ensure that any guidance is a response to the mentee's identified needs rather than, as in many in-house schemes, the possession of a reservoir of *tacit* organisational knowledge for simple 'downloading' from the more experienced to the less experienced.

The key lessons are:

- Although modern communication technologies have the capacity to overcome the challenges of global organisational structures by allowing mentors to be in different places and time zones (Hamilton and Scandura 2003), the quality of the relationship may not always remain intact or have the same impact.
- Although physical distance and technology can act as a shield by rendering physical or visible disparities neutral (Shpigelman *et al.* 2009), the distance and remoteness between partners increases the risk not only to the relationship, but a point is reached where the risk to the relationship *increases both sharply and disproportionately*.
- Management of down time/offline periods becomes more critical.
- Widely varying technologies, with many being financed and maintained by individuals, raises the risk of compatibility and reliability (Bierema and Hill 2005).
- The *voluntary* mentoring role may conflict with organisational priorities.
- The 'size' of the project team and the degree of support needs to be managed in order for the team to reassure themselves that the partnership is alive and well.
- As distance reduces the possibility of training mentors and mentees *in the same workshop*, this increases the requirement on the project team to ensure that training material has been received and fully digested/understood by all participants.
- Building wider relationship with the mentor's organisation may be a more sustainable model.
- Face-to-face, even a placement, can strengthen the relationship and employability outcomes.

References

BIEREMA, L. and HILL, J.R. (2005) Virtual mentoring and HRD. *Advances in Developing Human Resources*. Vol 7, No 4, November. pp556–568.

CLUTTERBUCK, D. (1998c) Mentoring diagnostic kit. Clutterbuck Associates.

HAMILTON, B.A. and SCANDURA, T.A. (2003) E-mentoring: implications for organisational learning and development in a weird world. *Organisational Dynamics*. Vol 31, No 4. pp388–402.

KLASEN, N. and CLUTTERBUCK, D. (2002) *Implementing mentoring schemes: a practical guide to successful programs*. Oxford: Elsevier Butterworth-Heinemann.

SHPIGELMAN, C., WEISS, P.L. and REITER, S. (2009) E-mentoring for all. *Computers in Human Behavior*. Vol 25, No 4. pp919–928.

ZEY, M.G. (2011) Virtual mentoring: the challenges and opportunities of electronically – mediated formal mentor programs. *Review of Business Research*. Vol 11, No 4.

Source: Contributed by Chandana Sanyal.

CASE STUDY

INTERNATIONAL BAR ASSOCIATION'S LAW FIRM MENTORING PROGRAMME

The International Bar Association (IBA), established in 1947, is the world's leading organisation of international legal practitioners, bar associations, and law societies. The IBA influences the development of international law reform and shapes the future of the legal profession throughout the world.

It has a membership of more than 50,000 individual lawyers and over 200 bar associations and law societies spanning all continents. The Law Firm Management Committee, with over 3,000 members, is the biggest committee of the IBA. Mentoring has always traditionally been at the heart of the legal profession. The Law Firm Management Committee has placed the Law Firm Mentoring Programme as one of its highest priorities.

In 2009, the Law Firm Management Committee decided to launch a Law Firm Mentoring Programme. The initiative links law firm partners with lawyers from around the world to help them start or grow their practice. Initially, the programme was aimed primarily at providing guidance and advice to IBA lawyers in emerging markets or developing economies who had no access to law firm management expertise.

With very little promotion, the programme rapidly attracted an impressive number of mentors who were respected members of the profession, from various parts of the world. The challenge that the programme encountered was to reach out to the mentees who either did not know of the IBA mentoring opportunities or did not know how to get involved.

In 2012, Rebecca Normand-Hochman, an IBA member and Franco-British former lawyer working in talent management, redesigned the programme to enable proper promotion, co-ordination and monitoring on a bigger scale. She made the initiative available to mentees whether or not they are IBA members and regardless of the jurisdiction in which they work (whether or not it is regarded as a developing economy).

To reach out to mentees around the world, the IBA is now partnering with local bar associations so that they can promote and co-ordinate the programme to their members directly. The first example of that is a partnership with the Costa Rican Bar, which is currently launching the initiative in six Central American countries.

Since the formal relaunch of the Law Firm Mentoring Programme at the IBA Annual Conference in Dublin in October 2012, a number of mentors and mentees are joining the programme on an ongoing basis and from a growing number of jurisdictions (we currently have a hundred participants from 35 jurisdictions).

At the beginning of the initiative, some senior partners were questioning whether distance mentoring could build meaningful mentoring relationships. Fortunately, and due to the attention and support that the programme has attracted, most of them have now been convinced that this can be achieved.

The challenge now ahead relates to providing sufficient mentoring skills for participants so that once they have joined the programme, the mentoring pairs quickly engage in strong mentoring relationships.

Source: Contributed by Rebecca Normand-Hochman.

CASE STUDY

MENTORING FOR EMPLOYABILITY

The Graduate Employability Support Programme (GESP) at Middlesex University Business School was part of a suite of employability provisions known collectively as *Platforms* provided by a large north London local authority. One of the Council's key corporate objectives was to ensure that the borough is a 'successful London suburb' and continues to be a prosperous place where people wish to live and work. The Council made a strategic commitment to achieve this through regeneration and promoting enterprise and employment. An essential part of achieving this is through the development of skills and employment initiatives to NEET (Not in Employment, Education or Training) university graduates, aged between 21 and 24.

The specific aims of this programme were to offer career guidance through themed employability workshops and interview practice, and to provide participants with additional resources outside the themed workshops. The unique element was to provide mentoring and coaching which wrapped around the employment workshops. The Business School has wide experience of mentoring and coaching and was engaged to provide a programme to support members of this particular group into employment.

NEET graduates were referred to the programme team by the four Job Centre Plus offices in the borough. A total of 23 graduates participated in the employability workshops in two cohorts over an eight-month period (2012–2013).

The Council's initial aim was for mentors to be sourced from the local business community. However, creating a pool of mentors with skills, experience, and credibility appropriate to the needs and ambitions of graduates proved difficult for the project team. A decision was made to strengthen the initially small pool by drawing on surplus mentors from another mentoring project being run simultaneously. These additional mentors were deemed appropriate, as they were recent graduates who had experience of successfully entering employment in the public sector via graduate schemes.

During the programme a number of the graduates either achieved employment or withdrew from the programme. Those who remained were provided with a development workshop, in which the concept of mentoring and the respective roles of mentor and mentee were introduced and explored, along with some theoretical frameworks to underpin their experience. They were then offered the opportunity to be matched and supported by a mentor and their preferences for particular mentor characteristics were invited to aid the matching process. These included age, gender, preferred method of mentoring communication, current field and experience.

This programme was funded by public money based upon outcomes in the form of registrations to the programme and conversions from NEET status into employment of at least 16 hours per week. To date, five participants have formally entered employment and a further seven continue with employability mentoring support.

Key lessons from this project

1 Clarity of the dimensions of mentoring is essential.

   That mentoring means different things to different people and the need to ensure that project sponsors and project team have a clear, shared understanding of what mentoring is, what it can achieve, and what is required to achieve successful outcomes at the outset of the project.

2 Matching mentees from diverse educational backgrounds and experience with mentors from their chosen sector was challenging, therefore managing expectations is crucial.

   The composition of the mentees was entirely random, beyond the control of the project team and as such was extremely diverse. Graduate degree disciplines ranged from Theatre Studies to Politics, Philosophy and Economics to Biomedicine, to Oceanography. As such their ambitions were largely shaped, and some might say constrained, by this degree experience. Finding skilled mentors with the mentees' expressed preference for experience in these fields proved challenging.

3 It is not always possible to train mentors and mentees together in the same space however, it is crucial to ensure that both parties receive the same training content.

   Another challenge to the project team was training or briefing mentors and mentees to achieve a common understanding of the programme and of the skills for success. Leading practice suggests that mentors and mentees should undertake this together. The diverse nature and sources of both mentors and mentees precluded this and required multiple individual conversations with mentors, plus the creation of tailored briefing documents. Also, the value of sharing theoretical mentoring frameworks with mentors and mentees to support their understanding of the experience enhances prospects of success.

4 A mentoring project is not just about a mentor and mentee; there are numerous actors involved and stakeholder management is key to the success of the project.

   This was *not* an in-house mentoring project in which mentors and mentees might identify with shared organisational goals. The multiplicity of stakeholders – local authority sponsors; Business School Project Team; employability workshop providers; Jobcentre Plus officers responsible for referring graduates and with targets to achieve; other competing providers of employability support initially unbeknownst to the project team or the local authority; the diverse group of graduate NEETs and a similarly diverse group of mentors – scaled up the complexity to unanticipated levels.

5 The value of working closely with colleagues running other mentoring schemes who could act as a sounding board and recommend

ways to strengthen the project. For example, the value of having a colleague dedicated to the evaluation elements of the project.

6 The value of having a dedicated administrator to manage and file sensitive personal data and information.

Source: Contributed by Chris Rigby, Senior Lecturer; Dr Julie Haddock-Millar, Senior Lecturer and Teaching Fellow; Chandana Sanyal, Lecturer, Department of Leadership, Work and Organisations, Middlesex University Business School.

CASE STUDY

PARTNERSHIP FOR POSSIBILITY, SOUTH AFRICA

The Partnership for Possibility programme started in 2010. It is an initiative of Symphonia for South Africa (a social enterprise). The programme partners business leaders with experience in organisational change with school principals of under-resourced schools in a creative co-action and co-learning partnership. To date, more than 113 business leaders have been partnered with principals across South Africa (in the Western Cape, Free State, Kwazulu Natal and Gauteng).

The programmes' objectives are:

- To develop the leadership skills of school principals and business leaders and to and increase their ability to employ collaborative leadership principles to lead effective change in schools, organisations and communities.
- To achieve improved education outcomes in under-resourced schools.

Structure

The Partnership for Possibility leadership development process extends over 12 months. Partnerships are grouped into leadership circles (eight to ten partnerships). Each leadership circle has a Learning Process Facilitator who facilitates the 12-month programme. The business partners and school principals commit to a minimum of 120 hours over the 12-month period. The programme consists of:

- Five days of formal training to be attended by the business partner and principal.
- Community of practice sessions every six weeks.
- The business partner and principal will typically spend a minimum of two hours every two weeks together where they share thoughts, reflect on experiences, grapple with challenges, and learn from each other.
- Monthly coaching conversation for the business leaders.

Content

Most school principals of under-resourced schools in South Africa have received little or no leadership training to equip them for the challenging task they face. These principals are expected to lead change in communities that are marked by unemployment, poverty, HIV/Aids and a host of other socio-economic challenges. The content of the programme therefore includes training in the art of community building, social contracting, problem solving, and collaborative leadership principles.

During the bi-weekly meetings between the business partner and school principal, co-mentoring takes place as they build the relationship and tackle practical challenges and issues at the school. This includes community engagement, collaboration with stakeholders, setting strategic objectives, and documenting their journey. Business partners often experience culture shock as they enter the world of the school principals. They are suddenly faced with challenges that they have never dealt with before in their corporate environments and this process creates a new level of consciousness and self-awareness. The monthly coaching sessions with the Learning Process Facilitators helps the business partners to make sense of what they are experiencing.

Every six weeks the partnerships in the leadership circle meet for two hours for a community of practice session. At these sessions tough issues are discussed and lessons learned are shared. This peer mentoring provides a powerful co-learning experience and often leads to broader collaborative action.

Benefits

The information that is used to track the benefits of the programme is in the form of journals, retrospective focus groups, coaching notes, and narratives as business partners and principals share their experiences. The Partnership for Possibility leadership development process provides the following benefits:

- Increases self-esteem of principals as they rediscover their gifts and capacity to lead the school community.
- Strengthens organisations by developing leaders who discover their capacity for citizenship through actively engaging with one of the toughest (and most critical) issues facing South Africa.
- Engages parents as active partners in education so that children are more supported and have a better chance to do well at school.
- Strengthens communities by building relationships with principals, learners, parents, teachers, and other people and organisations involved at the school.

Source: Contributed by Jenny Venter, Symphonia for South Africa.

CASE STUDY

GROUP MENTORING FOR YOUNG ENTREPRENEURS

Mentoring is widely recognised as a process that helps people develop their knowledge and skills through a relationship with another person. This person is often someone with greater experience than the mentee, and the relationships are almost always one-to-one.

At Middlesex University we have developed an Enterprise Development Hub (EDH@MDX) that provides a range of support for students. One of the types of support we provide is mentoring. However, due to the large number of students it is extremely difficult to provide one-to-one mentoring, particularly for students who are just exploring a business idea.

To resolve this we have developed a group mentoring format. The sessions are run for two hours as drop-in sessions where any student with a question about their business idea can come at any time. The number of students at these sessions range from 5 to 30. The sessions are facilitated by a person with significant experience in starting and running a small business. At the start of each session students are told that this is not personal, but about challenging the view they hold about their business idea. The intention being that they understand the issues relating to their business idea more deeply.

The main purpose of getting the students to think more deeply about their business idea is that they will come to certain conclusions about the business idea. This is critical as the students are never told that their business idea won't work. In fact they are told that the idea is a good idea, but the success or failure of the business is in the application of the business idea. The students need to come to that conclusion about the success or failure themselves.

Students are asked questions about their business by the facilitator as a way of getting a discussion started. As the student describes their business they are asked more challenging questions by the facilitator. However, the questioning role is not just left to the facilitator. Other students attending the sessions are encouraged to question the student talking. As a result discussion can become quite fierce.

The length of time students attend the sessions is dependent on their needs. Some exit having realised their idea won't work and some move on to one-to-one mentoring because their idea is being implemented. There is also a small number that never exit even though they have no idea what sort of business they want, or even if they want to run a business. This is because they see the sessions as a great learning process.

Source: Contributed by Julie Haddock and Chris Rigby.

CASE STUDY

THE ITALIAN AND AFGHAN AIRFORCES

One of the most basic applications for mentoring is the transfer of specific knowledge and skills. If that's all the relationship is about, however, it is not mentoring, but teaching or instructing. This case study of a mentoring programme to help the Afghan Air Force develop a centre of military aviation excellence, illustrates the extra dimension that mentoring brings to knowledge transfer.

Since 2010, NATO (North Atlantic Treaty Organisation) has supported a project by the Italian School of Mentoring to create developmental partnerships between Italian professionals in all aspects of military airport management (from food and refuelling to helicopter pilots) and their counterparts at the Afghan military airport of Shindand, which is intended to become the training school for the Afghan Air Force.

The project is unusual in a number of respects, but particularly in:

- the difficult operating political and social climate
- the substantial differences in cultural background
- the diversity of the mentees (Pashtun 45%, Tajik 21%, other 17% and Hazara, 5%)
- language complexities (translating from Italian to English to Farsi and back again!)
- the detail with which the mentoring relationships were analysed.

The last of these was made possible by requiring the mentors to keep and share with the programme manager regular diaries, which went well beyond the normal requirements of monitoring know-how transfer, to include a variety of facets relating to relationship quality and relationship dynamics.

In all, 170 mentor diaries provided a deep insight into what made these learning relationships work. Those relationships that worked best in terms of both knowledge transfer and relationship quality were those that were built upon the sharing of common meta-values that transcended cultural differences – values such as collaboration and trust, respect, friendship, devotion to family, attachment tradition, and desire for peace. Of religious values that might have been expected to have an impact on the relationship and on quality of learning, only one was significant – fatalism.

Among the lessons from this case study is the importance of focusing training of mentors and mentees on building trust and rapport through the sharing of such meta-values.

Source: Contributed by Matteo Perchiazzi.

CASE STUDY

MENTORING WITH PROJECTSCOTLAND

ProjectScotland is Scotland's national youth volunteering organisation. It places 1,000 volunteers with charity partners each year. Each volunteer spends three months with a local charity, giving their time in return for skills and experience. While volunteering they are offered a mentor to help them get the most from their experience. This is a formative time in a young person's life. The mentor helps the volunteer to think about their future and how to get the most from volunteering. The mentor shares their experience, skills and connections. The mentors themselves are trained by ProjectScotland and encouraged to reflect on their own learning.

How it works

Mentors apply through the ProjectScotland website and nominate two referees. Once the references have been received an initial telephone call is held. Expectations, assumptions and aspirations about being a mentor are discussed. The mentor then receives a ProjectScotland mentor manual and is invited to attend an upcoming workshop. Workshops often contain a diverse group with a variety of skill levels. ProjectScotland is looking for its mentors to feel able and confident to give volunteers the very best support. At the workshop a team of actors role play mentoring conversations giving participants the opportunity to observe, take part, and learn by asking 'how would I do this?' ProjectScotland then matches mentors to volunteers based on interests, aspirations and geography. Mentors meet or speak with volunteers for about an hour a week. There are opportunities for mentors to attend further workshops looking at specific tools and techniques they can consider using. There is a dedicated mentor manager at ProjectScotland to talk through any issues that arise.

Challenges

The initial 'introduction to mentoring' workshop focuses on potential challenges that the mentors will face.

Professional actors role play scenarios that highlight potentially challenging conversations. These include areas like building a relationship, maintaining contact, and difficult conversations about the volunteers' futures.

Mentors are encouraged to think about how they act, react, and interact with others, while getting the opportunity to explore how to create great mentoring conversations.

When working through scenarios participants form groups and become mentor 'brains', to help and support the person who is playing the role of the mentor.

Mentors can consult their brains to discuss how to create better conversations; 'brains' can make suggestions and give feedback on the conversation they are observing. This approach creates a responsive and collaborative learning situation.

Outcomes

Mentoring has been at the heart of what we do since we launched in 2005. We've worked with more than 550 adults to date: registering, supporting, training and then matching many of them to young people volunteering in charities throughout Scotland.

ProjectScotland mentors report that it has enhanced their CV, allowed them to see the world through the eyes of a young person and often comment 'you cannot mentor someone without applying the learning to yourself'.

Source: Contributed by Rucelle Soutar, Finance Director, ProjectScotland.

CASE STUDY

ACADEMIC MENTORING IN EDINBURGH

Mentoring in academia is usually done informally by experienced and enthusiastic individuals who are willing to give their time. In most cases those individuals have had no formal education or training in mentoring and gain no recognition for their work. The Edinburgh Napier Mentoring & Coaching Award (ENMCA) was developed to provide theoretical underpinning and skills training for mentoring and coaching for those engaged in teaching and the support of learning, and to provide an externally accredited qualification for programme participants. The ENMCA is mapped to the Staff and Educational Development Association (SEDA) Professional Development Framework (PDF) Award in Mentoring and Coaching (created by Edinburgh Napier in 2011) so all completers obtain a university and a SEDA certificate.

The programme was initially envisaged as a way to support applications to the university's teaching excellence recognition scheme, which requires the creation of an extensive reflective account of academic practice, supported by a mentor who is an established teaching fellow. However, it quickly became apparent that the scope for enhancement of academic practice through mentoring and coaching was much broader and could support staff at various stages of their careers by offering space and time for reflective dialogue in the context of one-to-one developmental relationship.

The programme runs as four, one-day workshops over an eight-month period, with ten hours of mentoring/coaching practice. Participants are also offered professional support and supervision. The workshops are highly interactive, designed to draw upon participants' existing experience, and are supported by online resources and discussions provided through Moodle. Assessments are reflective and map to the typical stages of the mentoring/coaching relationship and the participant's plans for future learning and development as a mentor/coach, all referenced to relevant literature.

The approach taken is non-directive and 'off line', encouraging each individual to develop their own style within a developmental model of mentoring and coaching. Experience to date indicates that the programme is seen as deeply significant for participants in a number of ways, including enhanced skill, self-knowledge and confidence, as well as the satisfaction of providing high-quality support to their colleagues.

Source: Contributed by Angela Benzies and Elaine Mowat.

CASE STUDY

MENTORING STUDENTS AT THE UNIVERSITY OF ILLINOIS SCHOOL OF MUSIC

First-year students from all backgrounds participate in the programme in order to decrease the likelihood they will perform poorly or drop out of undergraduate courses during the first semester. The School of Music programme was initiated by Tracy Parish, a research scholar and tutor, and student Emily Malamud, an experienced mentor. In its first two years, 50 mentees have been through the programme.

The programme was formally designed to last through the first semester (16 weeks) and as long thereafter as each dyad wanted. Many lasted all year and beyond, with deep friendships often developing.

Mentees and mentors were all volunteers, with mentors often being nominated by their tutors. Many mentors are music education majors in their second, third, or fourth year of university, so mentoring is good learning experience for them in their subsequent careers in schools. It also earns them credits towards their degrees.

The programme starts well before the beginning of the first semester, with an online training session at the beginning for mentors and an exchange of e-mails between mentors and mentees. Participants are matched on a number of factors: degree programme, age, gender, hometown community type, personal interests, and answers to series of other open-ended questions about personal background and preferences. During the first semester, mentors are enrolled in a hybrid music course, delivered both online and in person, specifically designed to provide mentor training and programme information.

Many mentoring pairs meet weekly, but the formal expectation is to meet fortnightly over the first semester. After each meeting, mentors are expected to send in to the programme manager reflection notes about their learning from the mentoring role. During the weeks when formal meetings are not required, mentors submit responses to discussion topics provided by the programme manager via an online course site.

Slides sent to mentors at intervals suggest topics they might like to explore with the mentee. This support is not meant to be prescriptive – rather, it ensures that the mentee is aware of issues such as communication, time management, academic resources (eg libraries, Academic Affairs Office), tutoring services, health and wellness resources, student affairs, and exam preparation. They might typically spend 15 minutes of the 60-minute session on a given topic and the rest on whatever the mentee wants to discuss. Mentors also receive guidance and suggestions for their personal reflections – for example, 'What was your most striking moment with your mentee?'

Mentors and mentees attend a reception at the beginning and end of the formal programme and go to cultural events together. They also collaborate on at least one community project.

Mentors also receive support from previous years' mentors. Sometimes they have a three-way meeting, with a current and a previous mentor, plus mentee.

Measurement

Data on the programme was gathered through interviews, questionnaires and analysis of grade scores and compared with a control group. The comparisons show that students within the mentoring programme have substantially higher grade averages and higher retention. Having a mentor to talk to made it easier to change their major, rather than drop out. They also showed stronger and wider social networks with other students (often hard to establish if you come from a disadvantaged background), greater attention to healthy lifestyles (exercise and diet), more focus on their studies, and better time management. Mentors in the programme showed increased levels of engagement in the university and the wider community, increased confidence, stronger leadership skills, and greater comfort with reflective learning practice.

Source: Tracy Parish, School of Music Mentoring Program, University of Illinois School of Music.

THE BODY SHOP

The Body Shop has taken an unusual approach to mentoring, in affording participants an exceptionally high level of support throughout their programme. This is based on the belief of the programme sponsor, Sarah Burns, that anyone launching a mentoring programme has a responsibility to maintain a similar level of support for their mentors as the expected level of supervision for a professional coach. The programme was designed to support the development of mentees (people at any level in the organisation) as well as equip the senior leadership team to have great mentoring dialogues.

All mentees joined the programme voluntarily and mentors were hand-picked based on each mentee's needs. Over 20 mentoring pairs were given pre-reading, joined a peer online learning network, and were asked to complete a reflection log prior to attending a mandatory, externally facilitated, two-day mentor workshop or one-day mentee workshop. These workshops provided a practical approach to the skills, knowledge, and protocols of mentoring. As part of each workshop, all participants discovered their mentoring match with mentors composing a handwritten welcome letter, and mentees receiving the letter. This served as a positive first step in organising the initial meeting.

Mentors were supported in their role through participating in an action learning set, meeting six times over the nine months of the mentoring programme. This afforded ongoing, peer supervision and a more structured, formal approach to receiving feedback for each individual with a focus on listening and questioning skills. Provision of reflection journals for each participant and a half-day booster/review session for mentors with a mentoring expert, were also part of the ongoing support.

Although this programme is labelled 'Mentoring' there is clearly a strong desire for all participants to transfer the classic coaching/mentoring skills of listening, questioning, summarising etc. into their wider role as leaders, and to embrace a coaching approach to everyday conversations. Burns claims: 'I'm a big believer in helping people see that learning is happening all the time around them – transferring this learning and experiencing the change that occurs as a result is very powerful.'

Mentees commented that their mentoring relationship helped increase their confidence and had been very empowering. One mentee described the experience as enabling them to 'have a better understanding about my emotions and how to take ownership and responsibility of my choices and actions'.

Feedback from mentors highlighted feeling valued because of the investment in their own development as well as gaining satisfaction in helping someone else develop. One mentor commented:

> Making the commitment to meet every month is hugely motivational. Having time for mentoring allows me to recharge my batteries and forces me to reflect on good practice. I have become a better manager because I'm considering how I communicate with others. A key learning for me is that I am not developing people when I am in directive mode.

Source: Contributed by Emily Cosgrove and Sara Hope, who continue to support The Body Shop programme.

CASE STUDY

JP/POLITIKENS HUS MENTORING PROGRAMME

JP/Politikens Hus was established on 01 January 2003 as a merger between Politikens Hus and Jyllands-Posten A/S. Morgenavisen Jyllands-Posten was founded in 1871 and Politiken in 1883, so a tremendous legacy of journalistic history combined. The main objective of JP/Politikens Hus is to create and disseminate news, debate, and entertainment. The group is one of Denmark's leading media companies in printed, digital, and mobile publications. JP/Politikens Hus publishes three national newspapers; Ekstra Bladet, Morgenavisen Jyllands-Posten and Politiken, which are Denmark's leading daily newspapers. Their activities also include free tabloids, local newspapers in Denmark and Sweden, a publishing house, TV production, operation and development of a range of digital activities and news services, and other business areas, which are attached to their primary activity: the creation and dissemination of news, debate, and entertainment to all media.

In recent years, JP/Politikens Hus has particularly invested in the development and expansion of digital and mobile platforms, and the group's newspaper activities now enjoy a leading position in print, on the Internet and on the mobile platform. The development of their newspapers' position on the mobile platform and in online television is their main focus area in the years to come, and significant resources have been reserved for innovation and development in these business areas. It is also a central tenet for JP/Politikens Hus that the group's three daily newspapers maintain their full editorial independence and special character.

Since 2008, Peter Borup and Pernille Ravn of the JP/Politikens Group have run a mentoring programme, where new and inexperienced managers (mentees) are paired with experienced leaders (mentors). This programme originated from a project called Women in Management and it particularly encourages women to participate.

The objectives of the programme are for new leaders to:

- acquire management skills
- have a better balance between the demands of work and personal life
- become more assertive
- be clearer about their career goals
- expand their networks in JP/Politiken Group
- and finally, that the leaders want to continue their careers in the company!

After a kick-off introduction day, the mentoring pairs meet four to six times over the next nine months. In order to achieve maximum openness and learning challenge between the parties, Peter and Pernille match mentor and mentee with as much organisational and academic diversity as possible. For example, a commercial director may therefore be a mentor for an editorial director. However, to aid the rapport building, they will match participants on the basis of life interests and personal profile.

At the initial kick-off event, the mentors and mentees spend a day together in a workshop, which includes a series of short one-to-one meetings between the mentor and mentee to discuss how their relationship will unfold and with special emphasis on building rapport and setting direction for the relationship. These events are facilitated by external consultant Lis Merrick and are held in inspiring venues such as the Royal Trotting Track and Copenhagen Zoo. Lis ensures that the relationships began as developmental mentoring relationships, rather than as sponsorship, and there is clear focus and energy in these new relationships. She then meets the mentors and mentees as separate groups two months later to check that the relationships are gaining momentum and to support the groups with any particular issues, such as keeping the mentor on the mentee's agenda, rather than their own agenda for the mentee, and encouraging the mentors to really listen to the mentees. Newsletters to the participants then reinforce these aspects and other key elements of mentoring good practice during the course of the programme. The Danish media culture enjoyed by JP/Politikens Hus engages best with focused, pragmatic and sense of fun activities, which Lis aims to create in the events.

The evaluation experience demonstrates that both parties have benefited greatly from the mentoring programme. The mentors enjoy the two-way learning they gain from their interaction with their mentees and as part of the continuing development of the kick-off day and support session; there has been a focus on developing mentors as leaders who embrace a learning culture around them as mentors and coaches.

Source: Contributed by Lis Merrick.

CASE STUDY

MENTORING AT THE EUROPEAN BANK FOR RECONSTRUCTION AND DEVELOPMENT

The European Bank for Reconstruction and Development (EBRD) was established to help build a new, post-Cold War era in Central and Eastern Europe. It has since played a historic role and gained unique expertise in fostering change in the region – and beyond.

The EBRD is committed to furthering progress towards, in the words of its founding articles, 'market-oriented economies and the promotion of private and entrepreneurial initiative'. This has been its guiding principle since its creation at the beginning of the 1990s and, new challenges and the welcoming of new countries to the EBRD world notwithstanding, will continue to be its mission in years to come. EBRD provides project financing for banks, industries, and businesses, both new ventures and investments in existing companies. They also work with publicly owned companies. The bank invests only in projects that could not otherwise attract financing on similar terms.

EBRD is a truly multi-cultural organisation, even in its London office where about 75% of the staff are based. The remainder of the internationally recruited employees are spread over 31 resident offices.

In the summer of 2011, EBRD launched its first mentoring programme, in conjunction with Lis Merrick. Now there are four programmes operating within the bank, each designed to the particular needs of the mentees involved, and with a view to opening up more mentoring across the organisation in the next few years.

International Professional's Programme

Each year 12 young trainees join this rotational two-year programme and move around the organisation in four rotations, including at least one rotation in a resident office. Their mentor remains with them for the whole two-year period to support them into the organisation, through their various transitions, and in finding the right role for their entry into the organisation at the end of the programme. This is not a sponsorship mentoring programme, but one of its biggest challenges has been to ensure the mentees do not treat it as such and understand the benefits of developmental mentoring as opposed to having their own sponsor. The programme has been particularly useful to the mentees during the transition phases between rotations.

Human Resources Programme

This programme provides career support to build confidence and potential for HR staff members at relatively junior levels by using the option of a mentor from a manager level (or similar) in the HR department. The positioning of the programme was important because of the selection process of the mentee pool. The HR management team submitted names for the initial pool of the programme in which they believed mentoring might be a good support for the mentee's career progression. It was key that the mentees did not feel that they had been selected due to poor performance but just the opposite – that managers have confidence in their employees and therefore want to help to build that within them. This point was difficult for some of the mentees to understand initially.

As the mentors are located within the department, the fact that the relationship is confidential and does not bear weight on performance ratings is crucial. Some of the building of rapport and trust has taken a longer period within the relationship due to the close proximity of the mentors and mentees.

'Open-Circles'

This mentoring programme has been designed to support the Career Management Programme for Women at EBRD. The mentoring has been developed to support women with; breaking through the 'glass ceiling', work–life balance issues, confidence, not having many visible senior women role models, to break the stereotyping of women and how to gain awareness and skill in navigating power and politics issues.

New Resident Office Heads

A small mentoring programme to supply new heads of the resident offices with a role model mentor who can support them through the transition of moving into a bigger leadership role. There is also the added difficulty of geographical distance from the Head Office in London and the cultural issues of settling into a new location, which can be potentially challenging.

Each of these different mentoring programmes within EBRD has been individually tailored to the key people issues they are supporting, the business needs they are satisfying, and with a very culturally sensitive approach from the centrally co-ordinated control for the programmes in London.

Source: Contributed by Lis Merrick.

CASE STUDY

MENTORING DISABLED STUDENTS IN UK HIGHER EDUCATION

Mentoring is often utilised to support disabled students in UK higher education institutions (HEIs). In the UK disabled students who attend higher education courses are able to claim grants (the Disabled Students' Allowances (DSAs)) to support them during their studies. One of these grants is often used to pay for the mentoring for these students. Disability is defined quite broadly in UK higher education and as a term covers physical conditions such as hearing impairment or mobility impairment, as well as psychological conditions such as mental health difficulties and specific learning difficulties (eg dyslexia).

Mentors work with students, usually in one-hour sessions, and provide support relating to the specific issues which the students present with. The mentors are usually recruited from within the student body or as a minimum requirement they need to hold a degree and to have experienced student life. Research evidence from within the UK has shown that students are more likely to stay on course if they have a sense of belonging to the institution. Also, various measures have shown the efficacy of the DSA 'package' of which mentoring is a part – although different aspects of the DSAs have not been disaggregated in any current research. Whilst support relating to study skills often occurs during these mentoring sessions, there is also a strong emphasis on life skills and acquiring the wherewithal to survive student life. Skills such as time management, planning for assignments, understanding course related information are covered, as well as issues to do with social skills such as self-esteem and relationships. Students benefit from a regular weekly appointment and from knowing that there is someone to check in with who is a familiar, friendly face. The ultimate aim is to keep the student on the programme and to achieve to the best of their abilities.

At York St John University the Learning Support Team Manager, Mike Wray, reached out to Lis Merrick and Roland Spencer to support the mentors with some further tailored training to enhance this mentoring support to the disabled students. We began the process by holding a focus day with all the mentors to ascertain what additional skills or competences they felt they needed on top of their initial mentoring training.

Some of the mentors felt out of their depth at times and welcomed the opportunity to learn more about:

- managing some common difficult scenarios with mentees
- how to support behavioural change and adopt new study habits
- managing student expectations and dependency building
- understanding non-verbal communication
- techniques and process models for supporting mentoring conversations
- self-harm awareness and response reaction, so they are better tuned in to any warning signals and can sign post mentees on to counselling etc
- coaching students with time management issues.

This training was provided for the mentors and the programme also introduced follow up group supervision with some learning input to support the mentors further and build their confidence in some of the situations they find themselves in.

The next stage is to evaluate the outcomes from this more sophisticated approach to preparing mentors and see what difference it has made to the service overall.

Source: Contributed by Lis Merrick.

CASE STUDY

MENTORING AFRICAN AND CARIBBEAN STUDENTS IN UK SCHOOLS

Since the 1970s, black British pupils have consistently ranked at the bottom of league tables measuring academic attainment in England. African & Caribbean Diversity, a charity, understood the solution involved an early-interventionist, holistic investment that takes account of the personal, cultural and social dynamic risk factors to deal with this long-term and consistent underachievement among these pupils. Here are some facts:

- Only 39% of black pupils achieve five or more A*–C GCSE grades (age 16 qualification). Pupils at fee-paying schools are three and a half times more likely than pupils from poor backgrounds to attain five GCSEs with grades A*–C including English and maths.

- Black pupils are four times more likely to be expelled from schools than pupils from any other group.
- 16% of pupils who are eligible for free school meals progress to university, in comparison to 96% of young people educated in fee-paying schools (Sutton Trust 2010).
- Unemployment among black youth aged 16 to 24 is 44% compared to 20% of their white counterparts (UK's Labour Force Survey 2012).
- Black pupils have limited access to social capital and therefore networking opportunities.

Logistics

This programme, now in its tenth year, focuses on achievement by:

- *Co-ordinating a four-year intensive programme:* Year 9 pupils are recruited and supported in their academic and personal development throughout the four years of their schooling with mentors, residential summer schools, workshops, career days and cultural visits. This highly intensive programme involves a yearly minimum of ten workshops by ACD and 20 mentoring sessions, on average, with corporate mentors.
- *Involving private sector employers:* Pupils are matched with mentors recruited from firms including Barclays Capital, Citigroup, Clifford Chance, Slaughter and May, Withers, and J.P. Morgan. These mentors are from a diverse range of nationalities and ethnicities. Mentoring sessions include: subject and university choices; effective CVs; and encouraging extra-curriculum activities. These sessions greatly enhance pupils' chances of junior internships and entry into their first-choice university.
- *Focusing on mentoring:* In order to optimise the mentors' contribution towards the pupils. Key logistic elements are:
  - The mentor registers online and the information provided is used for the police check and initial matching of the mentor with a pupil.
  - Training sessions take place twice a year at the mentors' workplace.
  - There is a 'formal' introduction involving the parents at the mentors' workplace.
  - The one-to-one mentoring sessions take place for 30 to 45 minutes at the mentors' workplace.
  - Mentors and pupils use the online database to manage their interactions and ACD provides ongoing support.

Successes

- ACD has contributed to narrowing the gap in the educational achievements of black British youth within the Government statistics and facilitated creative and practical routes into employment for this underrepresented group. Statistics demonstrating this impact: 97% of ACD students continued into post-16 education; 71% gained admission to universities, with 27% going to the top 30 universities. ACD has alumni present at the top 20 universities listed in *The Sunday Times* University League Table. ACD alumni take up leadership positions at university, either in the Student Union or the university's African Caribbean society or organising outreach activities or events such as TEDx. ACD alumni normally take a gap year giving back to the community by becoming assistant teachers or arranging information and motivational workshops sharing experiences. 95% attained the Government's benchmark of five GCSE passes, including English and maths (2010 average for black students was 43%). Over 90% of ACD alumni are in employment, with over 60% gaining employment in highly competitive graduate recruitment programmes where black British citizens are greatly underrepresented.

Aiming the most significant challenges for the programme have been that:

- The mentors need to focus on the young person's personal development and social skills – appropriate dress, importance of maintaining eye contact, as well as providing advice such as study tips, effective CVs, subject and university choices.
- Although most mentors will have received this guidance during their childhood, some believe that these skills come naturally as opposed to being developed.
- The majority of parents are fully involved, however, a significant minority are not engaged and this can make the difference between success or failure.

Lessons learned

- Mentoring must start at 13/14 years old, not post-16.
- Mentors need to be well briefed during training of the possible impact of inter-generational poverty.
- Parental involvement is critical.

Source: Contributed by Brenda King MBE, Chief Executive of African & Caribbean Diversity.

MENTORING SUPERVISION AT THE DANISH ASSOCIATION OF LAWYERS AND ECONOMISTS

One of the assets of mentoring is that it is a two-way learning process. If the match is right, and if the distance between mentor and mentee in experience is not too great the mentor will learn and appreciate what she is gaining from the conversations with the mentee. However, for the mentor there may be even more to gain if the programme offers them supervision. In the Association we have during the past ten years offered mentoring to those of our members who are managers and leaders and for our newly graduated members. On an annual basis we have 500 new tandems.

What supervision offers

A reflective person will soon learn the value of a partner to help them reflect – to add different perspectives, thoughts, angles to her own lines of thinking. A good supervisor does that, but will often focus the learning conversation in a more methodical direction, or at least on a different subject matter than occurs to the mentor from his own world of experience. Supervision thus offers insight into more process-oriented and interpersonal aspects of the learning conversation. In this case study we learned the following from our mentors when they had participated in supervision.[1]

On the role:

'Supervision is about having a professional, who observes patterns you aren't aware of.'

'Supervision means contact with a person, who doesn't take part in the daily issues – a person who can guide and inspire you in relation to your role as mentor.'

On the method:

'Supervision is a method to become aware of one's blind spots in conversations with the mentee.'

[1] The case study stems from a study made by Merrick and Stokes (2010) on the mentor programmes of the Danish Association of Lawyers and Economists, a programme that comprises about 500 mentors and has run for ten years.

'Supervision is feedback relating to form, contents, and relationships.'

'Supervision is a method to observe a situation from another perspective.'

Supervision has been offered to the mentors for five years now. What we had in mind when we were setting up supervision was a kind of mentor's mentor. We believe that it is what we have achieved. We have chosen right from the start to have a distance between the supervisor, the supervision offer, and the programme management, so that the mentors would not feel that we were controlling them. We had no reason to doubt the success and quality of what was going on in the mentoring conversations. It was more an initiative to give our mentors the chance to 'step back metaphorically ... so that they can take a meta-perspective, or broader view of their practice' – to quote Julie Hay (Hay 2007, p4) almost correctly.

The supervisor and methods

A supervisor needs to be an experienced person or a professional in the interpersonal professions. The supervisors in our programme have been just that.

During the five years we have offered supervision, we have had four supervisors. They have all had coaching training combined with a background in either psychology, HR, or pedagogy.

When asked about their approach to supervision, they state that they use a combination of methods from solution-based coaching, organisational development, process consulting, and regular advising. They all stress that one of the most important things for establishing good sessions has been the confidence and confidentiality between them and the mentors. Mutual respect is a prerequisite for the mentor to open up to reflecting on her own approach, learning, blind spots and so on. And that is no different from what we know from the mentoring relationship. No confidence – no depth in either reflection or learning. So the mentor and the supervisor also need to small talk and 'find' each other before results can be achieved.

Source: Contributed by Else Iversen, senior consultant at the Danish Association of Lawyers and Economists.

CASE STUDY

FIT FOR THE FUTURE – MENTORING FOR PEOPLE SUCCESS AT IDA IRELAND

IDA Ireland is the Government Agency responsible for attracting Foreign Direct Investment (FDI) into Ireland. The success of the agency is dependent on the quality of the staff in the way they carry out their roles. Securing FDI to Ireland has become more challenging with a higher degree of competition and an increasing number of agencies fighting for the business. IDA has demanding targets each year on job creation for the country and each year the organisation needs to be more strategic in its approach to job creation and sophisticated in its engagement with clients and in its ability to generate solutions that meet client needs. To ensure we build the organisation's capability to meet the future challenges in competitiveness and job creation, the organisational development strategy is clearly aligned to achieving this aim.

IDA's Organisational Development strategy

The organisation has had a Performance Management and Development Review (PM&DR) process in place developed against a competency model that consists of nine competences indicating the skills, knowledge and behaviours expected at each level in the organisation. The competences are:

1. Sales and Marketing
2. Networking
3. Leadership and Management
4. Influencing and Negotiation
5. Project Management
6. Communications and Personal Effectiveness
7. Creativity and Innovation
8. Knowledge
9. Client Focused Relationship Building.

Mentoring has always been a key feature of developing people in IDA and has tended to focus on supporting new staff into the organisation, helping them navigate the system, and has become an integrated part of the Leadership and Management competence. Some training has been delivered over the years to managers in how to be an effective mentor, but the demand for mentoring began to increase as staff saw it as a potential means to address gaps they had for promotion. What IDA observed over time was that, at the start of the mentoring process, rapport-building and general discussion on the needs of the individual was conducted very well, but the process and content following that initial connection was unstructured and not as effective as it could be. As the organisation bases its annual Learning and Development programme on the output of the PM&DR process, and the HR team tend to provide the development solutions, the team saw that a more structured and focused approach was required to develop the mentoring relationship in IDA. The team developed an in-house programme, supplying the participants (mainly senior managers) with materials to deliver an effective mentoring relationship. These included tools from the Clutterbuck series and those who attended the training were then matched against three needs – new starters, those with specific knowledge requirements, and those who needed to be supported to develop their careers. Matching did not take place between direct line managers, but always with someone who worked in a different department, but who had the experiences and the mentoring programme to manage the relationship. This became a very popular means of development and the HR team felt that there ought to be a more formal qualification associated with the mentoring arrangement to really highlight the importance of it and how engaged senior managers had become. Additionally, further requests were being made for a mentoring relationship. The organisation was also looking for an outcome that would be about increasing the overall management capability in the organisation more specifically to develop the future talent of the organisation.

The approach

A discussion on the potential of mentoring as a development opportunity in IDA took place at the executive level in the organisation, and it was agreed that if the executive got engaged with becoming qualified mentors, then that would raise the status of the process and encourage others to take part. The executive team took part in an external mentoring programme delivered by Kingstown College. The success of this programme gave the impetus and support to cascade it down into the organisation. Although modular mentoring workshops were being delivered, the success of the programme at executive level meant that the culture around the use of internal mentors became the norm and the value of the approach was easily recognised. This supported the introduction and delivery of the programme and this helped to embed the approach more smoothly into the organisation. The benefits of a top down management approach meant that the culture of mentoring, and later coaching, in helping people to deliver their objectives and ultimately the organisation's objectives was, and still remains, very powerful.

Outcomes

- There has been observable positive performance in behaviours. Those people who are mentored are able to handle situations better and can become more engaged in the organisation in a more effective way.
- Mentoring conversations around individual career progression and support offered to people have helped people to secure promotions.
- Individuals developed their knowledge in a more effective way through the use of mentors, learning where to get information from, and how to use it to best effect.
- Mentoring has become an even more important part of IDA's organisational development strategy for the management and development of its people for the future.

Source: Contributed by Breda O'Toole.

CASE STUDY

MENTORING YOUNG JOBSEEKERS

The Steps Ahead Mentoring scheme was established by the CIPD, the professional body for HR and people development, in 2011. It forms a core element of Learning to Work, an action-focused programme led by the CIPD to promote the role of employers in reducing youth unemployment. Young people benefit hugely from direct contact with employers and HR professionals are particularly well placed to help young people with the skills they need to find employment.

Steps Ahead Mentoring works by matching HR professionals, who volunteer for the scheme, with young jobseekers aged 18 to 24. The scheme offers young people, most of whom have never worked before, up to six one-to-one mentoring sessions to help them improve their employability, boost their confidence and find work.

The scheme is entirely not-for-profit, in line with the CIPD's charitable purpose, to champion better work and working lives and is delivered exclusively by volunteers (who are also CIPD members). The CIPD works in collaboration with local Jobcentre Plus offices, which refer the young jobseekers to Steps Ahead Mentoring. Attendance is not mandatory and young jobseekers register themselves with the scheme if they think it can help them in their job search.

The objective is to bring these young jobseekers closer to the labour market and improve their employability skills through individual face-to-face mentoring. During their involvement in the scheme, mentees receive advice and guidance on job search, CV writing and interview techniques. Mentors also help young people to identify their career prospects and build confidence.

The volunteer mentors come from a variety of backgrounds, but most of them have been on the front line of recruitment and have the relevant experience to help young jobseekers to increase their chances of successfully finding work. They draw on their professional knowledge and experience to help assist the young people. The CIPD supports volunteers by making useful materials, such as CV and interview top tips, available in an online resource area. They are also provided with a clear point of contact at the CIPD should they have any additional queries or concerns.

Since it launched as a pilot in 2011, Steps Ahead Mentoring has helped hundreds of young people into a job, apprenticeship or work-experience opportunity, and over 1,500 volunteers have signed up to take part. The scheme is currently operating in partnership with more than 300 Jobcentre Plus officers across central England, the north-east of England and the north-west of England. It will be rolled out across the rest of England and the UK in 2014, with the launch of a new online portal that will help to streamline the mentor matching process.

Many mentees have provided feedback to their mentors describing how useful they found the experience. As one mentee who successfully went on to get a job in his chosen field of work said recently: 'I still think back to the sessions we had and definitely feel that I am still implementing a lot of what you helped me to learn'.

Source: Contributed by Kelly Duncan and Katherine Garrett, CIPD.

Bibliography

ANON (1995) Mentoring: a positive action initiative for ethnic minorities. *Equal Opportunities Review*. No 60, March/April. pp11–15.

ALLEMAN, E. (1984) *What's really true about mentoring?* Leadership Development Consultants Inc. Mentor, Ohio.

ALLEMAN, E. (1994) Interpersonal perceptions in mentoring relationships. *Presented at the American Educational Research Annual Meeting, New Orleans*.

ALRED, G. and GARVEY, R. (1996) Approaching mentoring: becoming a semi-god. *Proceedings of 3rd European Mentoring Conference, London*.

ALRED, G., GARVEY, R. and SMITH, R. (1998) *The mentoring pocketbook*. Alresford, Hants: Management Pocketbooks Ltd.

ANDERSON, A. (2010) *Polarity coaching: coaching people and managing polarities*. Amherst, MA: HRD Press.

ANTAL, A.B. (1993) Odysseus' legacy to management development: mentoring. *European Management Journal*. Vol 11, No 4.

ANTON, P.A. and TEMPLE, J. (2007) *Analyzing the social return on investment in youth mentoring programs: a framework for Minnesota*. St Paul, Minnesota: Wilder Research.

ARYEE, S. and CHAY, Y.W. (1994) An examination of the impact of career-oriented mentoring on work commitment, attitudes and career satisfaction among professionals and managerial employees. *British Journal of Management*. Vol 5.

ARYEE, S., WYATT, T. and STONE, R. (1996) Early career outcomes of graduate employees: the effect of mentoring and ingratiation. *Journal of Management Studies*. Vol 33, No 1.

BAJNOK, I.J. and GITTERMAN, G. (1988) Nurses as colleagues and mentors. *Canadian Nurse*. Vol 84, No 2. pp16–17.

BARHAM, K. and CONWAY, C. (1997) Mentoring goes International. *Ashridge Journal*.

BARHAM, K. and CONWAY, C. (1998) *Developing business and people internationally – a mentoring approach*. Berkhampstead: Ashridge Research.

BAXTER, A.G. and CLARK, K.M. (1992) Positive and productive mentoring: inside views. *Mentoring International*. Vol 6, No 2/3.

BEATTIE, R.S. and McDOUGALL, M. (1995) Peer mentoring: the issues and outcomes of non-hierarchical developmental relationships. *Presented at the British Academy of Management Annual Conference*.

BENNETTS, C. (1995) The secrets of a good relationship. *People Management*. 30 June.

BENNETTS, C. (1999) Interpersonal aspects of informal mentor/learner relationships: a research perspective. *Proceedings of the European Mentoring Centre Conference, London*.

BENNETTS, C. (1998) *A pilot inquiry into current mentoring projects and programmes for unemployed youth in England, Scotland and Wales.* Hertfordshire: TEC.

BENNETTS, C. (1999) Mentoring relationships and young people: trend and tradition in mentoring. *National Youth Agency/DfEE/Rowntree, Research, Policy and Practice Forum on Young People, London.*

BERGLAS, S. (2002) The very real dangers of executive coaching. *Harvard Business Review.* 1 June.

BIEREMA, L. and HILL, J.R. (2005) Virtual mentoring and HRD. Advances in Developing Human Resources.Vol 7, No 4, November. pp556–568.

BLAKE, R.R. and MOUTON, J.S. (1964) *The Managerial Grid.* Houston, Texas: Gulf.

BROWN, S. (2000) The keys to successful mentoring in Smithkline Beecham. *Proceedings of the seventh annual European Mentoring Conference, Cambridge.*

BUREAU OF BUSINESS PRACTICE (1990) Being a mentor. *Management Letter* 304, February.

BURKE, R.J. and McKEEN, C.A. (1997) Benefits of mentoring relationships among managerial and professional women: a cautionary tale. *Journal of Vocational Behavior.* Vol 51, No 1.

BURKE, R.J., McKENNA, C.S. and McKEEN, C.A. (1991) How do mentorships differ from typical supervisory relationships? *Psychological Review.* Vol 68.

BUSINESS WALES (2003) Available at: http://business.wales.gov.uk/growing-business/welsh-government-support-1/mentoring [Accessed 14 November 2013].

CARTER, S. (1993) Developing an organisation mentoring scheme. *Professional Manager.*

CARTER, S. (1994) The development, implementation and evaluation of a mentoring scheme. *Industrial and Commercial Training.* Vol 26, No 7. pp16–23.

CARTER, S. and LEWIS, G. (1994) The four bases of mentoring. *Proceedings of First European Mentoring Conference.* European Mentoring Centre/Sheffield Business School.

CARUSO, R. (ed.). (1992) *Mentoring and the business environment: asset or liability?* Dartmouth, USA.

CHAO, G.T. (1997) Mentoring phases and outcomes. *Journal of Vocational Behavior.* Vol 51.

CHAO, G.T. (1998) Invited reaction: challenging research in mentoring. *Human Resource Development Quarterly.* Vol 9, No 4.

CHAO, G.T., WALZ, P.M. and GARDNER, P.D. (1992) Formal and informal mentorships: a comparison on mentoring functions and contrast with non-mentored counterparts. *Personnel Psychology.* Vol 45.

CLUTTERBUCK, D. (1992) *Top Manager Programme.* Oxford Regional Health Authority.

CLUTTERBUCK, D. (1993) *Mentoring – a key tool in training and development, current best practice.* London: The Industrial Society.

CLUTTERBUCK, D. (1994a) Blooming Managers. *Management Training.* February.

CLUTTERBUCK, D. (1994b) Business mentoring in evolution. *Mentoring.* Summer.

CLUTTERBUCK, D. (1994c) *Managing mentoring, how to avoid the common pitfalls.* Mentoring and Coaching. Deventer, Netherlands: Kluwer Bedrijtswetenschappen.

CLUTTERBUCK, D. (1994d) The mentoring game. *The Business Magazine.* October.

CLUTTERBUCK, D. (1994e) Uncovering the way a mentor does his work. *The Business Magazine.* November.

CLUTTERBUCK, D. (1995) *Consenting adults.* London: Channel Four Publications.

CLUTTERBUCK, D. (1996a) Developing learning teams. *Training Officer.* Vol 32, No 6, July/August.

CLUTTERBUCK, D. (1996b) How executives learn from each other. In: SADLER, P. (ed.). *International executive development programmes.* London: Kogan Page.

CLUTTERBUCK, D. (1996c) Will you be my mentor? *Modern Management.* Vol 10, June.

CLUTTERBUCK, D. (1997a) Are you getting in the way of the learning organisation? *Direction.* April.

CLUTTERBUCK, D. (1997b) Mentoring and the glass ceiling. *The Diversity Directory 12th Edition.* Diversity, UK.

CLUTTERBUCK, D. (1997c) *Power in the mentoring relationship.* Staff and Educational Development Association.

CLUTTERBUCK, D. (1998a) *Learning alliances.* London: Institute of Personnel and Development.

CLUTTERBUCK, D. (1998b) The rapid rise of executive mentoring. *Croner's Human Resources Briefing.* 12 January.

CLUTTERBUCK, D. (1998c) Mentoring diagnostic kit. Clutterbuck Associates.

CLUTTERBUCK, D. (1999a) Mentoring, developing two for the price of one. In: PRIOR, J. MBE (ed.). *Gower handbook of training and development, 3rd edition.* Aldershot: Gower Publishing Limited. Chapter 24.

CLUTTERBUCK, D. (1999b) Mentoring in business, executives and directors. *Mentoring and Tutoring.* Vol 6, No 3.

CLUTTERBUCK, D. (2000a) Ten core mentor competencies. *Organisations & People.* Vol 7, No 2, November.

CLUTTERBUCK, D. (2000b) Where next in mentoring? *AMED News.* October.

CLUTTERBUCK, D. (2000/2001) Quiet transformation, the growing power of mentoring. *Mount Eliza Business Review.* Summer/autumn.

CLUTTERBUCK, D. (2007a) An international perspective on mentoring. In: RAGINS, B. R. and KRAM, K. (eds). *The Handbook of Mentoring at Work.* California, SA: Sage. pp 633–655.

CLUTTERBUCK, D. (2007b) *A longitudinal study of the effectiveness of developmental mentoring.* PhD thesis. King's College, University of London.

CLUTTERBUCK, D. (2012) *The talent wave*. London: Kogan Page.

CLUTTERBUCK, D. (2013) *Making the most of developmental mentoring: a practical guide for mentors and mentees*. Coaching and Mentoring International.

CLUTTERBUCK, D. and DEVINE, M. (1987) *Businesswoman*. London: Macmillan.

CLUTTERBUCK, D. and HUSSAIN, Z. (2009) *Virtual coach, virtual mentor*. Charlotte, NC: Information Age Publishing.

CLUTTERBUCK, D. and MEGGINSON, D. (1999) *Mentoring Executives and Directors*. Oxford: Butterworth-Heinemann.

CLUTTERBUCK, D. and MEGGINSON, M. (2001) Winding up or winding down? *Proceedings of European Mentoring Centre Conference, Cambridge (UK), November.*

CLUTTERBUCK, D., POULSEN, K.P. and KOCHAN, F. (2012) *Developing successful diversity mentoring programmes: an international casebook*. Maidenhead: McGraw-Hill.

CLUTTERBUCK, D. and RAGINS, B.R. (2001) *Mentoring and diversity: an international perspective*. Oxford: Butterworth-Heinemann.

CLUTTERBUCK, D. and SCHNEIDER, S. (1998) Executive mentoring. *Croner's Executive Companion Bulletin*. October, issue 29.

CLUTTERBUCK, D. and SNOW, D. (1995) *BEAT – Beginning education and training, an evaluation*. Birmingham, BEAT Projects.

CLUTTERBUCK, D. and WYNNE, B. (1993) Mentoring and coaching. In: *Handbook of Management Development*. Aldershot: Gower.

COLLIN, A. (1979) Notes on some typologies of management development and the role of the mentor in the process of adaptation of the individual to the organisation. *Personnel Review*. Vol 8, No 1.

CONWAY, C. (1995) Mentoring managers in organisations. *Equal Opportunities International*. Vol 14, No 3/4.

CONWAY, C. (1998) Strategies for mentoring: a blueprint for successful organizational development. Chichester: John Wiley and Sons, Ltd.

CORPORATE MENTORING SOLUTIONS (CMSI) (2001) *Mentoring programme benchmark 2001 survey*. Vancouver: CMSI.

CRANWELL-WARD, J., BOSSONS, P. and GOVER, S. (2004) *Mentoring: a Henley review of best practice*. Basingstoke: Palgrave.

CROSBY, F.J. (1999) The development literature on developmental relationships. In: MURRELL, A.J., CROSBY, F.J. and ELY, R.J. (eds). *Mentoring dilemmas: developmental relationships within multicultural organizations*. New Jersey: Lawrence Erlbaum Associates.

CUNNINGHAM, J.B. and EBERLE, T. (1993) Characteristics of the mentoring experience: a qualitative study. *Personnel Review*. Vol 22, No 4.

DARLING, L.A. (1984) Mentor types and life cycles. *The Journal of Nursing Administration*. November.

DARWIN, A. (1998) *Characteristics ascribed to mentors by their protégés.* Doctoral thesis (p49). University of British Columbia.

DATA PROTECTION ACT (1998) Available at: http://www.legislation.gov.uk/ukpga/1998/29/contents [Accessed 11 December 2013].

DEANGELIS, K.L. (2013) *Reverse Mentoring at the Hartford: Cross-generational transfer of knowledge about social media.* May. Available at: http://www.bc.edu/content/dam/files/research_sites/agingandwork/pdf/publications/hartford.pdf [Accessed 18 December 2013].

DOUVASA, L. (2009) *Peer Mentoring and Health Recovery.* July. Available at: http://ezinearticles.com/?Peer-Mentoring-and-Mental-Health-Recovery&id=2620137 [Accessed 18 December 2013].

EBY, L.T. (1997) Alternative forms of mentoring in changing organisational environments: a conceptual extension of the mentoring literature. *Journal of Vocational Behavior.* Vol 51.

ENGSTRÖM, T. (1997/8) *Personality factors impact on success in the mentor-protégé relationship.* MSc thesis to Norwegian School of Hotel Management, Oslo.

FAGAN, M. (1988) The term 'mentor': a review of the literature. *International Journal of Mentoring.* Vol 2, No 12, winter.

FAGENSON-ELAND, E.A., MARKS, M.A. and AMENDOLA, K.L. (1997) Perceptions of mentoring relationships. *Journal of Vocational Behavior.* Vol 51, No 51. pp29–42.

FLEIG-PALMER, M. (2009) *The impact of mentoring on retention through knowledge transfer, affective commitment and trust.* Dissertations and Theses from the College of Business Administration. Paper 4. Lincoln: University of Nebraska.

FORRET, M.L., TURBAN, D.B. and DOUGHERTY, T.W. (1996) Issues facing organizations when implementing formal mentoring programmes. *Leadership & Organization Journal.* Vol 17, No 3.

GARDNER, C. (1997) Mentoring: a professional friendship? *Proceedings of the Fourth European Conference on Mentoring, European Mentoring Centre/Sheffield Business School.*

GARDNER, C.E. (1996) *Mentoring: a study of the concept, theory and practice of mentoring in the educational field.* Dissertation MA in Education at the University of Central England, Birmingham.

GARVEY, R. (1995) Healthy Signs for Mentoring. *Education and Training.* Vol 37, No 5.

GARVEY, R. (1998) *Mentoring in the marketplace: studies of learning at work.* Thesis submitted for the degree of Doctor of Philosophy, Durham University.

GARVEY, R. (1999) Mentoring and the changing paradigm. *Mentoring and Tutoring.* Vol 7, No 1.

GARVEY, R. and ALRED, G. (2000a) Developing mentors. *Career Development International.* Vol 5, No 4/5.

GARVEY, R. and ALRED, G. (2000b) Educating mentors. *Mentoring and Tutoring.* Vol 8, No 2.

GARVEY, R. and ALRED, G. (2001) Mentoring and the tolerance of complexity. *Futures.* Vol 33.

GARVEY, R., ALRED, G. and SMITH, R. (1996) First person mentoring. *Career Development International.* Vol 1, No 5.

GIBB, S. (1994a) Evaluating mentoring. *Education and Training.* Vol 36, No 5.

GIBB, S. (1994b) Inside corporate mentoring schemes, the development of a conceptual framework. *Personnel Review.* Vol 23, No 3.

GIBB, S. (1999) The usefulness of theory, a case study in evaluating formal mentoring schemes. *Human Relation.* Vol 52, No 2, August.

GIBB, S and MEGGINSON, D. (1992) Inside corporate mentoring schemes, a new agenda of concerns. *Personnel Review.* Vol 21, No 7.

GRAY, W.A. (1986) Achieving employment equity and affirmative action through formalized mentoring. *Conference Proceedings of the National Conference on Management in the Public Sector, Victoria, BC Canada, April 21–23.*

HALE, R. (2000) To match or mis-match? The dynamics of mentoring as a route to personal and organisational learning. *Career Development International.* Vol. 5, No 4/5. pp.223–234.

HAMILTON, R. (1993) *Mentoring.* London: The Industrial Society.

HAMILTON, B.A. and SCANDURA, T.A. (2003) E-mentoring: implications for organisational learning and development in a weird world. Organisational Dynamics. Vol 31, No 4. pp388–402.

HAY, J. (1993) A new approach to mentoring. *Financial Training Review.* October.

HAY, J. (1995) *Transformational mentoring: creating developmental alliances for changing organisational cultures.* Maidenhead: McGraw-Hill.

HAY, J. (1997) *Action mentoring: creating your own developmental alliance.* Watford: Sherwood Publishing.

HAY, J. (1998) Mentoring – traditional versus developmental. *Organisations and People.* Vol 5, No 3, August.

HAY, J. (2007) *Reflective practice and supervision for coaches.* Maidenhead: McGraw-Hill.

HIGGINS, M.C. and KRAM, K.E. (2001) Reconceptualizing mentoring at work: a developmental network perspective. *Academy of Management Review.* Vol 26, No. 2. pp264–288.

HODGSON, P. (1987) Managers can be taught but leaders have to learn. *Industrial and Commercial Training.* November–December.

HOFSTEDE, G. and MINKOV, M. (2010). *Cultures and organisations: software of the mind.* New York: McGraw Hill.

HOLINCHECK, J. (2006) *Case study: workforce analytics at Sun.* Stamford, CT: Gartner, Inc.

HOLLOWAY, A. (1994) *Mentoring: the definitive workbook.* Manchester: Development Processes.

HUGHES, J.E. (2003) A reflection on the art and practice of mentorship. *Journal of Wealth Management.* Vol 5, No 4. pp8–11.

HUNT, D.M. (1992) A longitudinal study of mentor outcomes. *Mentoring International.* Vol 6, No 2/3.

IBARRA, H. (2000) Making partner: a mentor's guide to the psychological journey. *Harvard Business Review.* Vol 78, No 2.

INDUSTRIAL SOCIETY (1995) Mentoring. *Managing Best Practice.* Vol 12. p3.

INDUSTRIAL SOCIETY AND THE ITEM GROUP (1990) *The line manager's role in developing talent.* London: Industrial Society.

KEGAN, R. (1982) *The evolving self: problem and process in human development.* Cambridge, MA: Harvard University Press.

KING, Z. (2012) The Goldilocks network. *New Scientist.* 26 May. pp37–39.

KIZILOS, P. (1990) Take my mentor, please. *Training.* Vol 4, No 27.

KLASEN, N. and CLUTTERBUCK, D. (2002) *Implementing mentoring schemes: a practical guide to successful programs.* Oxford: Elsevier Butterworth-Heinemann.

KRAM, K. (1980) *Mentoring processes at work: developmental relationships in managerial careers.* Doctoral dissertation, Yale University.

KRAM, K. (1983) Phases of the mentor relationship. *Academy of Management Journal.* Vol 26, No 4.

KRAM, K. (1985) Improving the mentoring process. *Training and Development Journal.* April.

KRAM, K. (1985) *Mentoring at work.* Lanham, MD: University Press of America.

KRAM, K. and ISABELLA, L.A. (1983) Much ado about mentors, not enough about peers. *Career Development Bulletin.*

KRAM, K. and ISABELLA, L.A. (1985) Mentoring alternatives: the role of peer relationships in career development. *Academy of Management Journal.* Vol 28, No 1.

KWOH, L. (2011) Reverse mentoring cracks workplace. *Wall Street Journal.* November 28. Available at: http://online.wsj.com/news/articles/SB10001424052970203764804577060051461094004 [Accessed 19 December 2013].

LEVINSON, D. (1978) *The seasons of a man's life.* New York: Alfred Knopf.

LEWIS, G. (1988) *The mentoring manager: strategies for fostering talent and spreading knowledge.* London: Pitman/Institute of Management.

LEWIS, G. (1993) *The mentoring manager.* London: Pitman.

LIKERT, R. (1961) *New patterns of management.* New York: McGraw-Hill.

MACLENNAN, N. (1995) *Coaching and mentoring.* Aldershot: Gower.

McDOUGALL, M. and BEATTIE, R.S. (1997) Peer mentoring at work. *Management Learning.* Vol 28, No 4.

McGREGOR, L. (2000) Mentoring: the Australian experience. *Proceedings of the 7th European Mentoring Conference, Cambridge, November.*

MEGGINSON, D. (1993) Three ways of mentoring. *AMED/Sundridge Park Conference Proceedings.*

MEGGINSON, D. (1994a) Images of mentoring. *EMC Research Conference, Sheffield.*

MEGGINSON, D. (1994b) Planned and emergent learning, a framework and a method. *Executive Development.* Vol 7, No 6.

MEGGINSON, D. (2000) Current issues in mentoring. *Career Development International.*

MEGGINSON, D. and CLUTTERBUCK, D. (1995) *Mentoring in action: a practical guide for managers.* London: Kogan Page.

MEGGINSON, D. and GARVEY, R. (2001) *Odysseus, Telemachus and Mentor: stumbling into, searching for and signposting the road to desire.* European Group for Organisation Studies.

MUMFORD, A. (1993) *How managers can develop managers.* Aldershot: Gower.

MUMFORD, A. (1985) What's new in management development. *Personnel Management.* May.

MURRAY, M. with OWEN M.A. (1991) *Beyond the myths and magic of mentoring.* San Francisco, California: Jossey-Bass.

NOE, R.A. (1988) An investigation into the determinants of successful assigned mentoring relationships. *Personnel Psychology.* Vol 41.

NOLLER, R.B. (1982) Mentoring: a renaissance of apprenticeship. *Journal of Creative Behavior.* Vol 16, No 1.

O'NEILL, R.M., HORTON, S. and CROSBY, F.J. (1999) Gender issues in developmental relationships. In: MURRELL, A.J., CROSBY, F.J., ELY, R.J. AND ERLBAUM, L. (eds). *Mentoring dilemmas: developmental relationships within multicultural organizations.* New Jersey: Lawrence Erlbaum Associates.

ORPEN, C. (1997) The effects of formal mentoring on employee work motivation, organisational commitment and job performance. *The Learning Organisation.* Vol 4, No 2.

PARSLOE, E. (1992) *Coaching, mentoring and assessing: a practical guide to developing competence.* London: Kogan Page.

PARSLOE, E. (1999) A selection of letters. *People Management.* 20 May.

PLAISTER-TEN, J. (2009) Towards greater cultural understanding in coaching. *International Journal of Evidence Based Coaching and Mentoring.* Special Issue No 3, November. p64.

PLAISTER-TEN, J. (2010) Adapt and survive. *Coaching at Work.* Vol 5, No 5.

POULSEN, K.M. (2008) *Mentor+Guiden.* Copenhagen: KMP+.

QUAST, L. (2011) *Reverse mentoring: what it is and why it is beneficial [blog].* Forbes. 03 Jan. Available at: http://www.forbes.com/sites/work-in-progress/2011/01/03/reverse-mentoring-what-is-it-and-why-is-it-beneficial/ [Accessed 15 November 2013].

RAGINS, B.R. (1997a) Antecedents of diversified mentoring relationships. *Journal of Vocational Behavior.* Vol 51, No1.

RAGINS, B.R. (1997b) Diversified mentoring relationships in organisations: a power perspective. *Academy of Management Review*. Vol 22, No 2.

RAGINS, B.R. (1999a) Where do we go from here? And how do we get there? Methodological issues in conducting research on diversity and mentoring relationships. In: MURRELL, CROSBY and ELY (eds). *Mentoring dilemmas: developmental relationships within multicultural organisations*. New Jersey: Lawrence Erlbaum Associates.

RAGINS, B.R. (1999b) Gender and mentoring relationships. In POWELL, G.N. (ed.). *Handbook of gender and work*. Sage.

RAGINS, B.R. and COTTON, J.L. (1993) Gender and willingness to mentor in organisations. *Journal of Management*. Vol 19, No 1. pp97–111.

RAGINS, B.R. and COTTON, J.L. (1996) Jumping the hurdles: the barriers to mentoring for women in organizations. *Leadership & Organization Development Journal*. Vol 17, No 3.

RAGINS, B.R. and COTTON, J.L. (1999) Mentor functions and outcomes: a comparison of men and women in formal and informal mentoring relationships. *Journal of Applied Psychology*. Vol 84, No 4.

RAGINS, B.R. and KRAM, K. (eds). (2007) *The Handbook of Mentoring at Work*. California, SA: Sage.

RAGINS, B.R. and McFARLIN, D.B. (1990) Perceptions of mentor roles in cross-gender mentoring relationships. *Journal of Vocational Behavior*. Vol 37, No 3. pp321–339.

RAGINS, B.R. and SCANDURA, T.A. (1993) The effects of sex and gender role orientation on mentorship in male dominated occupations. *Journal of Vocational Behavior*. Vol 43, No 3. pp 251–265.

RAGINS, B.R. and SCANDURA, T.A. (1994) Gender differences in expected outcomes of mentoring relationships. *Academy of Management Journal*. Vol 37, No 4.

RAGINS, B.R. and SCANDURA, T.A. (1999) Burden or blessing? Expected costs and benefits of being a mentor. *Journal of Organizational Behavior*. Vol 20, No 4. pp493–509.

RAGINS, B.R., COTTON, J.L. and MILLER, J.S. (2000) Marginal mentoring: the effects of type of mentor, quality of relationship and program design on work and career attitudes. *Academy of Management Journal*. Vol 43, No 6.

ROSINSKI, P. (2003), *Coaching across cultures*. London: Nicholas Brealey Publishing.

SCHRIESHEIM, C.A. and MURPHY, C.J. (1976) Relationships between leader behavior and subordinate satisfaction and performance: a test of some situational moderators. *Journal of Applied Psychology*. Vol 61, No 5.

SEGERMAN-PECK, L. (1991) *Networking and mentoring: a woman's guide*. London: Piatkus.

SHPIGELMAN, C., WEISS, P. L. and REITER, S. (2009) E-mentoring for all. *Computers in Human Behavior*. Vol 25, No 4. pp919–928.

SIEBERT, S. (1999) The effectiveness of facilitated mentoring: a longitudinal quasi-experiment. *Journal of Vocational Behavior*. Vol 54, No3.

SMIT, A. (2000) *Transformational mentoring: to implement an action learning process in developing effective mentoring practice.* Doctoral thesis. Australia, Southern Cross University.

SMITH, P. and WEST-BURNHAM, J. (eds). (1993) *Mentoring in the effective schools.* London: Longham.

STOTT, A. and SWEENEY, J. (1999) More than a match. *People Management.* 30 June.

STRUTHERS, N.J. (1995) Differences in mentoring: a function of gender or organisational rank? *Journal of Social Behaviour and Personality.* Vol 10.

SUTTON TRUST (2010) *The mobility manifesto.* March. Available at: http://www.suttontrust.com/public/documents/20100312_mobility_manifesto20102.pdf [Accessed 19 December 2013].

THOMAS, D.A. (1990) The impact of race on managers' experiences of developmental relationships (mentoring and sponsorship): an intra-organizational study. *Journal of Organizational Behavior.* Vol 11, No 6. pp479–492.

TROMPENAARS, F. and HAMPDEN-TURNER, C. (1997) *Riding the waves of culture, understanding cultural diversity in business.* London: Nicholas Brealey Publishing.

TURBAN, D.B. and DOUGHERTY, T.W. (1994) Role of protégé personality in receipt of mentoring and career success. *Academy of Management Journal.* Vol 37, No 3.

UK'S LABOUR FORCE SURVEY (2012) Available at: www.ons.gov.uk/ons [Accessed 15 November 2013].

VARNER, I. and BEAMER, L. (2010) *Intercultural communication in the global workplace.* New York: McGraw-Hill.

VIATOR, R.E. (1999) An analysis of formal mentoring programs and perceived barriers to obtaining a mentor at large public accounting firms. *Accounting Horizons.* Vol 13, No 1.

WALES, S. (1998) *Executive mentoring: a retrospective exploration of managers' experiences of external mentoring.* Dissertation for MSc in Change Agent Skills and Strategies, University of Surrey.

WILKIN, M. (ed). (1992) *Mentoring in Schools.* London: Kogan Page.

WRIGHT, R.G. and WERTHER, W.B. (1991) Mentors at work. *Journal of Management Development.* Vol 10, No 3.

ZEY, M.G. (1984) *The mentor connection.* New York: Dow Jones Irwin.

ZEY, M. G. (2011) Virtual mentoring: the challenges and opportunities of electronically – mediated formal mentor programs. *Review of Business Research.* Vol 11, No 4.

Index

100 Black Men 3
Accreditation (see Qualifications)
Advising v, 1, 7, 8, 9, 11, 13, 14, 16, 17, 18, 22, 30, 31, 32, 33, 34, 35, 37, 47, 48, 64, 65, 68, 78, 97, 101, 102, 103, 114, 139, 143, 148, 150, 152, 161, 163, 169, 184, 185, 187
Armed Forces 3, 174
Asda 92, 138, 139
Association of Danish Lawyers and Economists 64, 184, 185
Athena 7, 10

BAE Systems 26
Bank of England 113
Big Brothers, Big Sisters 20
Body Shop, The 178
BOOST 2
BP 34, 71, 93, 127
Brent, London Borough of 134, 135
British Telecom 2, 150, 151
Business case for mentoring 3, 31, 33

Cabinet Office, UK 20, 95
Career (planning) xii, xiii, 3, 5, 8, 9, 11–18, 25–45, 62, 63, 67, 69, 74, 79, 88, 99, 117, 123–5, 127, 129, 130, 134, 135, 137, 142, 149, 151, 152, 155, 160–3, 168, 170, 176–9, 186–7
Centrica Energy Renewables 35
CEO (being mentored by) 68, 94, 113
Cherie Blair Foundation 2, 143
Children's Society 92
Coaching v, ix, xiii, xv, 1, 5, 9–15, 21, 23, 38, 44, 51, 64, 68, 69, 72, 78, 87, 89, 90, 109, 119, 122, 137, 138, 139, 141, 153, 155, 163, 168, 170, 172, 173, 176, 178, 182, 185, 186
Coaching at Work magazine xi, 90
Code of practice 80, 88
Communication 8, 21, 26, 28, 42, 43, 51, 55, 58,62, 74, 75, 77, 93, 109, 113, 120, 122, 123, 130, 134, 135, 139, 147, 150, 152, 153, 156, 167–8, 171, 177, 182, 186
Competencies xiii, xiv, xv, xvi, 3, 10, 21, 39, 40, 42, 49, 58, 62, 66, 69, 70, 73, 79, 80, 84, 87, 89, 102, 111, 124, 125, 135, 141, 142–3, 160, 182, 185–6
Conceptual modelling 43
Confidentiality 27, 38, 65, 72, 76, 80, 81, 113, 142, 149, 155, 185
Contract(ing) vi, 12, 80, 81, 92, 101, 113, 116, 122, 126, 172
Cross-organisational mentoring vii, xvi, 155–7
Counselling 1, 5, 7, 9, 10, 11, 12, 17, 25, 29, 89, 124, 143, 144, 168, 182
Culture xiii, 5, 8, 9, 10, 12, 13, 23, 26, 27, 28, 30, 32, 37, 40, 42, 49, 57, 62, 71, 72, 77, 88, 90, 93, 98, 109, 112, 119, 120, 121, 122, 127, 130, 131, 132, 137, 138, 144, 145, 151, 155, 157, 168, 172, 180, 186

Definitions 1, 4, 6, 7, 99, 105, 111, 115, 120, 121, 125, 127, 128, 156
Dependency 80, 105, 116, 182
Dimensions of mentoring 9, 10, 17, 167, 171
Disability xii, 20, 181
Dissolution (see Ending) 13, 106, 125
Distance media xiii, 63, 147–153
Diversity xii, xv, xvi, 20, 21, 25, 30, 32, 36, 39, 40, 51, 58, 71, 84, 88, 93, 95, 96, 120, 122, 125, 127–136, 152, 157, 174, 179, 182, 184
Diversity awareness ladder 133
Domestic violence 164
Dominguez, Nora xvi

E-mentoring (see Virtual mentoring)
Employability 58, 166, 168, 170, 171, 187
Employment xii, xv, 2, 21, 29, 30, 31, 58, 62, 88, 89, 126, 170, 171, 172, 183, 187
Empowerment (see Power)
Ending the mentoring relationship (see Dissolution)
Entrepreneur xi, xii, 2, 30, 69, 130, 141, 142, 143, 173, 180
European Bank for Reconstruction and Redevelopment 180
European Mentoring and Coaching Council (EMCC) xi, xv, 13, 69, 75, 87, 90, 141

First meeting 82, 100, 101, 160
Football Association (UK) 163–4
Formal v informal mentoring xii, xiii, xvi, 7, 8, 17–23, 25, 26, 28, 29, 31, 37, 44, 53, 57, 61, 67, 68, 74, 75, 79, 80, 81, 83, 85, 90, 91, 92, 97, 98, 99, 100, 106, 107, 109, 111, 116, 123, 125, 126, 134, 135, 150, 152, 160, 165–7, 172, 176, 177, 178, 183

Gender 10, 20, 32, 40, 56–8, 71, 93, 96, 117, 121, 128, 132, 165, 171, 177
Goals (goal clarity) xi, 1, 2 3, 6, 7, 9, 10, 20, 21, 25–27, 29–31, 33, 37, 40, 42, 44, 49, 51, 58, 67, 73, 74, 78, 79, 81, 84, 85, 90, 91, 94, 95, 100, 101, 102, 105, 115, 116, 121, 123, 128, 129, 131, 145, 150, 153, 168, 171, 178

Graduates 2, 3, 20, 21, 26, 27, 29, 31, 32, 35, 37, 38, 48, 49, 50, 58, 62, 69, 83, 88, 113, 115, 123–6, 166, 170, 171, 176, 183, 184, 189
Ground rules 49, 53, 64, 65, 80, 81, 101, 149, 152, 160
Guiding (see Advising)

High potential employees xii, 17, 25, 49, 50, 53, 112, 123, 125, 126, 165
HSBC 36
Hofstede, Gert 121, 122
Humour 40, 42, 50, 107, 109

IDA (Irish Development Agency) 185
Induction 25, 26, 29, 31, 32, 91, 123
Industrial Society (now The Work Foundation) 35
Institute of Chartered Accountants in England and Wales 2, 35
Institute of Practitioners in Advertising 2
Institute of Leadership and Management 87
International Association of Mentoring Academies 69
International Bar Association 169
International Standards for Mentoring Programmes in Employment (ISMPE) xi, xii, xv, 21, 58, 75, 87–90, 111
Influence (see also Power) xii, 3, 6, 11, 13, 42, 47, 48, 59, 91, 93, 98, 100, 102, 105, 114, 123, 126, 129
International Mentoring Association xv
International mentoring programmes 4, 119–126, 143, 166, 169
IT support systems xiii, 64, 88, 120, 170, 179
Italy 174

Jobseekers 187
JP/Politikens Hus 179, 180

Keele, Reba 109
Kram, Kathy xii, xv, 4, 99, 100, 102, 104, 106, 107, 109, 116

Leader development xi, xv, 3, 26, 28, 34, 57, 68, 119, 123, 125, 128, 131, 145, 152, 172, 173, 180, 181
Leicester City Council 92
Line manager (role of) 4, 6, 7, 11, 14, 17, 18, 21, 25, 35, 38, 50, 55, 61, 62, 65, 67, 69, 70, 76, 77, 81, 87, 102, 110, 114, 119, 124, 135, 156, 165, 185
Living positive programme 92

Marshall, Judy 130
Maternity mentoring xiv, xvi, 92, 137–9
Matching xiii, 19, 22, 39, 49, 53–60
Maturity 2, 15, 54, 116, 167
Measurement xii, xiii, xvi, 21, 25, 30, 40, 62, 65, 74–6
Megginson, David 6, 95, 106
"Mentor from Hell" 48
Mentoring and Befriending Foundation 87
Mentoring Institute, University of New Mexico 90
Mentoring meeting xiii, 9, 23, 34, 38, 44, 49, 50, 56, 62, 64, 67, 77, 79, 81, 82, 84, 85, 95, 96, 97, 101, 102, 104, 106, 107, 110, 111, 114, 115, 116, 117, 145, 146
Mentoring quadrangle 61
Merrill Lynch 37
Middlesex University 54, 58, 60, 166, 170, 172, 173
Models of mentoring xvi, 5–18, 43, 68, 89, 109, 182
Motivation 1, 3, 26, 27, 34, 41, 47, 48, 57, 67, 68, 73, 82, 96, 104, 123, 125, 126, 135, 148, 152, 153, 178, 183
Mowgli 2, 143
Multi-country mentoring xvi, 119–122

Napier University 176
National Grid 26
National Health Service UK (NHS) 80, 91
Networking xiii, 1, 3, 8, 10–12, 13, 15, 23, 26, 28, 30, 31, 47, 48, 66, 69, 74, 79, 81, 84, 90, 106, 109, 113, 114, 123, 125, 126, 129, 137, 142, 143, 145, 151, 152, 160, 165, 166, 177, 179, 183 185
Non-verbal communication 42, 147, 182
Norway 2, 57, 144
"No fault divorce" 56, 82

Outcomes of mentoring xvi, 3, 4, 8, 9, 14, 18, 35, 38, 40, 44, 51, 59, 66, 75, 77, 79,84, 85, 97, 101, 106, 110, 114, 135, 145, 150, 166, 168, 171, 172, 175, 182, 186
Oxford University xii

Peer learning alliance 96–98, 144
Peer mentoring xiii, 2, 7, 13, 17, 20, 57, 66, 69, 76, 91–98, 133, 155, 159, 164, 173, 178
Personality 41, 54, 56, 59, 92, 149, 153, 161
Phases of the mentoring relationship xvi, 68, 73, 79, 99–107, 138
Pilkington 37
Power xii, 5, 6, 9, 13, 16, 31, 32, 34, 42, 44, 80, 83, 96, 102, 105, 113, 114, 120, 121, 122, 124, 127, 133, 142, 148, 164, 167, 181
Princes' Trust 143
Procter and Gamble 93, 94, 95
Professional mentors 69, 70, 88, 141–6
Programme coordinator (see Programme manager)

Programme manager xiii, xiv, xvi, 19, 21, 29, 51, 53, 61, 66, 70, 72, 76–78, 81, 85, 88, 90, 105, 111, 112, 145, 149, 150, 167
ProjectScotland 175
Pygmalion effect 103

Qualifications 69, 87, 141, 176

Rank Group 2
Rapport 19, 33, 41, 42, 44, 53, 54, 55, 57, 58, 59, 60, 67, 73, 74, 82, 85, 91, 97, 100, 101, 103, 107, 115, 124, 126, 135, 147, 148, 149, 167, 174, 179, 181, 186
Recruitment 3, 26, 76, 87, 123, 135, 151, 155, 156, 183, 187
Referee 163, 164, 175
Retention xvi, 2, 3, 26, 27, 29, 30, 84, 92, 95, 97, 126, 177
Reuters 95, 96
Reverse mentoring xiii, 39, 90–98, 115
Role model xiii, 1, 3, 12, 21, 22, 27, 28, 32, 36, 43, 45, 67, 93, 125, 129, 130, 139, 144, 165, 181

Sandia Laboratories 4
Schools, mentoring in 2, 3, 13, 20, 30, 90, 164, 166, 182, 183
Second Wave Mentoring xii, xiii, xvi
Selection xvi, 19, 25, 39, 49, 53, 87, 88, 88, 112, 126, 135, 181
Self-awareness 6, 40, 41, 69, 79, 85, 125, 143
Self-confidence 29, 32, 50, 51, 66, 126, 130, 137, 145, 152
Sheffield Hallam University 7, 18, 139, 143, 153
Shell 106
Small business mentoring 2, 142–3, 148, 153
Smithkline Beecham 29
Social inclusion xvi, 20
South Africa 172–3
Sponsor(ship) xii, xiii, 1, 4, 5, 9, 12, 13, 16, 17, 18, 21, 29, 33, 35, 47, 50, 74, 75, 91, 94, 99, 100, 104, 105, 105 107, 109, 110, 113, 116, 124, 129, 130 132, 156, 160, 165, 171, 178, 179, 180
Standards xi, xii, xvi, 21, 58, 75, 87, 88, 89, 90, 111
Steering group 21, 70, 76, 77, 134, 135, 136
Succession xii, 3, 25, 26, 28, 38, 50, 124, 125
Supervision 21, 41, 64, 68, 88, 110, 138, 139, 141, 176, 178, 182, 184

Trainer knowledge 73
Training xiii, xiv, xv, 2, 20, 21, 22, 23, 26, 29, 30, 43, 44, 51, 68–75, 76, 77, 78, 82, 83, 84, 85, 87, 88, 89, 93, 94, 95, 96, 97, 105, 107, 111, 115, 116, 120, 121, 122, 123, 124, 126, 133, 134, 135, 141, 143, 145, 146, 147, 150, 151, 152, 153, 155, 156, 157, 160, 165, 166, 167, 168, 170, 171, 172, 174, 175, 176, 177, 182, 183, 184, 185, 186

Unisys 33
University of Illinois School of Music 176–7

Values-based matching 55–7
Virtual mentoring xvi, 39, 68, 71, 125, 126, 147–153, 165

Wisdom 1, 6, 7, 10, 15, 16, 115